What people are saying about

WORKING FROM YOUR CORE

"**Working from Your Core** boldly tackles one of the most challenging disciplines of the learning organization—personal mastery—in both an elegant and engaging manner. It provides a practical guide to leaders for self discovery and organizational renewal based on universal, time-honored principles. This book offers inspiring reading for all who are seeking direction on the personal mastery journey and who wish to contribute to the learning organizations of the future."

> —**Steven Cavaleri**, coeditor, *Managing in Organizations That Learn*

"With irresistible exercises, **Working from Your Core** draws the reader immediately into the substance of his or her own core, then offers reams of valuable information about each core pattern. You can pick and choose particular morsels or consume the whole banquet. Either way, Sharon Seivert has written a wonderfully intelligent and authentic book."

> —**Carol Frenier,** author, *Business and the Feminine Principle*

"I've been involved in three significant health system mergers over the past five years and I strongly believe that the understanding and appreciation of corporate culture is key to the success, or failure, of a merger. This book is a very effective guide for an organization as it thinks through its cultural development or the prospect of a merger. It can help an organization define itself."

> —**Brian J. Osberg**, Senior Vice President,
> Managed Care, CareGroup

"I've found Seivert's work to be quite helpful in diagnosing organizational needs and for recommending specific improvements that are easily actionable. It has been interesting to observe just how quickly people understand and apply the archetypal models to their own experience at work. The descriptions give managers a common language for building effective business relationships and for consciously planning ways to improve real-world problem-solving."

> —**Kevin Bourne**, Team Leader, ManagerWorks

"The material in **Working from Your Core** is a special gift. The testing instruments provided insights into both our personal and organizational styles. Very exciting, powerful, and meaningful."

> —**Ronnie Herbst** and **Mary Ellen Coffey**, Educators,
> St. Peter's Hospital, Albany, NY

Working from Your Core

WORKING FROM YOUR CORE

Personal and Corporate Wisdom in a World of Change

SHARON SEIVERT

Butterworth-Heinemann

Boston   Oxford   Johannesburg   Melbourne   New Delhi   Singapore

Recognizing the importance of preserving what has been written, Butterworth–Heinemann prints its books on acid-free paper whenever possible.

 Butterworth–Heinemann supports the efforts of American Forests and the Global ReLeaf program in its campaign for the betterment of trees, forests, and our environment.

Library of Congress Cataloging-in-Publication Data

Seivert, Sharon.
    Working from your core : personal and corporate wisdom in a world of change / Sharon Seivert
        p.   cm.
    Includes bibliographical references and index.
    ISBN 0-7506-9931-0 (alk. paper)
    1. Organizational behavior.   2. Management — Employee participation.   I. Title.
    HD58.7.S44   1998
    302.3′5—dc21   97-29930
                                                                          CIP

British Library Cataloguing-in-Publication Data

A catalogue record for this book is available from the British Library.

The publisher offers special discounts on bulk orders of this book. For information, please contact:

Manager of Special Sales
Butterworth–Heinemann
225 Wildwood Avenue
Woburn, MA 01801-2041
Tel: 1-800-366-2665
Fax: 1-800-446-6520

For information on all Butterworth–Heinemann books available, contact our World Wide Web home page at: http://www.bh.com

10 9 8 7 6 5 4 3 2 1

Printed in the United States of America

Contents

A Guide to This Book

Working from Your Core is designed so that you can easily self-tailor your reading of it and make it immediately useful. You can (a) read this book straight through; (b) use only the parts of interest to you — personal, or organizational, or change; or (c) proceed immediately to the instruments, get your scores, and use the rest of the book as a reference. In fact, *Working from Your Core* is written so that you can pick it up time and again and easily find the material you need.

Preface and Dedication: Tells the story of how I came to this work and why I believe it can help you and your organization.

Chapter 1: Describes how to use this material as a stepping stone to learning, self-mastery, and organizational success. It provides the theoretical basis for the rest of the book. If you do not need to be convinced of the value of this material, you can skip this chapter and go directly to the instruments.

Chapter 2: Contains the Core Type Profile, which will help you determine your own preferred Core Types. This chapter will guide your reading of the chapter that follows.

Chapter 3: Details each of the ten Core Types, which are familiar models of human behavior. Included for each Core Type are illustrative stories, its gifts for and difficulties within the workplace, how to recognize this type in yourself and others, how to work with others of this type, how each Core Type responds to stress, and variations of this Core Type with which you may be familiar — from the least pleasant to the most noble.

Chapter 4: Contains the Organizational Culture Profile, which will give you a sense of how these same models of human behavior unconsciously affect the way your workplace does business.

Chapter 5: Describes ten different forms of Core Culture, including for each: illustrative stories; its strengths and weaknesses; what it's like when it's at its best and worst; how *you* are likely to find it, that is, your likely gifts for and difficulties within this culture; and how to best survive there.

Chapter 6: Looks at the three dynamic processes of change and how each Core Type and Core Culture can more gracefully "ride the waves of change."

Chapter 7: Discusses how each of the Core models and processes of change contribute to Wisdom. Describes the process of learning, specifically a heroic learning theory that can help you access the gifts of the Core Types. Also discussed here is wisdom — what it is and how to bring it into our lives and work.

Epilogue: Contains a concluding story and insights.

Preface

One afternoon, a few years ago, I was teaching a seminar. I heard myself say that I did this kind of work so that people would have more tools to help them heal their own workplaces. I stated that there was too much unnecessary suffering, pain, and stress in organizations, and that, as a result, people were literally dying from their work. Now, I had said this before. I knew it to be true. But that day an echo of this truth reached into a part of me that had been slumbering for many years. "John," I thought suddenly. "Oh, my God. I'm doing this work because of John."

My younger brother, John Seivert, was a laborer at a modern plant that treated sewage, sanitizing it into a sterilized sludge that was used for fertilizer. Although this Midwestern facility was up-to-date, the management was not. The plant had a history of accidents and near-accidents, one involving an ammonia leak, in which an explosion, which could have rocked the area, was narrowly averted. All this, plus uncomfortable labor-management relations, made John eager to find employment elsewhere. He was actively searching for a job in a similar facility when the following incident occurred.

One ice-cold February morning, John was standing in the back of a truck in an underground garage at the plant. He had been asked to fill in for another worker. The task was to load sludge from a large ceiling spout into a truck. His best friend, Roger, sat behind the wheel. As the truck container filled, John called to Roger to move forward a bit, so he could adjust the nozzle and complete the task. Roger thought John meant that it was time to pull out of the garage. As John saw the low-hanging cement ledge coming rapidly at him, he took what appeared to be the only exit available — diving as deeply as he could into the slight cavity left unfilled. A heartbeat later, the truck lifted its front wheels onto the sharply inclined driveway to ground level, heaving the container to within a few inches of the ledge. John was crushed. Roger didn't know what had happened until he heard my brother's screams. Workers came running from all directions. John was rushed to the nearest hospital, where he underwent several hours of emergency surgery.

Dad called me after John emerged safely from the surgery. He said there had been a terrible accident, but John was out of danger: he had pulled through the surgery, and was now resting comfortably. I was stunned by this close call. I talked with my father at length, pumping him for details and assurance. We determined that I should wait to arrange travel plans until we knew how long John would be in the hospital.

Very early the next morning, at 5:30 to be precise, I was awakened by a soft, cool touch on my shoulder. I stared into the pitch-black stillness of the room. It was John. He had come to say goodbye. Before I could form another thought, or find my voice to beg him to stay, he was gone. My mind was shocked into complete silence. I slowly laid down again, then turned over on my side to stare, without feeling or thought, at the clock. I was waiting for the phone to ring.

Dad called at 6:30 that morning with the news: John had died unexpectedly an hour earlier. I rose slowly, reluctant to meet my own grief and that of the rest of my family. At that moment it was little consolation that my brother had, with the greatest compassion imaginable, come to notify his sister that he was just fine, that he was at peace. All I knew then was that I ached inside and out because I could never touch my brother again.

* * * * *

I chose to begin *Working from Your Core* with this extremely personal story for several reasons. My brother's death changed my life, catapulting me out of the life I had designed for myself, and setting me on an entirely new path. And, John's accident was avoidable: it was a "systems failure." Management at the plant had been advised repeatedly that the combination of the sharp-incline driveway from the underground garage and the cement overhang was a death trap, an accident waiting to happen. Management had been told to change it, but they opted not to. The repairs would cost too much, they figured, particularly because the odds were so high that nothing would ever happen.

W. Edwards Deming, the American statistician, writer, and consultant who started the current worldwide quality revolution, was fond of saying that at least 85 percent of mistakes in organizations are systems failures, and no more than 15 percent result from human error. I have experienced this truth again and again. That fateful February morning, Roger was not at fault for hearing wrong, nor was John for giving an ambiguous instruction to his colleague. Such minor communication problems usually result in hurt feelings, not in bodies crushed beyond repair. Clearly, the system needed fixing, management was told it needed fixing, and they decided not to. My family forced the plant to fix the problem so that no one else would be hurt in the future. The cost of this system failure turned out to be very high for everyone involved.

After John's death, I changed my life completely — leaving my job as CEO of a successful group health plan, moving across the country to be with the man I loved, and eventually starting a new career in workplace consulting and writing. Ironically, John had made this life change possible, for (unbeknownst to me) he had named me beneficiary of his life insurance policy. With that money in hand, I set upon a path that led, over a great many years, to this book.

Working from Your Core presents a technology that approaches workplace problems simultaneously from the individual and the systems levels. Both we and the human systems in which we accomplish our work together need to learn and adapt to change. This book is intended to help individuals become stronger and smarter (so they can survive dysfunctional workplaces) AND simultaneously improve these systems so they don't crush their workers. This is the analogy I use: If a building collapses and people are trapped inside, two things need to happen at the same time. The people inside have to have the courage and will (and luck) to survive; and, the rubble has to be lifted off them, or they'll never make it.

This book then, is a call to the Quest — a quiet quest, a daily quest. It is a call to heroism in the workplace — a call for real transformation of yourself, your work, and your organization. Our systems must be changed by the people within them. And we, the workers, must change ourselves so we are equal to the task. It is difficult, but not impossible. I have seen many who are already doing it. You will find some of their stories herein. The cure to the workplace diseases that plague us — stress, apathy, fear, anger, greed — lie within each of us. You have in your *Core* (the very center of yourself), a great source of innate wisdom and heroism that is just waiting to be tapped.

The task before us is to uplift ourselves, our colleagues, employees, and organizations by first realizing, then bringing our very best natures from our Core into reality. This is "working from your Core." This book also serves as a call to organizations to work from *their* Core, rather than making us spin our collective wheels on the periphery, wasting our time, energy, power, and creativity. This is a call to smart workplaces that learn and thrive because the people within them learn and thrive. It is a call to all wise, heroic people who have the capability and daring to reshape their ailing organizations, thereby saving the minds, souls, and health of the workers and leaders within them.

No one of us can accomplish this daunting task alone. But, then, no one of us has to. And we need so much heroism today. Our problems are extremely complex, interwoven through industries and nations. It is difficult to see where one challenge begins and another ends. We are faced with labyrinths everywhere — our buildings, our organizational charts, our problems, even our proposed solutions. We need every form of wisdom and heroism available, every set of clear eyes on the difficulties before us, every good mind on the obstacles in our path.

Most of us are trained to look for solutions to our problems from experts who supposedly know more than we do. We rarely trust our own intuition, our own workplace experience. But this approach has not proven particularly successful. The truth is that we have all the knowledge and wisdom we need available to us when we tap into our own Core. The only difficulty is determining how we can access such wisdom in the midst of a full-speed workday. This book is an introduction to a colorful board of internal advisors who can help you with this difficult, but worthy task.

* * * * *

Dedication

To my beloved brother, John C. Seivert,
who taught me generosity, kindness, stick-to-it-ivism
in the face of adversity, and the real-life costs
of workplace dysfunction and
systems failures.

To the members of my family of origin:
my loving parents, Jack and Myra (McLaughlin),
my wonderful siblings, Irene Haley, Tom Seivert,
and Dorothy Ginnett,
their great spouses and terrific children.

With great gratitude for your love and support.

I treasure you all beyond words.

Acknowledgments

I would like to acknowledge Carol S. Pearson, with whom I developed the *Heroes at Work* and *Magic at Work* models. Carol and I started our work together in 1985 with the establishment of Meristem, a nonprofit think tank that provided the structure through which we brought our ideas into the workplace, received feedback about what worked, and developed testing instruments and applications of this material. These years were a time of great synergistic creativity, laughter, and collegiality — a time I will always treasure. Our collaborative work, *Heroes at Work: A Workbook* (1988) and the three-volume *Heroes at Work* (1996), provided the outline for much of this present book. Carol and I concluded our years of partnership with the writing of *Magic at Work: Camelot, Creative Leadership, and Everyday Miracles* (1995). Carol is also the author of *The Hero Within: Six Archetypes We Live By* (1986) and *Awakening the Hero Within: Twelve Archetypes to Help Us Find Ourselves and Transform Our World* (1991). I heartily recommend these two beautifully written books to readers who want to learn more about their personal heroic journeys.

I also would like to thank several people who contributed significantly to the development of this book. First among these is Steven Cavaleri, Professor of Management at Central Connecticut State University. Steve urged me to address many of the issues contained in Chapters 1 and 7. Steve has been supportive of my work since we met in 1990 and has acted as my personal mentor in systems thinking and organizational learning. Steve is the author of *Management Systems: A Global Perspective* (1993) and co-editor of *Managing in Organizations That Learn* (1996.)

Many other colleagues and friends contributed significantly to the early stages of the manuscript. These include Judith Lieberman, who has a gift for pressing gently but firmly with her relentless "So what?" and "Now what?" questions. *Working from Your Core* has evolved to become more practical and accessible as a result. Fred Reed taught me everything I know about autognomics learning theory and reviewed the learning theory in Chapter 7 to make certain it was "autognomically correct." Andy Hahn and Kathy Eckles also contributed their insights and wisdom to this book, particularly to the final chapter. Prema Popat brought her sharp skeptic's eye and her wordsmithing to this work. Thanks also go to my irreverent friend, Glen Koocher, who was the first person to propose the archetype of the "Jerk" — thereby triggering my contemplation of the less noble aspects of all the Core Types. And endless gratitude goes to Donna Sherry, to whom I owe a great debt for making this book possible, and who helped me bring it out into the world.

Lynnette Yount and her terrific associates provided me with years of stimulating, collegial work. They also taught me the basics of TQM and group dynamics, and were big fans of this work when it was in its infancy. I also would like to thank the staff and board members of the Central Minnesota Group Health Plan for giving their all to our shared effort, and for proving to me and the world just how wonderful an organization can be.

Jeremiah Cole has been supportive of this work from its inception and through our many years together. He edited *Heroes at Work: A Workbook* while I was completing it. As the fates would have it, Jerry was immediately thereafter called to jury duty for a sensational murder trial in New York City. As foreman, he used what he'd just learned to help hold together a sharply divided jury. Thanks also go to Michael and Elizabeth Cole for their long-time interest in this work and for their continued support of me.

This book and I have been blessed with a great editor, in the old style of publishing, that is, someone who loves books and who nurtures her writers. Karen Speerstra sought me out for this book. At our first meeting, we talked nonstop for four hours. I was completely captivated. Since that time we have become fast friends. Moreover, Karen went way beyond the call of duty to midwife this book during its final, difficult stages of labor.

Finally, I would like to thank the participants in my seminars, and the students who have been certified to do this work. It is through their eyes, ears, and candid feedback that this material has evolved, matured, and become much more useful to others.

PART I

Why Work from the Core?

1

The Paths to Learning, Self-Mastery, and Organizational Success

There are a thousand ways to go home again.
— JELUDDIN RUMI

Your Core, the center of your being, is your real home. It is the goal and the end of all your striving. *Working from Your Core* introduces you to an internal council of advisors who make their home in the Core, and who therefore can serve as guides on the path you choose to learning and Self-mastery. They can bring you to a greater understanding of both your personal Core and the Core of your organization.

Your Core is a treasure-trove. It contains your special gifts for the world, your unique piece of the puzzle. Your Core is your own personal holograph of the Whole. It subtly connects you to everyone with whom you live and work, and it also provides you with a link to the accumulated knowledge of humanity. Specifically, *Working from Your Core* will provide you with a greater understanding of:

- yourself,
- your co-workers,
- interactions with and differences among co-workers,
- your workplace's culture,
- your "fit" within your workplace, and
- the forces of change which affect all of the above.

Working from Your Core is designed to help you, your co-workers, and your organization become the best each is capable of becoming — that is, to "optimize" yourself and your workplace by bringing the unique gifts of each into the world. It can help you execute the advice that Quality advisor W. Edwards Deming encoded in his fourteen management points — in particular, to "drive out fear"; "break down barriers" between yourself, other people, and parts of the organizations; "institute leadership" and "continuously improve" workplace systems.[1]

Working from Your Core will be especially useful if you are willing to treat your own work as a path — one which can lead you on a journey through learning to personal, and possibly also corporate, Wisdom. It contains tools to repair any organizational dysfunction *you* have inadvertently created due to your own behavior. *Inc. Magazine*, in an article entitled "The Zero-Defect CEO," describes a growing phenomenon: how many business leaders, having worked so hard to remove defects from their businesses, are now trying to do the same for their psyches. By becoming more self-aware, we all can remove our own blind spots, see the choices we do have, and contribute less frequently to the difficulties around us.[2]

My colleagues and I have used this material in a variety of workplace settings: health care, government, high-tech, education, manufacturing, retail, unions, small business, etc. We have worked with many kinds of people within those diverse organizations: from CEOs to grocery clerks; from organizational change-agents to beleaguered workers who merely hope to survive the latest storm of change; from internal to external consultants; from management professors to their students; from psychologists treating highly-stressed workers to workers who are looking for relief themselves.

The concepts contained in this book are what Deming would have called *profound knowledge*. Deming classified profound knowledge into four areas: knowledge about systems, variation, theory, and — of particular relevance here — *the psychology of individuals, society, and change*. As such, the models contained in *Working from Your Core* have a great many applications. For example, they can help you deal better with workplace stress, increase your effectiveness as a leader, improve your sense of connection to and your relationships with colleagues, determine your organization's current culture, increase the likelihood that change efforts will be effective, reduce conflict among staff members or departments, and remain true to yourself if you are in a workplace culture that is somewhat "foreign" to you.

YOUR INTERNAL BOARD OF DIRECTORS — GUIDES ON THE PATH

> I know there are reservoirs of spiritual strength from which
> we human beings thoughtlessly cut ourselves off.
>
> — HENRY FORD

Your internal board of directors is already helping to manage your affairs from behind the scenes. *Working from Your Core* makes you more aware of the effects of this colorful cast of characters on your life, relationships, work, and your workplace's culture. These powerful guides have both individual and organizational forms — Core Types and Core Cultures. They are the:

Innocent	Seeker	Caregiver	Magician	Lover
Orphan	Jester	Warrior	Ruler	Sage

The Core Types are described in detail in Chapter 3 and the Core Cultures in Chapter 5. The instruments which indicate your preferences for each are contained in Chapters 2 and 4, respectively. If you are already convinced of the value of the Core material, or are not particularly interested in its theoretical underpinnings, you may move on now to the chapters that most interest you. However, if you would like to better understand the derivation of the Core model, please read on.

The ten advisors described in *Working from Your Core* are *archetypes* — identifiable energy patterns, natural templates, which give Life its many diverse forms.* They are *human* models, patterns, or instincts — your human birthright. As such, these ten models have familiar human faces which can be easily recognized. They exist simultaneously within both your personal psyche (last night's dreams) and also within the collective mind you and I share as members of the same species. For this reason, they can help you and I relate on a whole new level by understanding our similarities and respecting our differences.

The Core Types embody profound knowledge about human nature. Each of these symbolic codes can be found throughout the world, and each is a comprehensive package which describes the different ways we know how to be human. The Core Types affect every aspect of our lives and work: (1) our identity, (2) the way we view the world, (3) our behavior, (4) our interactions with others, and (5) the habits and structures we create in our lives. (Please refer to Appendix A for a description of how the Core Types reflect the five fields that underlie and unify all living systems.)

These human models have been called *the eternal ones of the dream* (Aborigine Australian) and *subjectively known forms* (Hindu). Cicero, Pliny, and St. Augustine described such human patterns in their writings. Adolf Bastian called them *elementary ideas.* Psychologist Carl Jung popularized the term *archetypes,* which he defined as: "Forms or images of a collective nature which occur practically all over the earth as constituents of myths and at the same time as in-

---

*An archetype is "the original pattern of which all things of the same species are representations or copies; original idea, model, or type." Not discussed in this book are many other kinds of archetypes such as natural templates (spiraling galaxies, a DNA strand, or a fractal), geometric patterns, or systems archetypes (such as elaborate, recurring, and often counter-intuitive work patterns.) *Working from Your Core* addresses only the archetypal models of human beings, the human systems within which we work, and the dynamic forces of change which affect both.

dividual products of unconscious origin."[3] Indeed, these models of humanity are so pervasive that at any given time you can see their familiar faces on TV soap operas, the front page of newspapers, and as characters in great literature or cartoon shows.

> The Self is the Actor . . . the supreme Truth or Consciousness, [who] wears different costumes and appears to change His nature. Assuming different roles, He continues His play in the world.
> — THE SHIVA SUTRAS

We can see this play of this great "actor" in the Core Types, as different ones of our advisors emerge from behind the curtain and enter the stage of our lives to speak their lines and teach us a particular lesson. Because the Core Types are archetypes, you will find it easy to recognize this cast of colorful characters. Indeed, it is because you are merely naming and recalling what you already know, that the Core methodology is so easy to learn and apply.

The Core Types are both *images* and *metaphors* — conceptual structures humans have used for millennia to make sense out of life — like language itself. Metaphors can help us both to name our experiences and then communicate the complex realities of our work life with a rich symbolic language. (Metaphors are so powerful that Aristotle called them "the mark of genius."[4]) The Core model provides vivid, easily memorable imagery for the workplace. And, although these archetypes are ancient constructs, this model of human behavior and systems can give us fresh, revitalizing insights into our workplace problems today.

> New imagery, signaled by new words, is as important as new theory; indeed new theory without new imagery can go unnoticed.[5]
> — CHARLES HANDY

As you become more aware of these Core Types, they will become increasingly visible to you. Indeed, you will start to notice them everywhere. They may appear to take on a life of their own as you watch them move fluidly not only in yourself but also in your colleagues and workplace systems. As one seminar participant so aptly put it: "These archetypes are as real as your fingernails." The Core Types *feel* tangible. Each is a distinctive pattern of energy that moves us, invisibly but powerfully, from within.

The Core Types serve as guides into, through, and back out of our own vast, complex inner landscape. As our companions, they make journeying into our Core a less formidable task. They also provide us with a conceptual vehicle to carry our insights back out into the world and put them to work. The Core Types therefore can help us with the task of *individuation*, becoming our full unique selves, even within the difficult — some would say inherently hostile — context of our workplaces. Paradoxically, the Core Types can also help us with the task of *connectedness* — bridging differences, seeing the ways we are the same, and improving our relationships with others.

The journey to Self-mastery is well worth the effort, for extraordinary treasures are hidden inside you. No matter how smart you are, your conscious intelligence is only a tiny fraction of the Intelligence you can access when you activate the bridge between your Conscious and Unconscious minds. As you gain "innerstanding" the bridge changes from a walkway into a super-highway. *Indeed, here lies genius.* The following analogy may illustrate my point.

> *I sit now in my office, inputting this book via my personal computer. My PC is VERY smart — it stores several books and countless letters, and will display any one of them for me with only a few seconds notice. It also hooks up to my music system, allowing me to input, record, and transcribe the songs I write. Moreover, it plays them immediately with more instruments than I could master in a lifetime. It has more gigabytes of memory than I can comprehend, and it effortlessly executes commands far beyond my personal ability.*
>
> *However, when I compare my PC to the international Internet, I can see immediately that, although powerful, it has only an infinitesimally tiny fraction of one percent of the Internet's capability. Fortunately I can use my small, but quite-capable PC to log into the Internet's vast, hidden, and collectively-linked capability.*

OTHER TYPOLOGY MODELS

The Core Types are one way of better understanding ourselves, the similarities and differences we have with others, and workplace culture. The Core Types are not the full you, but they reflect real parts of you. Other excellent Typology modalities exist.

For example, I am very fond of the Myers-Briggs Type Indicator, which is the most widely used personality inventory in the world. It gives information about how we perceive the world, what energizes us, how we make decisions, and how ordered or flexible we prefer our lives to be.

Another Typology system, rediscovered and popularized in recent decades is the Ennea-Type. The Ennea-Type provides an in-depth understanding of the primary psychological wounding that keeps us separated from our essence, our core, our best selves; it is an excellent therapeutic tool.

The Core Typology system differs from these two other classifications in that it is fluid, that is, you change your preferences depending upon the challenges you have to meet in your life and work. These three Typology systems provide different insights — all valid — that can help you increase your Self-mastery. I have found that their impact can be augmented if they are used together.

This analogy provides a way to think about the comparative ratio of your conscious knowledge to the Wisdom you can access by linking up with the vast collective Unconscious, which is always ready, waiting for you to "log in."

A similar comparison can be made to the ratio of the *unfolded* (visible) order to the *enfolded* (invisible) order, as these are described by physicist David Bohm. Bohm described the world as a *holomovement* between the reality we can see and the vast potential lying just below that surface. We link our conscious (unfolded) world to our unconscious (enfolded) world when we tap into our Core, thereby connecting our ordinary life with the extraordinary life force always available to us. Wisdom comes from moving easily, like a holomovement, between these visible and invisible worlds. But that is not where we start. The very first form of wisdom, then, is our willingness to set upon the path of learning and open ourselves to whatever life has to teach us. This is the route we travel to Self-mastery. All it takes is a little heroism.

HEROES AND ANTIHEROES

The Core Types are *heroic* archetypes. They are models of behavior, ways of being, that en*courage* us first to learn about ourselves, then to act increasingly with courage and nobility. In *Leading from the Heart: Choosing Courage over Fear in the Workplace,* author Kay Gilley defines courage as infusing your work with *life* by putting your whole heart into what you do. She quotes Lao Tzu, who calls the heart the "first treasure" and the source of courage. Gilley challenges leaders to choose courage over fear — to look inside and develop a loving relationship with themselves. Then, she says, they "can stop needing to get from others what they most need to give themselves."[6]

The greatest act of courage known to humanity is the willingness to learn about one's Self. Indeed, it is the stuff of legend. Self-learning is the ultimately heroic, even Herculean, task. After all, in mythology the dragons and heroes who challenged each other were only symbols, respectively, of the fears and doubts lurking inside the complex maze of our inner selves, and the nobility and strength inherent in each of us. The reward for the hero's daring actions in these stories from all times and places is a great treasure. This represents the rich wisdom just waiting for us in our depths — the realization of who we really are and an unshakeable sense of Self-worth.

One example of this inner treasure is the *emotional intelligence* we so value in bosses, coworkers, and subordinates. Daniel Goleman described emotional intelligence as including *interpersonal* intelligence (such as empathy, recognizing others' emotions, handling relationships well) and *intrapersonal* intelligence (self-awareness, knowing what you are really feeling, handling your emotions appropriately). Both of these intelligences increase when you learn and work from your Core. And the pay-off is substantial: research indicates that such emotional intelligence is a better predictor for success in life, work, and even education, than IQ scores.[7]

Each one of the Core Types provides different tools that help us face our problems and give our best gifts to our workplaces and the world. When made conscious, these heroic models are paths to nobility. When ignored and left unconscious, however, they act *on* us, rather than *with* us and become paths to ignobility. (Think of what happens when you ignore a board member, staff person, spouse, or child. Of course: they act out.)

The Core Types, therefore, enfold not only our potential successes, but also the pits we can so easily fall into. That is, they contain our full human capacity for both heroic and antiheroic behavior. Participants in my workshops often ask: "So. . . . Where's the archetype of the Jerk?" The answer is that each of the Core Types ranges all the way from the truly noble to the "I'm having a bad day," to the really, really ugly.

You always have a choice. In every moment you can move toward or away from learning about yourself. The good news is that the rewards are great for every step you take as you travel this route. A great teacher, Swami Chidvilasananda, once said, "The study of your own true nature frees you from the habit of blaming others for your condition in life. This inner study creates a haven that gives you the power to overcome your faults. Knowing the great Self is the secret of supreme peace."[8]

HEROES AT WORK?

Working from Your Core focuses on the Core model as it plays out in the workplace because (1) we can witness such a kaleidoscope of human behavior on the stage of our workplaces, (2) work acts as a bridge between our talents and the rest of the world, (3) work is where many of us have the greatest need for heroism, and (4) because these models apply to both individuals and systems, they can help us relate better to each other and our workplaces.

Work is an alchemical fire that transforms us. It burns, it hurts, it *works on us* as we are working. Rather than thinking of our workplaces as arenas where "the men are separated from the boys," we would benefit from thinking of them as places where the heroes are separated from the antiheroes. Work is filled with daily stress, challenges that range from minor to mind-boggling. Work tests our souls and minds and wills and hearts and bodies — often sorely. As Studs Terkel said in his classic *Working*, "To survive the day is victory enough for the walking wounded among the great many of us."[9]

This is precisely the problem that Carol Pearson and I tried to address by launching our collaboration. Just as Carol was completing the manuscript for her best-selling *The Hero Within*, we made a pact to combine our skills in order to address the workplace difficulties we saw.

We were both painfully aware that many of our friends and acquaintances were suffering excessively in their organizations. The fruit of our labors was *Heroes at Work: A Workbook*, which contained in outline form these ten models of individual and organizational heroism. Over the years, we brought *Heroes at Work* into many kinds of organizations and designed testing instruments, courses, and materials. We learned that these heroic models of human behavior were inherently *democratic* and *ennobling* — that they did indeed help people move from fear to courage, from separation to relationship, from acting like jerks to becoming more wise.

THE JOURNEY TOWARD SELF-MASTERY

Self-mastery is the ability you gain when you learn about your Self, and then move from that core of your being into the world. The fruit of Self-mastery is Wisdom — the ultimate form of human knowledge. Wisdom is defined as "deep, thorough, or mature understanding . . . the ability to make sensible decisions,"[10] and "the capacity to judge soundly concerning what is true or false"[11] (especially relating to life and right conduct). To attain *mastery* at something requires that you learn all about that topic, gain knowledge and skill, become an expert. The word *Self* has been defined variously. For example, it is "an individual's awareness of what constitutes his or her essential nature and distinguishes him or her from all others: a strong sense of self." (A synonym for ego).[12] Indeed, this is the common usage of Self, and the material contained in *Working from Your Core* can help you attain this first form of Self-mastery.

Moreover, the Core material can take you to other levels of Self-mastery. *Self* comes from the Anglo-Saxon *self, seolf, sylf,* which meant "same; identical — having its own or a single nature or character, as in color, composition."[13] In this way, Self means that you are "saturated" with who you are: that you have the same identity all the way through, that you are congruent, integrated, whole. Carl Jung defined the Self as "the ordering and unifying center of the total psyche."[14] He believed that this part of us helped us become fully human — a process he labeled *individuation*. Italian psychiatrist Roberto Assagioli, Jung's contemporary and the founder of Psychosynthesis, defined the Self as "the unifying center" of a human being, "the very core of the human psyche."[15]

Working from Your Core is written so that you can choose the ways in which you wish to use this material and which level of Self-mastery you seek. Clearly, attaining any form of Self-mastery takes concerted effort. And, reaching the higher levels of Self-mastery is an ongoing, life-long journey. Fortunately, the Core models can help you along the way, as they are ingrained human patterns that form a link between "our ordinary consciousness and the shining peak of Self-realization." Assagioli described such ideal models as "intermediate phases, plateaus at various altitudes on which a man may rest or even make his abode . . . if [he] does not choose a further ascent."[16]

INTO YOUR CORE

Your Core is your home, a place of comfort, contentment, and ease. It is like a palace — with room enough to contain the complete you, everything you are now and everything you can be. The Core is also the meeting ground between your Conscious and Unconscious minds. It acts as a bridge between what you currently know and what you can learn, between what you see as "reality" and the latent possibilities which are now hidden from your view.

Your Core contains your complete identity. This includes your *persona* — who you or others think you are, the qualities of personality that make you obviously different from the person in the next

THE CORE TYPES AS STEPPING STONES TO SELF-MASTERY

Roberto Assagioli described the human personality as "pluridimensional," having all the components in Figure 1–1. When all these different parts of ourselves are integrated around a unifying, synthesized psychological center, he says, we attain Self-mastery. The Core Types exist in every dimension of the personality. Therefore they can be used as connecting links between the various parts of yourself, and also as stepping stones to your higher Self and a more integrated, stable personality. The Core Types can help you in your own evolutionary process, taking you to your higher Self, by acting as mirrors that reflect both what exists in the outer world and what exists in the unexplored parts of yourself. (Figure 1–2.)

1. The Lower Unconscious

2. The Middle Unconscious

3. The Higher Unconscious or Superconscious

4. The Field of Consciousness

5. The Conscious Self or "I"

6. The Higher Self

7. The Collective Unconscious

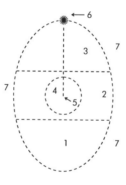

Figure 1–1
Roberto Assagioli described the human personality as "pluridimensional."
Source: *Psychosynthesis: A Collection of Basic Writings*, Roberto Assagioli, p. 17.

1. The Conscious Self or "I"

2. External Unifying Center

3. Higher Self

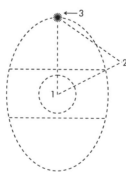

Figure 1–2
The Core Types act as mirrors that reflect both what is in the outer world and what exists in the unexplored parts of yourself.
Source: *Psychosynthesis*, p. 26.

office. It also includes many limited "identities" that are only a small part of the full you. (For example, "I am a stockbroker," or "I am a mother," or "I feel unequal to the task.") These external identities do not remain constant; they change as you change. If we allow ourselves to overly identify with such externals and we then lose that job or mate, we suddenly feel as if we are without clear definition or that we no longer exist.

It is in the Core that you store everything you've ever learned. Some of these things you can recall. Other data, ranging from expert knowledge, to trivial matters, to things in your past that you would rather forget, are stored in your *Personal Unconscious*, just waiting to be retrieved. Your Core also provides a link to the *Collective Unconscious* of the human species, which Jung defined as: "the deposit of all human experience right back to its remotest beginnings . . . a living system of reactions and aptitudes that determine the individual's life in invisible ways . . . a living fountain of instinct [from which] flows everything that is creative."[17] In many ways, individual humans exist in human communities much as cells exist in our bodies — with permeable membranes. Assagioli described our unconscious interchange and connection with those around us as being *psychological osmosis*.

Our Unconscious affects our daily work by invisibly directing a good deal of our behavior. It provides us with energy, insight, "gut" reactions, good instincts, and intuition. It helps us figure out what's *really* going on, interact well with others, make the right decisions, roll with the punches, and deliver excellent services and products. In other words, it is a great source of Wisdom.

Moreover, if you ignore the power of your Unconscious, it can seriously sabotage your change efforts — ranging from a personal diet to a company-wide reorganization. In short, you need to have *both* your Conscious and Unconscious working for you while you do your work. Otherwise, no matter how smart you are, no matter how good your intentions, you will often not be able to accomplish what you intend to because it will be invisibly undermined. And there you will sit, incredibly frustrated, stymied, and unable to figure out what went wrong.

You can use every event at work, every new challenge, every stressful situation to take another step towards learning and adaptation. If your organization allows, you can also contribute what you have learned to its success. The final chapter of this book describes how the Core learning process plays out, step by step. It shows how, when we learn from our Core, we become more capable — individually and collectively — of meeting our challenges with courage and competence. Chapter 7 also addresses how modern science, particularly *autognomics*, supports learning and working from your Core.

Autognomics ("self-knowing") is the study of how autonomous, intelligent systems — including you and your organization — learn. It defines learning as the ability of an intelligent system to adapt to a changing environment while *self-referencing*, that is, maintaining its core identity. As a science of learning, autognomics dances happily with the mythology of the hero's journey, because both assert that to find your best Self, you must choose your own path of learning. Unfortunately, many workplaces tell us the exact ways we need to work if we are to be a "good" employee and do a "good" job. As a result, we lose contact over time with our own internal compass, the source of our power and energy. This is a tragedy for all concerned: worker, leader, workplace, and society.

ORGANIZATIONS AS (MORE OR LESS) INTELLIGENT SYSTEMS

> Organizations learn only through individuals who learn.
> Individual learning does not guarantee organizational learning.
> But without it no organizational learning occurs.[18]
>
> — PETER SENGE

One of the most powerful aspects of *Working from Your Core* is that not only you, but also human systems such as your *organization* can be better understood with its templates. Therefore, this comprehensive Core archetypal system provides a framework with which you can dovetail your professional development and organizational improvement efforts.

Much as an individual can only attain Self-mastery by becoming aware of the workings of the inner self, a workplace learns by tapping into its Core. Effective organizational learning depends upon increasing an organization's *consciousness* of itself. This self-awareness, in turn, increases an organization's viability by creating and maintaining an internally generated, self-referenced cohesion and integrity.

The case for organizational consciousness has been made by biologists Humberto Maturana and Francisco Varela. In *The Tree of Knowledge*, they describe human social systems as *metasystems*. Human social systems, they say, are "metasystems of components with maximum autonomy, that is, components with many dimensions of independent existence."[19] This level of autonomy is in contrast to animals or plants, where individual cells do not have a life outside the organism. (And, as much as some of us may protest to the contrary, we do "have a life" outside the workplace.) Organizations *are* aware of themselves, to greater or lesser degrees. They can distinguish themselves from other systems, and they can articulate these differences. Most are also conscious of their boundaries; for example, who is inside the system and who is outside it, who fits well within it and who does not.

I find it useful to employ the metaphor of organizations as organic, living systems capable of adjusting themselves. I find it more helpful than the prevalent metaphor of organization-as-a-machine that we constantly have to control and adjust. Increasingly, other students and observers of organizations agree. As Steven Cavaleri and Krzysztof Obloj stated in *Management Systems: A Global Perspective*, organizations behave in many ways that are "dynamic, lifelike, and shaped by the human components."[20]

In human systems, as in other living organisms, the health of any one part and the health of the whole are related. One of the reasons it is so important for each of us to try to improve the well-being of our workplaces is that, quite literally, our own health and the health of everyone within the system are directly affected. Physicist David Bohm argued that, no matter how separate and distinct things or people appear, they are all connected into a seamless holographic fabric. A holographic image is remarkable in that, no matter how often it is divided, it still contains the whole image.

The holographic phenomenon was used by biologist Karl Pribram to describe how specific memories could be stored throughout an individual's whole brain, and by Bohm to explain why, once individual electrons were in plasma, they "stopped behaving like individuals and started behaving as if they were part of a larger and interconnected whole."[21] In organizations, we work as part of a tightly woven holographic fabric. This is why our learning can help our organizations — and vice versa. The holographic metaphor also helps explain why our workplaces have so much power to change us — and we them.

ORGANIZATIONAL CONSCIOUSNESS AND LEARNING

Bohm believed that consciousness and matter were not really separate, and that consciousness was present, to some degree, in all matter. However, some people and some organizations have a lot more ability and willingness to learn than others. Organizational consciousness ranges dramatically, as I am fond of saying, "from rock to ameba to puppy." Frankly, many organizations seem to have very little life or consciousness. They act as if they were learning-disabled.

What separates the potentially smart organization from the clueless one, is the degree to which it knows that it also has an Unconscious — hidden aspects of itself — about which it is willing to learn. These include its own culture, its collective core identity. The smart organization digs as deeply as possible to learn what the shared values, beliefs, hopes, and fears of its people *really* are. It then truly knows "who" it is.

I believe that this level of organizational self-consciousness is a *prerequisite* for organizational learning. I do not think it is overstating the point to say that a "learning organization" begins by becoming conscious of its identity. First we need to identify where we already are on a given map before we can chart the way to another destination. Most organizations really do not understand where they are before they embark on organizational improvement. Rather, they have an idealized, or hoped-for, identity. It's not hard to pick up on this; for example, workers roll their eyes when their organizational values, vision, and mission statements are read aloud.

The degree to which an organization can self-reference as it changes, the degree to which its members' beliefs and actions are integrated with the culture's identity, determines the degree to which the organization will be able to learn and successfully adapt. This is because organizational identity is "the most compelling organizing energy available."[22] I once heard William O'Brien, former CEO of Hanover Insurance Company, describe how he and his managers changed their organization by clarifying and redefining Hanover's cultural Core.

> *William O'Brien was one of the guest lecturers for the final session of an organizational intervention in which I was involved. This management group of a manufacturing company had spent the past couple of months learning about "learning organizations," then were set into teams to design their own. I noticed that they were listening attentively to Bill as he described his organizational experiences in his disarmingly homespun style.*
>
> *Bill described the early Hanover as typical of most organizations. Politics, bureaucratic behavior, and verbal gamesmanship produced a work environment that impeded Hanover's success. People were learning, he said, but they were learning all the wrong behaviors. As CEO, he searched for ways to make real change. He brought in Chris Argyris and other organizational experts. Eventually, he and his management team decided that the only antidote for their culture's diseases was to define, then adhere to strong cultural values.*
>
> *The management team set out to determine what core values they wanted to establish at Hanover. After spending some time delineating this list of values, he and the other managers worked very hard to make certain that, from that point on, every decision they made passed the test of being congruent with these values. At first people were skeptical. Others were resistant. However, over a period*

of years the steady application of these principles developed a cultural cohesion. Trust increased. Moreover, the cultural revamping process had very tangible, bottom-line results: the value of Hanover's stock grew from $5.70/share in 1979 to $39/share in 1991.

This act of becoming conscious of itself, this defining of a positive cultural core, a clear identity from which it could self-reference, set the stage for Hanover to become the successful learning organization which was described at length by Peter Senge in *The Fifth Discipline*. As Margaret Wheatley and Myron Kellner-Rogers argue, "Identity is the source of organization. Every organization is an identity in motion, moving through the world, trying to make a difference."[23]

INTO THE CULTURAL CORE

The identity of the organization resides in its Core. This identity includes its *culture* — a term that is a bit confusing, as it is defined so variously. Edgar H. Schein, in *Organizational Culture and Leadership*, argued that "the only thing of real importance that leaders do is to create and manage culture."[24] He argued that the culture operates *unconsciously*, and that it includes deeply held, basic assumptions and beliefs shared by the members of an organization, which they then tend to take for granted. Schein states that other common definitions of organizational culture are really just reflections of it: behavior, norms, values, philosophy, rules, and "feeling" or climate.

It is in the Core of the organization that its own Conscious and Unconscious meet. Unless leaders work to bridge these, the invisible forces which unconsciously influence the system will remain hidden, subtle, pervasive, and, sometimes, perverse. Indeed, most of us are completely unaware of the degree to which our culture affects our every action. It is like the air we breathe — we can't see it, but we depend upon it for life. If it is toxic, we suffer. Because we tend to take our organization's culture for granted, we often cannot see clearly whether it is healthy or unhealthy, nor where it could be improved. (This is why it is often useful to have outsiders help us examine our organizational culture.) As we saw was true in the personal psyche, the Unconscious contains a wealth of potential good and potential danger. When the organization deliberately reflects upon itself, it is as if all the people in a village, not just its leaders, become responsible for carrying torches into the night. As a result, everyone in the group is a lot less likely to fall into unseen holes.

Without a clear, agreed-upon cultural definition, our workplaces act in crazy, unintegrated ways. One department moves in one direction, another in the opposite. An executive makes one decision on Wednesday afternoon, and by Friday morning it is reversed. In crazy systems, the people trapped within become crazy too. As Wheatley and Kellner-Rogers state: "Organizations with multiple personality disorder confuse us with their incoherence. Our innate process of self-reference breaks down . . . [yet] when they go inside to find themselves, there is only one self there. We can resolve [organizational schizophrenia] only with coherence — fundamental integrity about who we are."[25]

Unfortunately, there is often great confusion about who or what the organization is. I see this all the time when I interview executives. It never ceases to amaze me that members of the same management team, many of whom have been working together for years, can describe their organization so variously. My experience is that gathering perceptions from throughout the *whole* system can reveal the truth — the Core cultural identity, the current state of the organization, the system's real strengths and real weaknesses. Surprisingly few leaders ask their organizations to reflect upon themselves. This is a shame, since our workplaces contain so much talent, insight, and inventiveness just waiting to be tapped. And, no matter how smart any manager is, he or she will never be able to provide the comprehensive knowledge that only full system feedback can provide. This ancient story explains why:

> *Four blind men, traveling together on the back roads of India, bump into an elephant who is blocking their path. Together they try to figure out the nature of this obstacle. One feels the elephant's trunk, another a tusk, the third a leg, and the last blind man, the elephant's tail. Their individual experiences seem to be contradictory. Only when they are put together do the puzzle pieces form a picture of reality.*

It is not surprising that many organizational leaders are adverse to discovering the real strengths and weaknesses that lie at their organization's Core. The Truth — both organizationally or individually — often hurts before it sets us free. Often pain and disruption are required to release us from the costly, debilitating illusions that keep us stuck. This is true for both individuals and workplaces. However, like individuals who seek to transform their lives, human systems have to first take "a long, hard, unblinking look" at themselves before they can exchange their current reality for a better one.[26] Otherwise, leaders and workers get caught in a perpetual loop of self-delusion, and are never able to escape the undertow of unconscious cultural influences. Only system-wide self-examination can lead to system-wide learning and adaptation.

Organizational success is the fruit of discovering, then moving into the world from, the organization's Core. An organization that self-references in this way is a learning organization. It increases its chances of survival by remaining open to the messages of its environment. Because it has a strong Core, it will not be easily tossed around by the vagaries of fate. Such an organization is likely to be successful because it is intelligent enough to tap the extraordinary intelligence, talent, and creativity contained within it. Its members tend to work enthusiastically on its behalf. Consequently, it is more likely to be able to determine the size, the shape, and the nature of the various obstacles it bumps into. Such an organization will be able to move consciously throughout its world, adapting appropriately to whatever changes it encounters.

MAKING CHANGES

Any individual or organizational intervention that does not take its core identity into account is doomed to failure. It will be unconsciously sabotaged. This is not only inefficient and frustrating, it is also costly. Unfortunately, we often just throw ourselves and our resources at change. Not only do we usually not know who or where we are before we begin moving things around, we also employ only a fraction of the talent and energy available to help move from here to there. Sometimes I feel that this is a bit like trying to move a mountain by busily shifting around all the boulders near the top.

In order for our personal or systems changes to be successful, we also need to know what change processes are available to us. This is why, in addition to the ten Core Types and Core Cultures, *Working from Your Core* describes the three dynamic processes of change: *Creation, Sustenance,* and *Destruction.* Each Core model employs these three processes, each in its own way, to make and manage change. When we consciously attend to these dynamic processes of change, our work and life transitions tend to be a bit smoother.

SUMMARY

> All models are wrong — but some are useful.
> — W. EDWARDS DEMING

Working from Your Core describes a system of thought — one with which I have worked for a long time, and of which I am particularly fond. However, because all ideas, models, and metaphors are by their nature arbitrary (i.e., maps of the territory and not the territory itself), the only measure of the "truth" of any one of them is its effectiveness. *Is it helpful?*

I think you will find that the concepts contained in this book are helpful, and that they will provide you with many insights into yourself, your relationships with others, and a fresh, revitalizing perspective of your workplace. Indeed, it is my fervent hope that you find this material as useful as I have found it.

Read on to decide for yourself. Have a wonderful journey.

NOTES

1. Mary Walton, *The Deming Management Method*, Perigee Books/Putnam Publishing, New York, 1986, p. 33–36.
2. Joshua Hyatt, "The Zero-Defect CEO," *Inc: The Magazine for Growing Companies*, June 1997, pp. 46–57.
3. C.G. Jung, "Psychology and Religion." In *The Basic Writings of C.G. Jung,* edited by Violet de Laszlo, Random House, New York/Toronto, 1959, p. 515.

4. Verna Allee, *The Knowledge Evolution: Expanding Organizational Intelligence*, Butterworth-Heinemann, Boston, MA, 1997, pp. 162–163.

5. Charles Handy, *The Age of Unreason*, Harvard Business School Press, Boston, MA, 1979, p. 25.

6. Kay Gilley, *Leading from the Heart: Choosing Courage over Fear in the Workplace*, Butterworth-Heinemann, Boston, MA, 1997, p. 7.

7. Daniel Goleman, *Emotional Intelligence*, Bantum Books, New York, 1995, p. 97.

8. Swami Muktananda and Swami Chidvilasananda, *Resonate with Stillness: Daily Contemplations*, SYDA Foundation, South Fallsburg, NY, p. August 30.

9. Studs Terkel, *Working*, Avon, New York, 1972, p. xiii.

10. *Roget's II The New Thesaurus*, Houghton Mifflin, Boston, MA, 1980, p. 1057.

11. *Webster's Collegiate Dictionary*, Merriam, Springfield, MA, 1937, p. 1158.

12. *Roget's II The New Thesaurus*, p. 824.

13. *Webster's Collegiate Dictionary*, p. 902.

14. Jean Dalby Clift and B. Wallace, *Symbols of Transformation in Dreams*, The Crossroad Publishing Co., New York, 1985, pp. 133–134.

15. Roberto Assagioli, *Psychosynthesis: A Collection of Basic Writings*, Arkana/Penguin Group, New York, 1965, pp. 24, 35.

16. Ibid., p. 24.

17. Joseph Campbell (ed.), "The Structure of the Psyche," *The Portable Jung* (reprint of Carl Gustav Jung's *The Structure and Dynamics of the Psyche. Collected Works*, Vol. 8, 1930), Viking Press, New York, 1971, p. 44.

18. Peter M. Senge, *The Fifth Discipline: The Art and Practice of the Learning Organization*, Doubleday/Currency, New York, 1972, p. 139.

19. Humberto R. Maturana and Francisco J. Varela, *The Tree of Knowledge*, Shambhala, Boston and London, 1992, p. 198.

20. Steven Cavaleri and Krzysztof Obloj, *Management Systems: A Global Perspective*, Wadsworth Publishing Company, Belmont, CA, 1993, pp. 14–16.

21. Michael Talbot, *The Holographic Universe*, HarperPerennial, New York, 1992, p. 38.

22. Margaret Wheatley and Myron Kellner-Rogers, *A Simpler Life*, Berrett-Kohler, San Francisco, CA, 1996, p. 58.

23. Ibid.

24. Edgar H. Schein, *Organizational Culture and Leadership*, Jossey-Bass Publishers, San Francisco, CA, and Oxford, UK, 1985, p. 2.

25. Wheatley and Kellner-Rogers, p. 60.

26. Stanilas Klossowski de Rola, *Alchemy: The Secret Art*, Thames and Hudson, London, 1973, p. 14.

PART II

Ten Paths to Self-Mastery

2

Determining Your Own Core Types

The Core Type Profile (CTP)* gives you a snapshot of your dominant Core Type, your key issues in the workplace, as seen through the lens of type, and how the Core Types affect your response to stress. The CTP is designed to help us better understand ourselves and those with whom we work by identifying the different — and sometimes contradictory — plots that shape our lives. Specifically, the CTP includes questions reflecting the world views of the:

Innocent	Orphan	Seeker	Jester	Caregiver
Warrior	Magician	Ruler	Lover	Sage

The CTP gives you a numerical score, which indicates your degree of identification with each of these ten distinct ways of interpreting events and seeing the world. Each Core Type has an important contribution to make to your life. You have access to all of these

---

*The CTP is an expansion of the Heroic Myth Index (HMI), which was originally designed by a team including Sharon Seivert, Mary Leonard, and Carol Pearson. Testing of the HMI included studies in both content validity and test-retest reliability. The HMI was first published in *Heroes at Work: A Workbook* (Meristem, 1988).

types, with stronger preferences for some than for others. No Core Type is better or worse than another. Each contains within it a wide range of behavior — from the most to the least noble. The CTP aims at the midrange of each Core Type. To reiterate: all ten Core Types are valuable, each brings special gifts, and we all have access to all of them. *Therefore, there are no right or wrong answers in the CTP.*

Once you have your CTP scores, please move to the analyses, which are designed to help you self-tailor your reading of the rest of this section of *Working from Your Core*. Look to Part A of the analysis to reveal your *dominant* Core Types and give you a snapshot of your preferences now. Part B of the analysis examines how the Core Types influence you in the key workplace issues of *security, autonomy, agency, power,* and *motivation*. Part C of the analysis looks at the *effects of stress* on you and your Core Types, that is, what your type preferences are when you're at your best — and at your worst! The chapter ends with a brief introduction to each of the ten Core Types.

DIRECTIONS

The 60 statements that follow express different ways in which people see themselves. Please use the following scale to indicate the extent to which you agree or disagree with each statement as a description of yourself. When you have responded to all the items, turn to the self-scoring sheet.

1	2	3	4	5	6	7
Strongly Disagree	*Disagree*	*Mildly Disagree*	*Neutral*	*Mildly Agree*	*Agree*	*Strongly Agree*

___ 1. I look on the bright side of life.
___ 2. I give to others before asking them for anything.
___ 3. People look to me for direction.
___ 4. I am willing to take personal risks in order to defend my beliefs.
___ 5. If I expect too much from life, I will be disappointed.
___ 6. My presence is often a catalyst for change.
___ 7. I accept other people just as they are, with all their imperfections.
___ 8. I like to find my own answers.
___ 9. I believe in the old saying: "Rules are made to be broken."

___10. Love is the most powerful force on earth.

___11. I have a hard time saying no.

___12. I try to manage situations with the good of all in mind.

___13. I assume people I meet are trustworthy.

___14. In the world, there are real enemies that must be faced.

___15. I am trying to discover what I want out of life.

___16. People who love their work are most productive.

___17. Others sometimes see me as fun but irresponsible.

___18. I am often struck with inspiration.

___19. Life is one heartache after another.

___20. I keep a sense of perspective by taking a long-range view.

___21. Few people can be trusted.

___22. I try to show others the humorous side of life.

___23. I put the needs of others before my own.

___24. Imagination is more powerful than reason.

___25. I am looking for greener pastures.

___26. I can count on others to take care of me.

___27. Courage is putting your fear aside and doing what needs to be done.

___28. I love life.

___29. In the big scheme of things, I am no different from anyone else.

___30. I match abilities with tasks to be done.

___31. I have good reasons for feeling cynical.

___32. I like to "lighten up" people who are too serious.

___33. When I care for something, I care passionately.

___34. I cannot sit back and let a wrong go by without challenging it.

___35. I am an intuitive person.

___36. Although I love many things in my life, I could give most up without regret.

___37. I enjoy bringing order out of chaos.

___38. I do not feel right about spending money on myself.

___39. I believe that "every cloud has a silver lining."

___40. I am breaking away from an important person in my life (e.g., supervisor, spouse).

___41. I stand up to offensive people.

___42. The world is a safe place.

___43. I am so attached to some people that I cannot imagine life without them.

___44. I feel restless.

___45. I enjoy making dreams into realities.

___46. I wish people were more sensitive to my needs.

___47. Sacrificing to help others makes me a better person.

___48. I identify with the statement: "The buck stops here."

___49. I work hard but am not overly attached to the results.

___50. Instead of solving problems directly, I prefer to find a clever way around them.

___51. I have learned that life is not fair.

___52. I thrive on competition.

___53. I do not believe that people really mean to hurt each other.

___54. It is essential for me to maintain my independence.

___55. Change should happen in an orderly fashion.

___56. I have sacrificed personal opportunities for people I care about.

___57. When life gets dull, I like to shake things up.

___58. I have found inner peace.

___59. I trust my hunches.

___60. It is better to have loved and lost than never to have loved at all.**

SCORING DIRECTIONS

Now move to the CTP Self-Scoring Report Form (Table 2–1), which follows. Please fill this form out completely, transferring the score of 1 to 7 you gave on each question to the number that corresponds to the item number. Then add up the columns to discover how active each Core Type is in your work life.

After completing the Self-Scoring Report Form, you can graph your CTP scores on the chart that follows. This will give you a visual representation of your CTP results.

The midpoint (24) indicates either neutrality or ambivalence about that Core Type. If you consistently answer 4 (neutral), it would suggest that it is of little interest to you. If conflicting responses of 6s and 7s versus 1s and 2s cancel each other out, this indicates ambivalence. Scores of 36 or higher suggest that this Core Type is active in your life in a conscious way. Scores of 12 or lower suggest either repression of or aversion to that Core Type. (It can also mean you've previously overdone that type and are now moving on to other life lessons.)

**No copying or reproduction of CTP permitted.

Table 2–1 CTP Self-Scoring Report Form

In taking the CTP, you were asked to rate items on a scale of 1 to 7, with 1 meaning "strongly disagree" and 7 meaning "strongly agree." The instrument includes six questions for each item. Therefore, in each category scores range from a low of 7 to a high of 42 points. Fill in your score (1 to 7) for each question, then add the columns.†

Item No.	Your Score	Item No.	Your Score	Item No.	Your Score	Item No.	Your Score	Item No.	Your Score
1.	____	5.	____	8.	____	9.	____	2.	____
13.	____	19.	____	15.	____	17.	____	11.	____
26.	____	21.	____	25.	____	22.	____	23.	____
39.	____	31.	____	40.	____	32.	____	38.	____
42.	____	46.	____	44.	____	50.	____	47.	____
53.	____	51.	____	54.	____	57.	____	56.	____
Innocent Total ____		**Orphan** Total ____		**Seeker** Total ____		**Jester** Total ____		**Caregiver** Total ____	

Item No.	Your Score	Item No.	Your Score	Item No.	Your Score	Item No.	Your Score	Item No.	Your Score
4.	____	6.	____	3.	____	10.	____	7.	____
14.	____	18.	____	12.	____	16.	____	20.	____
27.	____	24.	____	30.	____	28.	____	29.	____
34.	____	35.	____	37.	____	33.	____	36.	____
41.	____	45.	____	48.	____	43.	____	49.	____
52.	____	59.	____	55.	____	60.	____	58.	____
Warrior Total ____		**Magician** Total ____		**Ruler** Total ____		**Lover** Total ____		**Sage** Total ____	

† No copying or reproduction of CTP permitted.

PART A: ANALYSIS OF CORE TYPE RESULTS

You can graph your CTP scores in Figure 2–1.

Figure 2–1 *Mark in each column your degree of identification with that Core Type. Feel free to use different colors to represent the different Core Types.*

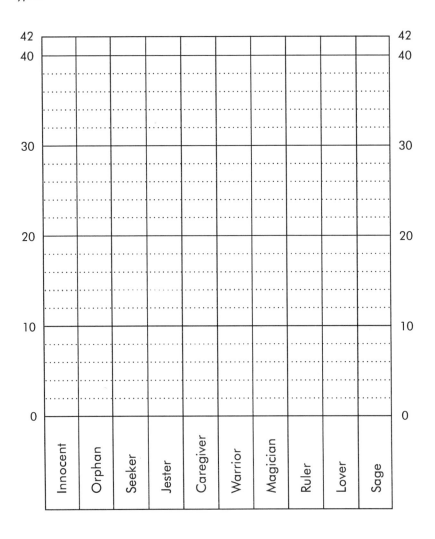

PART B: KEY WORKPLACE ISSUES

The ten Core Types can be grouped into five pairs, which provide a profile of your attitude, style, or orientation towards the following critical work issues: security, independence, agency, power, and motivation. In each of these categories, you are likely to have one archetype that "leads" and another that is less active and "follows." The difference between your scores indicates the magnitude of the disparity between your preferred and less preferred modes in each pairing (Table 2–2).

Table 2–2
For each issue and pair of Core Types:
1. Circle the Core Type which has the higher score on the CTP.
2. Write in the scores of both pairs—the higher score on the first line and the lower score on the second line.
3. Subtract the two scores to get an indication of the disparity between these Core Types in your work life. The more disparate the scores, the greater the likelihood that you may lead with one Core Type at the expense of the other. The more similar the scores, the greater the likelihood that you are using both equally in your work.

Workplace Issue	Circle higher scoring type	High minus low equals
SECURITY: TRUST IN THE WORKPLACE Both the Innocent and the Orphan help us to accurately assess situations so that we know when and where it is safe to trust. If your Innocent is dominant, you tend toward optimism and are trusting of others, and perhaps also of life itself. You may even be overly trusting and oblivious to many dangers. If your Orphan is dominant, you are more aware of dangers and threats but perhaps less able to trust, even when trust is warranted. In short, if your Innocent leads, you are likely to be an optimist. Conversely, if your Orphan leads, you tend toward pessimism.	Innocent Orphan	___ – ___ = ___
INDEPENDENCE: BEING TRUE TO YOURSELF Seeker and Jester are two styles of independence in the workplace. In the Seeker, independence is linked with finding and following your own ideas, values, and doing work that is your true vocation. In the Jester, it is expressed as playfulness, cleverness, and <div align="right">(continued)</div>	Seeker Jester	___ – ___ = ___

Table 2–2 (continued)

Workplace Issue	Circle higher scoring type	High minus low equals
a capacity to manipulate the system. Both aspects are important to success in today's world. On the down-side, if you lead strongly with your Seeker, you may be overly earnest and lose your joy in your work. If you lead with your Jester, you may become some-what frivolous and neglect the "great questions" of identity and vocation.		
AGENCY: MAKING A DIFFERENCE The Warrior and the Caregiver are two modes of agency; i.e., acting to make a difference. If your War-rior leads, you will prefer to act through competition, assertion, and achievement. If your Caregiver leads, your preferred way of acting will be to give to, care for, or empower others. If your Warrior strongly leads, you may "win" at the expense of others. If your Caregiver strongly leads, you may help others at your own expense.	Caregiver Warrior	__ – __ = __
POWER: CLAIMING YOUR POWER Magician and Ruler are two modes of expressing your power in the world. The Magician's power com-bines vision, creativity, and the will to transform existing reality or to create something that has never been before. The Ruler's power lies in making order out of disparate elements. If the Magician in you leads strongly, you may seek the new at the expense of organizational harmony and balance. If the Ruler leads strongly, you may achieve order but at the ex-pense of innovation.	Magician Ruler	__ – __ = __
MOTIVATION: FINDING JOB SATISFACTION If your Lover leads, it is important that you like (or even love) your work and respect your coworkers. If your Sage leads, it will be more important to you that you have an overview, a context, which gives your work meaning. If your Lover strongly leads, you may have trouble becoming or remaining committed to tasks or to people who do not interest or excite you. If your Sage strongly leads, you may become de-tached and disconnected from coworkers and from the day-to-day aspects of your job.	Lover Sage	__ – __ = __

Key Workplace Issues: Summary

1. Overall, do you tend to be more of a generalist (fairly even scores) or a specialist (high scores on a few types with lower scores on most of the others)?

2. Note which of the five pairings seem important to you in your work. List all pairings in which you have one (or both) Core Type(s) over 30.

3. List the job issues in order of importance to you by adding the scores of the two Core Types in the pairing (Table 2–3). For example, if your Warrior score was 26 and your Caregiver score was 18, your agency style score is 44.

4. Turning now to exploring Core Types that may be underdeveloped in your work life, list any type(s) that received a score under 18.

Table 2–3

List the job issues in order of importance to you by adding the scores of the two core types in the pairing.

Job Issue:				
Security	Independence	Agency	Power	Motivation
Core type:				
Innocent/Orphan	Seeker/Jester	Caregiver/Warrior	Magician /Ruler	Lover/Sage
Subscores:				
___+___=	___+___=	___+___=	__+___=	___+___=
Total Score:				
_____	_____	_____	_____	_____
List ISSUES in order (high to low):				
_____	_____	_____	_____	_____

5. Look at their companion types. If you scored under 18 on those as well, note (and list below) what job issues you are de-emphasizing. Are there ways that this has resulted in difficulties for you or your coworkers?

6. Are there any Core Types that you feel you need to develop more fully? If so, list them below.

7. Are there any Core Types that you dislike or find objectionable? In what ways? What redeeming aspects of this type(s) do you think you could appreciate in others or in yourself?

PART C: STRESS ANALYSIS

In the first part of the CTP you discovered your dominant types under most circumstances. This last section examines your preferences when you are under the least stress (optimal conditions) versus the most stress (the most difficult conditions); that is, when you are likely to be at your best and at your worst, respectively. You may find that you stay the same as your dominant type, or that you change under either of these extreme conditions. Interestingly, each Core Type finds different kinds of conditions more stressful than others. Often what is difficult or painful for one Core Type is easy for another.

Directions

Simply check the one answer that best completes each sentence below.

I. The work condition that I would find the most stressful is:

____ a. losing a good boss.

____ b. being taken advantage of.

____ c. having to do work that has little meaning for me.

____ d. being stuck in a boring job with boring people.

____ e. being unable to help the clients I'm supposed to serve.

____ f. having my hands tied, being forced to be inactive.

____ g. being able to see the future, but unable to move towards it.

____ h. a loss of rank, power, or prestige.

___ i. having to work on a project (or with people) I really dislike.

___ j. excessive activity or distractions that keep me from being able to think.

II. When I am at my best at work I:

___ a. can see the good in every person.

___ b. feel compassionate towards myself and others.

___ c. feel I've finally found what I've been looking for.

___ d. have great fun entertaining myself and/or others.

___ e. serve others in ways that are easy for me and truly helpful for them.

___ f. am strong, focused, and get a lot accomplished.

___ g. feel balanced, whole, and as if energy is moving through all of me.

___ h. have my own work and circumstances around me under control.

___ i. feel passionately alive.

___ j. am calm and peaceful.

III. When I am under too much stress at work, I tend to:

___ a. go into denial about the difficulties facing me.

___ b. become convinced that there's no hope.

___ c. escape to a better situation.

___ d. take it out on others by making fun of them.

___ e. try to make things better by giving to the point of exhaustion.

___ f. get more competitive and combative.

___ g. "persuade" people to do things my way.

___ h. protect the advantages I have so they won't be changed.

___ i. lash out at anyone criticizing me or my efforts.

___ j. emotionally detach and remove myself from the stressful situation.

Scoring Directions

Mark your answers from the above questions in Table 2–4.

Table 2–4

Mark your answers from questions I, II, and III here.

Core Type	a. In	b. Or	c. Sk	d. Js	e. Cg	f. Wr	g. Mg	h. Rl	I. Lv	j. Sg
Question I ✓										
Question II +										
Question III −										

Now transfer these stress symbols to the bar graph in Figure 2–1. Use the symbol ✓ to note which of the ten Core Types inside you is most likely to become stressed at work. This is the "hot button" that people around you have probably learned to avoid.

How well or poorly you respond to that stressor, of course, is a separate issue. You may respond with more or less wisdom at different times to this and other difficulties. Use the symbol + to note the Core Type that is likely to appear when you are feeling at your best, and the symbol – to note the Core Type that surfaces when you're feeling at your worst.

This information can prove helpful as you read Chapter 3, which contains descriptions of how each Core Type responds under stress. Start to observe how you act when you are stressed, and what circumstances trigger that felt stress. The Core Types can give you a lens through which you can (1) observe your own behavior, then (2) determine strategies to improve it.

INTRODUCING THE TEN CORE TYPES

Below is a description of the ten Core Types. Each makes significant contributions to — and has significant difficulties within — the workplace. Because each type has its own special strengths and weaknesses, each is important at different times of our lives. All have gifts that can significantly enrich our lives and work. This, then, is your inner council of advisors.

Innocent. The Innocent lives — or believes it is possible to live — in Eden. The Innocent's gift to the world is trust, optimism, belief, and a contentment with life as it is. The Innocent in each of us has a kind of pristine faith, an incorruptibility that others try to protect. The Innocent's contentment and optimism, however, may be somewhat dependent upon a tendency to denial.

Orphan. The Orphan wants to live in a safe world — but feels this is impossible. Orphans feel betrayed, abandoned, prematurely on their own, and powerless to help themselves. They tend to distrust life itself, expect the worst, and be prone to cynicism, which they may call "realism." The Orphan in each of us reminds us of our interdependence with others who do sometimes let us down. It also teaches us compassion and empathy.

Seeker. The Seeker's journey is about identity and finding one's vocation or mission. The Seeker's plot usually begins with a feeling of entrapment or restlessness and then a resulting escape — from a relationship, a job, a way of thinking or living. Then comes a solitary journey to find oneself. Seekers travel light (usually alone) and often avoid commitment in one or many parts of their lives.

Jester. The Jester lightens us up by finding clever, fun ways around obstacles — intellectual or physical. At worst, Jesters are irresponsible. At best, Jesters free us from convention to see things afresh. In either case, the Jester always undercuts order, even our own sense of individual identities.

Caregiver. Caregivers try to make the world a better place. Often, they will even sacrifice their own good for the sake of others. Caregivers are those ordinary individuals who aid or empower others through their genuine selflessness, care, and generosity. At the lowest levels, Caregivers can be manipulative or guilt-tripping; but at the highest levels, the act of giving is its own reward.

Warrior. The standard Warrior plot has three characters: the Hero (Warrior), the Villain, and the Victim to be rescued. It is a story about having the courage, will, and discipline to confront the enemy, within and without. Warriors are competitive, and they have high standards. Warriors are stoic and value toughness and team spirit in themselves and others. Their worst fear is being weak or cowardly.

Magician. The Magician creates what has never been before by opening us up to inspiration and then by manifesting new ideas into concrete reality. The Magician may be an inventor, an artist, or anyone who comes up with a new way of doing things, and then makes it happen. Like the ancient alchemists, Magicians strive to transform lesser realities into better realities (symbolized by changing lead to gold).

Ruler. The Ruler establishes and maintains order by taking diverse, seemingly chaotic, elements and making them into a harmonious whole. At worst, the Ruler can be a despot who creates order by subjugation, fear, or exclusion of less desirable elements. At best, the Ruler has the creativity to find the use for all, or almost all, elements in the kingdom. In our own individual lives, it is the Ruler within us who understands that we are responsible for both our internal and external realities.

Lover. If the Warrior, the Caregiver, and the Magician try to change reality, the Lover simply accepts and appreciates it. Lovers choose their work because they fall in love with it. At a lower level, the Lover may love only a few people or things; at a higher level, the Lover may love everything that exists. In the workplace, the Lover is associated with passion for work, for appreciation of self and others.

Sage. The Sage's journey requires the ability to let go, to rid the self of attachment to people, things, ideas. At the lowest level, the Sage has little ability to empathize with ordinary people (loves humanity but hates people). At the highest level, the Sage loves, but without ego attachment. In the workplace, the Sage may take on an explicit teaching function, may act as an elder statesperson or general advisor, or may choose to retreat to some variety of "ivory tower" for contemplation.

*   *   *   *   *

Now turn to Chapter 3 for detailed descriptions of each of these Core Types, including information about:

- primary issues for each Core Type
- its gifts for and difficulties within the workplace
- how to recognize that Core Type in yourself and others
- tips for improving working relationships, including handling conflict and power issues
- major stressors for that Core Type, and the ways it tends to respond
- faces of this Core Type with whom you may already be familiar

3

The Ten Core Types in the Workplace

Each of the Core Types is an internal advisor who can help you with challenges that arise in your life and work. Now that you've completed the Core Type Profile, you have an idea of your preferred types. You may wish to turn first to the descriptions of these. Or, you may prefer to read this chapter straight through in order to learn all about each of the types. Remember that the Core Types are fluid; your profile will change over time, as you do.

This chapter can also be used as a reference. Keep it at hand, so you can more quickly figure out how to approach difficult work situations, better understand someone who is very different from you, or deal more effectively with conflict among colleagues.

THE INNOCENT

As the early-morning flight took off, I watched the Norfolk, Virginia airport become smaller and smaller behind me. I was still trying to shake off the morning "blahs" which matched what was promising to be a misty grey day. The trip had been productive but exhausting. I settled more deeply into my seat and closed my eyes, hoping to rest a bit more before landing miles away into the next segment of a busy day.

My eyelids were suddenly blasted by raw white light as the plane changed course to fly north — just when the sun was breaking into the day beneath the plane's east wing. The sunrise was nothing short of spectacular. Gold and rose shafts of light streaked through cliffs of white and grey cloud banks. Sunlight poured into the ocean and lit up the rolling green hills. I was riveted by the stunning beauty of this glorious new day.

At that moment I was sure that I had never seen such a beautiful sunrise. I felt as if I were rising with the plane to touch heaven! My mood had shifted dramatically in only an instant. Not only was I awake now — I was thrilled to be alive. I remember thinking: "The world is so very beautiful. What a gift, to be living at a time when humans can fly into the day. My life is great! There is no place I would rather be."

The Innocent is acting as your internal advisor whenever you feel: "This is perfect. There is no place I would rather be." The Innocent Core Type offers the gifts of *hope* and *optimism*. It helps you not only to *notice beauty*, but also to *see the silver lining* in difficulties, often helping to *reframe problems* so you can solve them. Other gifts of the Innocent include *trust* and *faith*. These are generally placed in a higher authority (e.g., a good employer, God, the nation, or explicit rules) that provides a strong structure and boundaries. The Innocent's faith and trust, in turn, lead to a sense of *stability* and *contentment* — even *joy* — that others find enviable.

The Innocent's power comes from its ability to *hope*. It takes courage to retain your enthusiasm, idealism, or a *pleasant, cheerful demeanor* when discouraged. It takes guts to hold on to faith when staring into the face of your own doubts or others' cynicism. The Innocent Core Type supplies us with the heroism we need to engage in life despite its many obstacles and disappointments. After we've been scarred a few times by close encounters with the business world's nastier members, it can become almost impossible to *see humanity's better side*. Sometimes, in fact, it takes an act of will by the Innocent inside us to remember the possibility of paradise. During such bleak times, the Innocent contributes mightily to our personal wisdom.

The Innocent's Story

> The bird sings of the dawn when the night is still dark.
> — TAGORE

A great many legends, fables, and epic stories begin with the hero or heroine as an Innocent, living in a perfect (and perfectly stable) world. This idyllic world provides a logical foundation for the Innocent's sunny worldview.

The Innocent Core Type believes that "God's in his heaven and all's right with the world." In the workplace too, the Innocent often views supervisors as benevolent authorities who keep the best interest of their employees in mind. The Innocent feels protected from outside harm. Nothing can go wrong; everything is being taken care of. Interestingly, that belief is often self-fulfilling, because the Innocent draws to it the protection of others. (Indeed, biologists have discovered that the reason the infants of all species are "cute" is so they will not be abandoned. Innocence, then, has proven itself across all species to be a very successful survival strategy.)

In the workplace, varieties of the Innocent's story play out daily. Often brand-new employees (or employees given an exciting new assignment) display traits of the Innocent: a lively interest in the details of their new job, a fresh perspective, a spring in the step, a willingness to ask "naive" questions. Sometimes we see our Innocent surface in the trust we place in a superior or the workplace itself. For example, "My boss will protect me from those creeps in that other department," or "We will never have a layoff here."

Recognizing the Innocent in Yourself and Others

- *Eyes*: Wide open, bright, reflecting a transparent wonder; an honest, unashamed direct gaze.
- *Face*: Uplifted; expressions reflect whatever the feeling is at that moment; what you see is what you get — an open book; guileless.
- *Body*: Unguarded, not sophisticated; unthinking in motions, considerable energy.
- *Walk*: Bounces (like a puppy); skips; free movement.

- *Talk*: Happy, a higher or lighter voice than normal for age, naive, isn't aware of effect on others; feels free to ask questions; doesn't necessarily notice others or their needs.
- *Dress*: Immature, youngish, or old fashioned (e.g., flowery dresses or shapeless shifts for women, bow-ties for men), or unwittingly sexy outfits.

Contributions to and Difficulties within the Workplace

Each Core Type's contributions to and difficulties within the workplace form two sides of the same coin. Both spring, respectively, from its *goals* (what it wants from the workplace) and its *fears* (or challenges, the lessons that Core Type needs to learn). Clearly, the primary goal of the Innocent is to remain safe and protected in its ideal environment. Its worst fears are that change or the unknown will intrude into this perfect state. In general, the Innocent in us willingly does what is expected in the workplace. Its major challenge is to think for itself.

From the Innocent's vantage point, it is logical to assume that any change means things are going to get worse. In the workplace, then, the goal of Innocents is to keep things the same. This part of us wants security, stability, strong guidance, appreciation for being as "good" as we truly are, and reassurance that everything is going to be OK. The Innocent in us relies absolutely on the authorities in whom we have placed our faith. If this trusted person or institution is somehow taken from us, or if it abandons or betrays us, we experience a severe trauma.

The Innocent in each of us appreciates guidance and will usually cheerfully do whatever a trusted authority says to do. It is unlikely to "rock the boat." The Innocent pretty much accepts things as they are. This is not the aspect of us that will demand higher wages or better working conditions. Unless expressing its thoughts on a utopian state, the Innocent will not be among the change agents in the organization. Indeed, by and large, this Core Type will need significant support in making any necessary changes.

The Innocent's contributions to the workplace include: a trust in the organization, its leaders, and co-workers; a willingness to follow; an unquestioning acceptance of authority. Its enthusiasm, optimism, and positive energy can be contagious, "infecting" others, so that the best (rather than the worst) happens. By looking at the organization, colleagues, or projects with a fresh, unjaded eye, the Innocent can often see potentialities that others miss. It sometimes notices value, beauty, skill, and talents that are overlooked by others, and is often quick to praise these same traits. On the other hand, the Innocent tends to NOT notice problems. With a self-absorption that is typical of youth, this Core Type actually may not even see that others are in pain or need help.

Innocents can have a rough time in the "jungle" of corporate life. Once, as I was describing the Innocent Core Type to an executive group in a manufacturing firm, one person blurted out, to peals of laughter from his colleagues: "Oh, that. We beat that out of people within their first 24 hours here!" If the workplace environment is, in reality, very bad for the Innocent, we may deny what's really going on, thereby avoiding any confrontation that could change the system for the better. Interestingly, the Innocent tends either to fear change *or*, because of its naiveté, to be fearless at times when fear may be quite justified.

The Innocent may be overly dependent upon others to do its thinking and decision-making, preferring to remain childlike and not take responsibility. This part of us easily accept limits and constraints that would make others chafe, and often acquiesces to authority without having us think for ourselves. The Innocent can be very conventional in the way it behaves *or*, conversely, so starry-eyed that it is summarily dismissed. Because of the Innocent's tendency toward denial, we can unknowingly enable the addictive or truly bad behavior of colleagues, employees, or bosses, for whom we tend to make excuses. In addition, the Innocent part of ourselves can be so naively out of touch with reality that we make devastating business miscalculations.

Working with the Innocent in Others

- Remember that their key workplace issue is security; above all, make them feel safe.

- Avoid surprises and unnecessary changes, or cushion these as best you can.
- Be clear what you expect from them.
- If they are in denial, gently help them understand and face hard realities.
- Involve them in solving their own problems until they become more adept at doing so.
- Don't treat them as if they were stupid; don't make fun of them.
- Let them know you're there if they need help.
- Encourage them to ask questions; make it safe for them to do so.
- Use their fresh perspective, their beginner's mind, to see matters anew.
- Be aware that they may "truth-tell" and unwittingly break unwritten rules from a place of innocence (like the child who announced that "the emperor has no clothes").

When in conflict with Innocents: Assure them that, even though you disagree about a specific issue, you will not abandon them. Engage them in the process of seeking mutual solutions; sometimes they can find the silver lining that others overlook. Explain that problems will not go away if ignored, that this usually causes bigger problems later on. Help them learn that conflict is a natural stage in the evolution of a relationship, just one of the steps on the way to a deeper security.

Power and empowerment: The Innocent believes that power is what your bosses have to protect you and your job, to keep you and your organization safe. Many Innocents prefer to be taken care of by others. Consequently, they do NOT want to be empowered, as that would increase their responsibility. More mature Innocents are eager to venture out on their own. They sometimes empower themselves (and at other times get in over their heads) by rushing in where angels fear to tread.

If your boss is an Innocent: Innocent leaders tend to either be conservative, doing only the tried and true, OR they follow a utopian vision.

In the former case, check in regularly so s/he understands what you're doing and why. This is especially true if you're making changes. If your boss is a utopian, make certain that the vision you both are moving towards is well grounded rather than naive. Most Innocent bosses appreciate regular updates and explanations about what you're doing and why.

Innocents You May Have Met in the Workplace

All the Core Types discussed in this book have more mature forms and less mature forms. These range from the unpleasant and unwise to the very noble and wise. Because we are always learning, sometimes we respond with maturity and grace to our workplace challenges, and at other times we completely lose it.

For the Innocent, *security* is the key workplace issue. What this means is that the Innocent part of ourselves becomes significantly stressed when its security is threatened in any way. It is most vulnerable when the boss is transferred, or rumors circulate about a pending strike or lay-off. The Innocent's strategies for reacting to stressful conditions range from a low of denial and escapism ("This is *not* happening. I'm going to think about something else.") to an enlightened optimism ("No matter what happens here, I'll still be OK. Things have always worked out for me after the dust settled.").

All the Core Types have a variety of strategies for dealing with the challenges and stresses of life and work. These different strategies result in many forms of each Core Type, like prisms of a crystal. The Aspects of the Innocent listed below all have the same goal of maintaining the Innocent's sense of security.

A less well-developed Innocent can choose *not* to engage in a difficult or unpleasant task by denying — and thereby escaping — reality. "The world is as I pretend it to be," says the **Escapist**, not as the facts indicate. This strategy ranges from turning on the tube (and off my mind) after a hard day at work to drinking excessively every night because I hate my job and want to forget it. Another form of escapism is when we turn away from the suffering of others. In the workplace, we do frequently participate in the denial of pain, both ours and that of others. We turn a deaf ear to real complaints. We ignore our own stress levels. In such ways, we disempower ourselves and truncate the possibility of long-term solutions.

In the workplace we are often situationally **Naif** (naive because we have a new job, new duties, a new project). The Naif who is willing to learn is a charming student. However, showing one's lack of knowledge can constitute a heroic action in many organizations. (Numerous executive clients have confessed to me and my colleagues that they feel they have to know everything in order to justify their position and salaries.) However, if we are to model learning in our organizations, we all must become more comfortable with a deliberate strategy of Innocence, which is sometimes called *Beginner's Mind*. Consciously turning oneself into such a **Beginner**, a newbee, is one of the most highly adaptive learning strategies imaginable, a heroic form of Innocence in which we see the world, or a specific aspect of it, as if for the first time. It is a form of vigilance that guards against malaise, apathy, and indifference. Beginner's Mind also sets the stage for innovation, constant learning, fresh insights, and the joy of good work experiences. This form of Innocence is helpful in building learning organizations in which fearless questioning is rewarded.

Often the **Start-up Entrepreneur** is blessed with a shroud of ignorance that serves as a merciful protection. I frequently hear successful entrepreneurs say, "If I had known how difficult this was going to be, I probably never would have tried it." This was true of the startup of the Central Minnesota Group Health Plan, where I served as CEO. Had we really understood what we were up against — the aligned power of the then-hostile doctors and hospital, the ratio of our money to theirs, the slowness of the community at that time to this innovation — we would have soberly assessed the obstacles, then decided that this HMO would never fly. We didn't, and it did.

Sometimes, then, the impossible dream is not only attempted, but also is accomplished in Innocence. As futurist Joel Barker says of his (often Innocent, sometimes successful) paradigm pioneers: "Those who say it can't be done should get out of the way of those who are doing it!"[1] Clearly this strategy is not always successful, and the business world is littered with the corporate failures of Innocents who slammed into brick walls they didn't even know existed. (Then, again, if we pick ourselves up, this becomes just one stage in a larger learning process.) Those Innocents who manage to survive seem to agree with the old adage, "What doesn't kill us, makes us strong."

Under prolonged circumstances, the Naif can become either the Eternal Child or the Dupe. The **Puer Eternis** is a charmingly childish adult (like Peter Pan) who refuses to grow up. This form of Innocent often attracts Caregivers who cater to our needs, cover for us, or even do some of our work. This enables the Puer Eternis to climb the corporate ladder based on, for example, youthful charm, infectious enthusiasm, and good looks (remember the tried-and-true multi-species survival strategy of "cuteness").

The **Dupe**, on the other hand, is usually not so lucky. This kind of Innocent seems to be begging for others to take advantage of it. The Dupe tends to not have a long life span in the workplace. Clearly, people are not going to find it endearing if it's their money you've just lost, nor is your employment likely to extend much past such an error.

Another aspect of the Innocent is the **Conformist**, who tends to be rewarded by traditional business. The Conformist makes us steady employees who do exactly as we are told, conforming willingly to the rules of the institution. The **Traditionalist** often acts as guardian of the old ways, for example, the enforcer of the rules. "Doing things this way has always worked for us," these two will agree. Indeed, the Conformist and Traditionalist contribute significantly to making the ideal of stability a reality. However, these Innocent parts of ourselves may block necessary organizational changes in order to keep things just the way they are.

The **Pollyanna** arrives at work smiling like sunshine, greeting everyone with a melodious, "Good Morning!," which sounds a lot like "Zip-a-dee-doo-dah. Zip-a-dee-aye. My, oh my, what a wonderful day!" This form of Innocent can infuse energy and a fresh way of seeing things into stagnant or dying environments. Whereas many forms of Innocent react poorly to change, the Pollyanna embraces it and can bring about necessary change by putting others in touch with their own optimism and hope. However, to those who have lost touch with their own inner Innocent, the Pollyanna's relentless cheerfulness can be downright aggravating.

The all-too-common negative backlash to the Innocent Core Type is something that must be addressed particularly by trainers, consultants, or others who move quickly into and out of other people's work environment. It is an irresponsible action to "spread sunshine and light," that is, to blithely offer hope where little is to be had. Sometimes an intervention that raises people's expectations as a preamble to having them dashed again is in truth a careless activity that leaves only increased hopelessness in its wake.

The **Idealist**, **Utopian**, and **Visionary** parts of ourselves put forth our ideas of what a perfect world looks like, our dreams of

---

PERSONAL AND PROFESSIONAL ASSESSMENT

Your Core Type Profile Score for Innocent: _____

Aspects of the Innocent with which you identify:

_____

Aspects of the Innocent with which you do not identify:

_____

Situations that bring out the Innocent in you (and which form of Innocent?):

_____

_____

_____

Work colleagues (or friends or family members) in whom you see the Innocent:

Person   *Form of Innocent*

_____   _____

_____   _____

_____   _____

paradise, and sometimes even present reasonable plans about how to get from here to there. These categories of Innocent are more or less mature, depending on how "grounded" we are, how tempered by real-life experience. This makes our ideas worth investigating, perhaps even worth gambling the present comfortable situation on the future paradise we so clearly envision.

The seasoned Innocent comes in many forms, the most noble of which is the **Realist-Saint**. This is a very mature form of Innocent who has encountered life's difficulties, and through force of spirit, managed to re-create paradise in our day-to-day life and work. An example of this kind of Innocent would be the highly ethical CEO who insists on working by a strong code of principles, even though he knows the competition is not. "Truth," he insists, "will win out. Time is on my side. People will eventually figure things out." More jaded onlookers may consider this an overly optimistic strategy, perhaps even a grave miscalculation that seriously jeopardizes the welfare of the organization.

This highest form of our internal Innocent has been *informed* by its experience with the other Core Types, yet has consciously chosen the Innocent's worldview, because it has discovered a startling truth: *the world is already perfect, just as it is.* We just have to see the hidden reality of what lies right below the surface of what we call "reality." This profound understanding makes all the gifts of the Innocent effortless. Hope, optimism, trust, faith, and contentment are the most logical — indeed, the only possible — attitudes in a world that has been tested and found to be good at its core.

The Innocent's joy and enthusiasm are surprisingly powerful attitudes; they can melt cynicism in their wake and act as magnets that attract good fortune. This is little wonder; the word *enthusiasm* comes from the Greek *enthousiazein*, which means "having God inside, being inspired or possessed by God." The power of the Innocent Core Type, therefore, comes from its insistence upon seeing the good that *does* exist around us, inside us, and in our organizations. The Innocent's force of believing in that good (despite the skepticism of more sophisticated others) manages to make the "perfect" world it lives in a bit more real for everyone else.

THE ORPHAN

Nathan is a third-year analyst at a Wall Street brokerage house. For the first time in his 25 years, he finds himself with people to supervise. He notices not only that the first-year employees take his direction easily, but also that they bring him their questions without fear of embarrassment or repudiation. The contrast with his own first-year experience is significant.

Nathan was a Harvard graduate with a degree in government, keenly interested in, but relatively unschooled in finance. He was hired as a "poet" (a Wall Street term for non-finance types who are thrown into the hiring mix as a deliberate strategy to broaden the makeup of the organization). Nathan was initially assigned to a work group that, as it turned out, had serious internal problems. Although he regularly worked 90-hour weeks, his supervisors were less than supportive. Not only did they not coach him as part of his first-year learning process, they blamed many of the group's errors on him. (Only later did Nathan learn what was obvious to others in the firm — that the group's failings were due to the limited experience of the superiors in the group.)

On and off during this first difficult year, Nathan wrestled with resigning. Maybe finance wasn't right for him. Maybe this firm wasn't right for him. Maybe he didn't have the right stuff. Certainly that was the feedback he had been given. He decided to apply for a transfer to another work group within the same company. As it turned out, he was granted this transfer just as his own group was disbanded due to poor performance.

The next months were busy, but so successful that he was asked to stay on past his initial commitment with his new group. And, as his own star rose, he did not forget how miserable he had been during those early days. So now whenever Nathan has the opportunity, he makes a point of letting newcomers know that their questions are not stupid. "There's no reason," he says, "for them to suffer the way I did."

The Orphan is the part of you that has been victimized, taken advantage of, mistreated, yet has survived to see another day. This Core Type has been hurt by, yet is adept at making its own way in, the real world. People sometimes ask me why I consider the Orphan a "heroic" archetype. My answer: there is no part of ourselves that is more heroic! What takes more courage than to admit you are *vulner-*

able, to realize and face the difficulties around you? To get out the door to work when your personal life is in shambles (or vice versa)? What act is more kind than to *acknowledge your own humanity*, to view your own or others' flaws with *compassion*, to *forgive* yourself or others for mistakes? The Orphan is critical to Self-mastery because it helps us develop the *empathy* that is a cornerstone of emotional intelligence.

The Orphan shares with the Innocent the key workplace issue of *security*. It wants the same safe world and trustworthy authority figures that the Innocent aspect of ourselves thinks it already has. Our inner Orphan emerges whenever we feel betrayed, abandoned, powerless, or thrown into dangerous situations where we have to fend for ourselves. Consequently, this part of our psyche is very *vigilant*, warning us, as part of our survival strategy, about whom we can and cannot trust. It has learned how to prepare us to expect the worst.

The Orphan helps us *see real problems*. It reminds us of our *fallibility* and of *our dependence on and interdependence with others* (who will sometimes let us down). It turns our eyes away from the silver lining so that we can focus on the dark clouds themselves. It urges us to remove our rose-colored glasses so that we can develop the *discernment* we need for survival.

The Orphan is the part of ourselves that is willing to *voice our fears*. The Orphan whispers into our inner ear that something is wrong here: Danger! And it is often right. Indeed, to ignore the Orphan's voice is to court tragedy. Whereas the Innocent sings, "My, Grandma, what big teeth you have!," the Orphan counters in a loud voice: "Big teeth? Hey, that's not Grandma. I'm outta here!"

The Orphan's Story

The heart that breaks open can contain the whole universe.
— JOANNA MACY

In a great many legends and myths, the same child who started out as an Innocent in Act I becomes an Orphan in Act II. These children are left behind by good parents who die or are somehow taken from them. The Orphans now need to find their own way in a frightening, hostile world.

We all know this vulnerable place. We have lost paradise. We do not know where we are now, nor can we find the way back. We must move on; somehow we must find our way by ourselves. The world, once so sunny and full of promise, has suddenly become a very dangerous place. *In the Orphan's world, only villains and victims exist.* This worldview, although painful, is the Orphan's reality. It is also key to the Orphan's resilience and extraordinary ability to survive against great odds.

Today's workplaces are calling up the Orphan Core Type in a great many of us. Mergers, takeovers, buyouts, and bad management practices all can create an "us versus them" environment that justifies the Orphan's bleak worldview. These corporate versions of war zones spawn Orphans (usually in its lower forms) where other forms of heroism once existed. The international success of Dilbert cartoons, the eruption of workplace violence, and lack of employee trust of management are all manifestations of the felt powerlessness of this aspect of ourselves. The Orphan keeps an emotional distance, and is skeptical of management promises. It gives only partially of itself, because it is unwilling to commit to a workplace that does not commit in turn. We also see the mature Orphan come forth in these difficult workplace situations to help others who are similarly wounded — as tough but fair leaders, union organizers, or empathetic colleagues — anyone who tries to make things better for "the little people." In this way, the Orphan helps us evolve to become *wounded healers*. When we know how to survive, we can turn our attention to helping others do the same.

When the Orphan believes there is no hope, this part of us may give up entirely — abandon and betray itself before anyone else has the chance to do so (a self-destructive form of first strike). Or, the Orphan can decide that if the choice is between being a villain or victim, a villain sounds much better, thank you very much. Ironically, we then create the very world we wish to escape. The Orphan often has had (or feels it has had) more than its share of life's problems. (Its theme song could be "Nobody Knows the Trouble I've

Seen".) The Orphan is prone to *cynicism*, which it insists is actually *realism*. This Core Type characterizes other worldviews as pathetic (and dangerous) self-delusion.

Recognizing the Orphan in Yourself and Others

- *Eyes*: Down and hurt, *or* averted and masked. In either case alert, watching others for safety. Sometimes Orphans make compassionate connections with others, indicating they understand.
- *Face*: Down and hurt, or sensitive, *or* masked/defended.
- *Body*: Vulnerable looking and tired from having endured so much for so long, *or* defensive/offensive as a survival strategy. Sometimes depressed: shoulders collapsed, given up.
- *Walk*: Alert, checking for safety. Aware of surroundings. Either a victim walk *or* a false toughness/ bravado.
- *Talk*: Focused on real or perceived problems. Compassionate comments, sensitively connecting *or* complain/blame. The latter often also includes side comments or gestures, whining, accusatory "you" statements, and passive-aggressive interactions, including gossip.
- *Clothing*: Is used as a shield, which says "I'm tough, don't mess with me," *or* is used as a cloak (that is, for safety purposes, dress within cultural norm, take care to not stand out in any way).

Contributions to and Difficulties within the Workplace

The goal of the Orphan is to be rescued, to find its way to safety, to home, to the paradise it lost or to another paradise that is just as good. The key workplace issue for the Orphan, like the Innocent, is *security*. Part of the Orphan's challenge is to use discernment to sort out those people and institutions in which trust and hope is well placed, and then to risk these feelings. Clearly, the work situations this Core Type would find most stressful are those in which it is taken advantage of or otherwise harmed by someone it trusts. Orphans are often motivated in the workplace by guarantees of corporate survival; depending on the culture, this could be title, salary, union membership, tenure, or other protections from the vagaries of an assumed hostile management.

One of the most interesting qualities of the Orphan part of us is that it can become a bottleneck Core Type in which we get stuck in our personal and professional life journeys. If we do not learn its lessons, we are then capable only of play-acting the other archetypes. For example, we may pretend to be whatever Core Type our workplace culture prefers, but if our key workplace issue is still the security that we find so elusive, we really are Orphans who have put on another Core Type's garb as a way to buy that security. For example, if Warriors are prized in our organization, we may act tough on the outside, but inside we do not feel the Warrior's focus, discipline, or secure boundaries. We are not eager to launch into action. Instead we rattle our sabers, bully others because we fear becoming victims, and hide our vulnerability behind a psychic suit of armor. The Orphan, who believes the world to be unsafe and is so good at survival, can easily put on the robes of any other type that it sees as being more acceptable. But inside the veneer of this other Core Type, the Orphan is stuck, hiding out, unable to learn its lessons and contribute its gifts, much like the little man who pretended to be the Wizard of Oz.

This is a shame, because the Orphan in each of us has a great many gifts for our workplaces. It knows how to name real fears, constraints, and limits. The Orphan complains when necessary, often when others are unwilling to. In this way, it serves the role of the canary taken into coal mines to warn of inadequate oxygen or deadly gases. (The not-subtle signal was its own demise.) The Orphan recognizes the downside of issues. It names or anticipates problems, often acting as "the squeaky wheel" — an unpleasant and usually thankless task as witness the "No whining" signs plastered all over corporate walls. Granted, whining *is* very annoying. So is a siren, an infant's piercing cry, or other alarms, all of which do serve a survival purpose. Viewed this way by attentive leaders, an Orphan's whining can be a gift similar to that of the canary in the mine.

Perhaps this Core Type's most important workplace gift is its compassion for human frailties and vulnerabilities. In most workplaces, we play high-stakes games of blaming others before we ourselves are blamed. The Orphan in each of us needs to redirect its energy into fixing the problem rather than fixing the blame. The Orphan can also help us remember our prior difficulties and retain the common touch as we rise from the rank-and-file to positions of power (so that we can redress the situations about which we previously could only complain).

The Orphan has many significant difficulties in the workplace, all of which tend to erupt during times of high stress. These include a tendency towards complaining, then self-pity if its complaints go unheeded. The Orphan can also develop an "attitude" (i.e., a bad attitude) over time as a protective device, while it becomes increasingly callous to work, colleagues, and clients. If our Orphan feels very unsafe, we will not complain publicly but instead will avoid discussing difficult issues or dealing with difficult people entirely. Moreover, we may resort to blaming as a defensive strategy. The Orphan's rationale: in a world of villains and victims, it is better him (who gets fired) than me. An "us versus them" mentality sets in — labor versus management, finance versus operations, one racial group versus another.

Over time Orphans can fall prey to cynicism and/or despair. "There is no hope," we conclude. No reason to try. We feel powerless and can become extremely apathetic. Then, even if a wonderful new management team replaces the old awful one, we remain in a rut of distrust and fear: "Let them prove themselves trustworthy. I bet they're no better than the last crew. I'll just bide my time until they give me a good reason to believe otherwise." This attitude becomes a handicap for Orphans if hope is actually warranted by the changed situation. Soon this Core Type is seen to be dead weight by the new leaders, and the Orphan's fears and mistrust become self-fulfilling.

When Working with the Orphan in Others

- Remember that their key workplace issue is security.
- Be caring and reassuring; move slowly; building trust takes time.
- Let them know what you're doing and why.

- Let them know you've heard what they said; paraphrase discussions for clarity.
- They may excuse not following the rules ("Everyone does it"), so make limits and rules clear, and enforce them evenly so as to be fair to all and not create new Orphans.
- Be specific about how their cooperation is in their own best interest.
- Be aware that they are unlikely to trust you (don't expect them to be open).
- Stay alert; because they have so little trust, they can turn on you.
- Encourage collaboration to help them learn interdependence and responsibility.
- Refer them to employee assistance if you suspect personal problems.
- Once you have gained their trust, under NO circumstances betray it.

When in conflict with Orphans: Show that you have heard the concerns they voice; involve them in forging alliances that can solve common problems. Be caring and reassuring. Be honest about areas of disagreement; show where you can build bridges. Be firm about what you will and won't do. Be on the alert for gossip. Build a fence of truth around Orphans while working through the conflict, so as to minimize the spread of alienating rumors. Make certain that communication elsewhere is clear, because Orphans may, in desperation, try to justify their own worldview and behavior.

Power and empowerment: In a world with only victims and victimizers, power is in short supply. Power is what you have over others (or conversely what they have over you). For many Orphans, all this talk about empowerment is a scam. The bosses are just trying to get you to do their work! With more mature Orphans, empowerment is sharing power with others who are similarly disadvantaged.

If your boss is an Orphan: He or she may be able to define problems clearly and see them coming before others do. If significantly stressed or immature, your boss may be cynical, and more concerned with personal gain than the organization's good. This often manifests as turf battles with other departments. Don't try to cheerlead this boss into a rosier worldview. The more mature Orphan leader is often "of the people," someone who has a healing influence in the organization because everyone's best interests are kept in mind, and subordinates are dealt with fairly and compassionately.

Orphans You May Have Met in the Workplace

All of these forms of the Orphan are more or less mature reactions to this Core Type's key workplace issue: *security*. Two primary aspects of the Orphan are the **Victim** and the **Victimizer** (or **Villain**). Both of these come in many forms. The Victim, for instance, could be a bereaved person, lost soul, a constant complainer, or a Survivor. The Villain also comes in many forms: the abuser, paranoid person, or cynic.

Although the Villain and Victim appear to be polar opposites forms of the Orphan, in truth, these are often combined in the same person. In the workplace we experience this frequently as the **Bully**, who is often a yes-man to the boss (who has power over us), but verbally abusive to its subordinates (over whom we have power). Whether on the playground or in the boardroom, fear of those with power over you and a desire for power over others (which it thinks is necessary for survival) are the motivators for the Bully. One reason we have so many bullies in the workplace is that this form of Orphan can easily hide within the structure of our hierarchical systems. Our complex systems often hide other **Abusers**, who psychologists tell us, were usually abused in similar ways themselves. This pattern spills out from dysfunctional family systems to dysfunctional workplace systems, where abuse comes in the form of tongue-lashing, capricious policies, cutting remarks that erode others' ability to do good work. The relatively new practice of 360-degree leadership evaluations often pulls the cover off anyone who relies on silence to keep such secrets safe.

All of us reconnect with our inner Orphan when we experience loss. This can range from having a really bad day, to our computer's crashing, to the resignation of a colleague, to the literal loss of a job or loved one. We are in these cases, at least temporarily, the **Bereaved person.** Unfortunately, very few modern institutions help us cope with our minor or major losses. It is not acceptable for us to scream at the computer or throw it out the window. It would be considered inappropriate for us to cry at our colleague's going-away party. Nor are we given sufficient personal leave to recover from serious life losses. Instead, we tend to carry our unfinished grief as an extra burden inside our own bodies.

The **Lost Soul** is a variation of Orphan who considers itself a victim of Life, and often gets stuck in this spot. In fact, this perspective is a self-reinforcing loop that can turn into a way of life. It can even become a career for artists, musicians, poets, moviemakers, and writers who make a living illustrating the dark side of life. We

---

PERSONAL AND PROFESSIONAL ASSESSMENT

Your Core Type Profile Score for Orphan: _____

Aspects of the Orphan with which you identify:

_____

Aspects of the Orphan with which you do not identify:

_____

Situations that bring out the Orphan in you (and which form of Orphan?):

_____

_____

_____

Work colleagues (or friends or family members) in whom you see the Orphan:

Person   *Form of Orphan*

_____   _____

_____   _____

_____   _____

small home on the eastern shore, where she has envisioned herself far from the bustling crowd, with a thriving counseling and bodywork practice.

The Seeker is the internal advisor who emerges in your life and work when you need to move on, to explore, to set out on a new path (these travels can be external or internal). The Seeker's journey is about *identity* and — as one important aspect of identity — *finding your vocation or mission*, whatever work you're best suited to do. The goal of the Seeker in each of us is to help us to find our own truth, to determine how we are unique, the ways we are different from the rest of our community. If we are too different, the Seeker urges us to find a community that fits us better.

The Seeker helps you by getting you to *leave unhealthy situations*. For example, in Margaret's case, it's not that her workplace was unhealthy, it's just that she had stayed there too long. The Seeker also helps each of us *clarify who we are*, and it helps us *redefine who we are as we change and grow*. By making us leave places that offer our Innocent and Orphan the security we crave, the Seeker helps us gain Self-mastery by becoming *more independent, autonomous, capable, and competent*. It is the Seeker in us who demands that we discover and employ our special skills, our unique talents. The Seeker pushes us to develop our competencies, learn a trade, study for an advanced degree, invent a tool, open a brand new market, or write the novel that's been burning inside us. It is the Seeker who *challenges us to be all we can be*, to stretch, *to answer the call to the Quest, to ask hard questions* at work and of life itself, and to not give up until we have the answers that quench our thirst.

THE SEEKER

The Seeker's Story

Thirst was made for water; inquiry for truth.

— C.S. LEWIS

The Seeker's story usually begins with a feeling of entrapment or restlessness, and then an escape (from a bad job, a difficult relationship, an old paradigm, an outdated way of living). The Seeker then takes a solitary journey to find whatever it is we are looking for. This inner restlessness often translates to outer turmoil, to turning our own — and sometimes others' — lives upside down. The Seeker may urge us to leave our jobs, careers, homes, communities, spouses, or families when we enter this phase. Or, we may decide to not travel physically but rather internally (to seek knowledge, for example). The worst possible choice for the Seeker is to stay wherever we feel alienated — an outsider trapped within a job or a life that no longer fits. (The danger here is very real: i.e., the Seeker may unconsciously sabotage our work efforts or make us ill as a way out of our entrapment.)

If Seekers travel to new places, we may do so joyfully *or* with angst, dwelling on our isolation from others. The errant knights of the Round Table, yogis searching for a spiritual master, struggling actors determined to become stars, and the cowboys of the American wild west are all colorful examples of Seekers. Such adventurers tend to travel light (usually alone) and on a path they carve out for themselves. For example, when the legendary knights of the Round Table set off in search for the Holy Grail, they decided "it would be a disgrace to go forth in a group." Therefore each knight "entered the forest at a point that he, himself, had chosen, where it was darkest and there was no path."[2]

Because Seekers constantly move on until we find that ideal we're looking for, we tend to spend much of our time en route. Hence, we avoid commitments or entanglements that would slow us down or put an end to our seeking. Eventually, this Core Type learns how to be true to itself while living in a community of its choice, one that "fits" well, for example, a workplace that uses our special talents. Interestingly, it may wind up being our old community or workplace, which because of our journeying we now see with new eyes. T.S. Eliot described the Seeker's journey in the poem, "Four Quartets":

> We shall not cease from exploration
> And the end of all our exploring
> Will be to arrive where we started
> And know the place for the first time.

Recognizing the Seeker in Yourself and Others

- *Eyes*: Looking off in distance, or up toward an invisible ideal; unfocused on what is in front or present; instead focused on our own thoughts or on vision of future.
- *Face*: Looking off into distance, slightly up and away.
- *Body*: Sets self off from others; for example, sits in the back at lecture, with own belongings all around so no one else can get close.
- *Walk*: Focused on distant goal, not noticing where you are now, meandering, easily distracted. Can get lost because thinking of other things.
- *Talk*: Of ideals, meaning of life, or projects. Tends to be serious, considerable angst, no matter what the topic. An emphasis on "my" truth, ideas, what's of interest to "me." Talk not always connected to topic at hand. Future or other-place oriented.
- *Clothing*: Absent-minded professor look *or* clothing that expresses distinction from group norm, that is, clothes, haircut, accessories, cars that make a strong statement about that person's separate identity.

Contributions to and Difficulties within the Workplace

Because the Seeker in us wants to be left alone, to be allowed to solve our problems in our own way, its goals in the workplace are autonomy, independence, the ability to do meaningful work (with whatever exploration that might entail). This Core Type's major challenge is to define who we really are (so we can commit to the right work and/or people). Its worst fear is being stuck in a job, life, relationship, or town where we can't really be ourselves, where we have to "live a lie" by pretending to be, or by conforming to, something we are not.

The Seeker in us contributes to the workplace in a great many ways. It helps us examine accepted truisms or ways we are not working up to our ideals. In this way Seekers can help develop new and better products, materials, and solutions to problems. Perhaps more importantly, the Seeker helps us find meaning in our work, hold fast to our personal ideals and organizational values, and do our work in ways that are congruent with our own ethical standards. It also challenges those around us to do the same.

Many Seekers like to play "devil's advocate," challenging accepted policies and procedures, particularly those that in any way restrict our freedom or do not meet our ideals. In this way, the Seeker offers a fresh perspective and voice. Although the Seeker is very concerned with issues of meaning, truth, and integrity, these same may be narrowly defined, that is, in our own image. However, its quality of independence can push a lot of buttons because the Seeker will often speak its own truths despite peer pressure to the contrary. This Core Type is least likely to be among the smiling "yes men" of a corporation. This quality makes the Seeker one of the best possible safeguards against lapsing into the dangers of group-think.

The Seeker in each of us also has many workplace difficulties. Its truth-telling is often so serious that the valuable content of the message is lost in the gravatus or tactlessness of our delivery. Moreover, the Seeker's truth-telling can sound a bit like whining. Others accuse Seekers of not being "team players," of keeping too much to ourselves to be interested in the good of the organization. Because many managers and organizations do not really want to hear unpleasant truths, the Seeker can quickly find itself *persona non grata.* Understandably, Seekers then feel alien, not fully involved. In response, we often "check out" by emotionally distancing ourselves from the individuals or problems around us. In this way we can be absent even when present in body: "nice house, nobody home." In these circumstances, we will not risk sharing our true perceptions. Moreover, if we have determined that the job we occupy is not our "real work," we will act as uncommitted as does any drifter who is "just passing through town."

When Working with the Seeker in Others

- Give them as much freedom as possible to do things their way.
- Don't expect them to be team players.
- Don't "kill the messenger" when they bring bad news.
- Acknowledge their special contributions, their unique talents, their expertise.

- Make certain they understand your expertise and authority, or they will ignore you.
- Be aware that they will challenge rules that are not consistent or meaningful.
- Let them know you see and hear them; give (+ & -) feedback on their work.
- Challenge them to get involved, to say what they think and feel.
- Do whatever you can to give them work that expresses their full, unique selves.
- Use their perspective to avoid "group-think," to challenge existing opinions and paradigms.
- Keep a free rein AND keep in touch, so they don't go too far afield.
- Encourage them to challenge yourself and others to find meaning in your work, to uphold ideals, to work from shared values, to keep personal integrity intact.

When in conflict with Seekers: Realize that their message may be valid, or at least true for them. Acknowledge their competence and individuality. Let them know you respect their autonomy and will try to preserve it as long as they meet the requirements of the job. Use their perspective as "outsiders" to get a different view on the issues. Conflicts with Seekers may arise because they feel they cannot be "real," and therefore they're not fully at work. Talk as candidly as you can; put all the cards on the table.

Power and empowerment: The Seeker views power as the ability to discover who we truly are, then to be fully ourselves and do our own unique work. Empowerment, then, is when a supervisor trusts your competence enough to give you the resources and backing you need, then leaves you alone to get your work done in your own way.

If your boss is a Seeker: Seekers who are leaders tend to be individualistic, iconoclastic, and allow great freedom for their staff. They may also be so distracted by fascinating ideas, or so focused on their own specialized work that they are inattentive to staff issues, deadlines, or inconsistent with management policies.

Seekers You May Have Met in the Workplace

The key workplace issue for the Seeker is *autonomy*. There is nothing more stressful for the Seeker in us than not having the freedom to do the work that has meaning for us, or being forced to be in a work group where we have nothing in common with our co-workers. The Seeker can respond to workplace stresses of all types either maturely (searching for our ideal while minimizing repercussions on others, reminding others of their own ideals) or immaturely (bailing out completely and leaving others stranded, using our expertise to put down colleagues, laying our own personal angst on anyone who's around).

The Seeker comes in a great many forms. This Core Type can manifest as someone who chooses to be, or is labeled as, an **Outsider**. This can be the benign odd duck, the Ugly Duckling who is really a swan, someone with a different expertise or worldview, or someone with a different accent or skin color. When people act in ways that are not tolerated within the group norm, they then become **Outcasts** or **Misfits**. In ancient days, this was no small matter. When an individual was cast out of the safety of a community, it often resulted in a premature death. The workplace equivalent could easily spell the premature demise of a career, or a significant downturn in a person's fortune. In such cases, when we are thrust unwillingly into a life or job transition, we may opt to spend some time as an Orphan before picking ourselves up and moving on as a Seeker into the unknown territory that looms ahead. However, even in these cases, we often wind up with improved circumstances — new lives or careers that we otherwise would not have attempted.

A popular form of the self-defined Outcast or Misfit (particularly in middle age or adolescence) is the **Rebel**, with or without a cause. If co-workers suddenly appear on Monday morning with, for example, radically new haircuts, a flashy red convertible, or talking enthusiastically about a weekend meditation retreat that's changed them forever, you can reasonably assume that the Seeker has become active in their lives. You can also reasonably expect the Seeker to appear soon in their work, as the spirit of inquiry spills over into all parts of their lives.

Tumultuous world events can create the Seeker Core Type en masse: political or intellectual escapees, fugitives from oppressive governments. This drama also plays itself out in organizations, in which those Seekers who tell unsolicited truths wind up as outcasts. Indeed, the Seeker in us can claim to our spouses that "I told the truth and they set me free" as we arrive home unexpectedly midafternoon with the contents of our desks in a cardboard box. **Iconoclasts** are those Seekers who dare to shatter the cherished beliefs (the icons) of a group. The Seeker's subsequent survival after delivering such a forbidden message within a given group is determined by many factors: mutual trust, timing of the message, communication skills, the group's receptivity to unwelcome news, and the Seeker's desire to stick with the group.

Many legends and myths describe **Gypsies** and **Traveling Minstrels** as Seekers. In the workplace, there are similar travelers who wander from one job to another. In these cases, our "day job" is nowhere near the center of our lives. Many Seekers find meaning, and clues to our identity, as **Artists** (and poets, writers, and musicians). And there are a great many more artists in the workplace than those who are assigned such tasks. Many of us have one job for the body, and another for the soul.

Indeed, I have come across an extraordinary number of "ordinary" people with breathtakingly special gifts that would remain unopened unless the Seeker brought them out into the world. Such individuals are legion in the workforce — competent professionals, executives, and laborers who earn their living by day and at night or on weekends are transformed into community volunteers, Little League coaches, or jazz musicians. My financial advisor, I recently discovered, is a talented painter. Another colleague is a traditional Reiki Master who sees clients during evening hours. A goodly number of my friends use their Seeker to infuse their children with the ideals and values that will make the world a better place.

The Seeker is the internal advisor who helps us clarify our *complete* identity. By becoming all we can be, we fill what would otherwise be empty and unused parts of ourselves. It helps make us more real, and also larger, as diverse aspects of our lives influence and enrich each other. For example, I find that my writing improves if I spend time making music before I sit at the computer. It is my experience that music somehow fills my business writing with "overtones," making it more rich, less dry. The same can be said of executives I've met. The off-hours poets fill their reports with nuance, the avid readers with literary or historical references. In this way the Seeker enriches our work by cross-fertilizing it with seemingly unrelated material.

It is not uncommon for Seekers to fulfill our regular duties, then delve into other tasks at work that are outside our job description, but of particular interest to us. In this way, we sometimes develop special areas of expertise that lead to new assignments. The **Expert** is a form of Seeker who has, after many years of study and

---

PERSONAL AND PROFESSIONAL ASSESSMENT

Your Core Type Profile Score for Seeker: _____

Aspects of the Seeker with which you identify:

_____

Aspects of the Seeker with which you do not identify:

_____

Situations that bring out the Seeker in you (and which form of Seeker?):

_____

_____

_____

Work colleagues (or friends or family members) in whom you see the Seeker:

Person   *Form of Seeker*

_____   _____

_____   _____

_____   _____

experience, managed to develop a special competency that is valued by that workplace: a university professor who knows more about giraffes than just about anyone in the world, an internal consultant who teaches statistical process control to her colleagues, a manager who has studied systems thinking and coaches his peers.

Seekers can serve the workplace as **Scouts** who are adventurous enough to try new assignments or to check things out before the rest of the organization ventures forth (e.g., to benchmark with other organizations, to research new markets). Such Scouts can be **Explorers** and **Experimenters** who test and then launch new ventures. Seekers often serve the workplace as **Paradigm Pioneers** — challenging our old ways of thinking and sometimes dragging us behind them into new insights. Because the Seeker Core Type tends to travel ahead of the group, it often warns us and others of what's just around the corner. In this way it acts as a **Herald** or **Prophet** of coming things. (Clearly, the Seeker is often not thanked for the warnings it gives.)

And finally, the **Questor** is a well-developed form of Seeker who is in pursuit of the highest goal, which is symbolized in mythology as the magical Grail. Each one of us has our own version of what the Grail is — whatever makes life worth living and work worth working, whatever helps us create our ideal of heaven right here on earth. The most mature Seekers learn (as did Sissy, the world's greatest hitchhiker in *Even Cowgirls Get the Blues*) that: "Heaven and Hell are right here on earth. Hell is living your fears. Heaven is living your dreams."[3]

THE JESTER

Dave is an administrative member of AFL-CIO's Food and Commercial workers. He served previously as a union steward in the meat processing plant in which he worked. His job was to use a huge circular saw to cut off the hind quarters of cattle, then send the flank down the assembly line where others would chop it further into the pieces we find, sanitized, wrapped in plastic, under bright white lights in the meat departments of our grocery stores.

Dave's station was on a platform above his crew. After completing each task, and before starting the next, Dave would dance some silly jig, much to the entertainment of everyone. Laughter abounded. Productivity on his line was higher than anywhere else in the factory.

Enter the overly serious supervisor, who found Dave's antics inappropriate and ordered him to stop. This worked only during those moments when the supervisor had Dave fully in his sights. In retaliation for spoiling their fun, Dave and his group decided to play with the supervisor. As it was that time of year, they started singing Christmas carols. The supervisor, as they predicted, did not get into the spirit of the season. He ordered them to stop. They then, with much delight, engaged in "guerrilla" tactics. One person, on the opposite end of the line from where the supervisor then stood, would burst into whistling "Jingle Bells." As the supervisor rushed to find the culprit, another whistler would pick up the tune elsewhere. The supervisor rushed about madly, trying to trace the echoing tones to their source. This added greatly to the fun — and chaos. Finally in frustration and exhaustion, the supervisor threatened to discipline Dave as a way of punishing the lot.

The supervisor called in the factory owner in order to push his case of insubordination. The owner spent several hours walking around and talking with people. He also looked at the productivity figures. Finally he made his decision. "Let them sing and dance, for God's sake," he declared. And, because the humorless supervisor could not let the subject rest, he was fired.

There was much dancing and singing on the production line that day.

The Jester is the internal advisor who can help you *find clever, fun ways around obstacles*, be they intellectual, physical, or organizational. Your Jester shows you ways through otherwise-impossible situations. It makes you *notice irony*, *paradox*, and therefore *laugh at yourself*, others, or situations you've gotten yourself into. It *whistles while you work*, lightening you up so you don't take yourself — or anyone else — too seriously. It is a guide to *finding joy in your work* and the rest of your life.

The Jester brings us *brilliant breakthroughs*. It opens our minds to what others (or other parts of ourselves) would consider outrageous suggestions. The Jester is *highly creative*, seeing the world from unusual vantage points (think, for example, of the mind-boggling illusions of the visual artist Escher). The Jester is the part of us that is *inventive, paradigm shattering, dreams up daring new options*, and is a genius at *brainstorming*.

It is also a great Core Type to call upon for *relieving stressful situations*. Under high stress, our Jester can save our jobs, even our lives, by presenting us with alternatives to the fight or flight dilemma. To workplace options of (a) standing your ground in a fight, (b) working harder, or (c) just giving up, it may add something you've never tried before. "What the heck," says your Jester, "Lets try it. What have we got to lose?" The Jester employs laughter and humor as survival tools. It is convinced that no matter how bad things are, there's something funny about it. For example, it can bring down your blood pressure when you desperately want to throttle a colleague, but opt for imagining him in a clown's outfit instead.

I learned this lesson about the Jester's survival abilities from my Minnesota neighbor, Bill Cusack, who, as a downed American flyer in World War II, managed to survive not only a German prison camp but also a death march. Bill held me spellbound one day as he described how he and his fellow POWs kept up each other's spirits by joking despite the grimness of their plight. What he recalled from those days was not the pain, starvation, or tragedy of having to leave behind those who were too weak to take another step. He remembered how the prisoners helped each other, moment to precious moment, by laughing, quite literally, in the face of death. (And you think survival in your workplace is tough!)

Like the Seeker, the Jester's key workplace issue is *autonomy, freedom*. Both Core Types dread being "normal." The Jester differs from the Seeker, however, in that it wants that freedom not to find the meaning of life, but rather to have fun. ("What meaning?" the Jester would ask). Moreover, this desire for fun is not limited to its off-hours. This is the part of us that believes that work and play *do* mix, and that rules were meant to be broken. If it feels too confined, the Jester will find a way to act out, to stir the pot, to play jokes on others — *anything* to make life more interesting. There is nothing worse for the Jester than being confined someplace where it has to endure work or colleagues who are dull, serious, or pompous. (Look out! This situation is likely to bring out the prankster, or worse, in Jesters.) If no one will engage in play with the Jester, it will probably do the equivalent of picking up its marbles and going home; that is, it will find (or create) some other workplace where it can be its most innovative self.

The Jester's Story

> At the height of laughter the universe is flung into a
> kaleidoscope of new possibilities.
>
> — JEAN HOUSTON

In the Jester's story, he or she is a little hero who manages to defeat a much bigger opponent through cleverness. "Please, please, PLEASE don't throw me in that briar patch," the Jester manages to say with a straight face, thereby saving itself from imminent defeat.

In legendary olden days, each court had a Jester whose responsibility was dual: he was to entertain the bored nobility during dull days, AND he was called upon to use humor to tell the king any "unspeakable" truths. This was his job. Certainly no one else wanted to tell the king, for example, that his troops were deserting en masse or that the queen was having an affair with his best knight. But as soon as the Jester could verify the whispers, it would become a silly song or riddle that would be trotted out at the next opportunity. All others in the court who tried this (e.g., the more serious Seekers of the truth), would surely lose their heads while delivering the message. I imagine that Jesters kept their own heads on their own shoulders depending on their wit, daring, and probably also their quick feet.

Recognizing the Jester in Yourself and Others
- *Eyes*: Dancing, mischievous, alert; clowning.
- *Face*: Sides of mouth often up; deliberately makes rubbery faces and imitates others.

- *Body*: Flexible and disjointed, like a rag doll; can fall and get right back up, unhurt. Not graceful, but comic. Moves here, there, everywhere simultaneously. Likes to imitate others' motions, too, *or* can masquerade as cultural norm and "trick" others by pretending to fit it.
- *Walk*: Free, loose, fast; flexible, floppy; light on feet.
- *Talk*: Lilting, laughing, darts in and out; fast; focuses on idea generation, tries to engage others for play. Likes jokes, puns, pokes fun at others. Slippery — difficult to pin down. If it doesn't like the topic at hand, will just change it before others notice what's happened. Speech is often interspersed with jokes, puns, self-deprecating remarks, or other clever commentary.
- *Clothing*: Very irreverent (e.g., fish ties) or more subtle pokes at authority figures, *or* sloppy "computer geek" look, *or* flamboyant "I'm a free spirit" look. If can get away with it, will wear play clothes, such as T-shirts and shorts, to work.

Contributions and Difficulties within the Workplace

There is no doubt about it: Jesters have more fun. Workplaces that repress the Jester — as many do — are deadly dull. The Jester Core Type ranges from the brilliant inventor to the slick salesperson who counts on the adage "there's a sucker born every minute." At worst, the Jester is dangerously irresponsible — cutting corners, ignoring deadlines, playing at times when hard work is required. At best, the Jester breaks us out of our own mental bonds or accepted policies or social conventions to see these things completely anew. In either case, the Jester tends to challenge whatever we have accepted as existing order.

A major lesson for this Core Type, then, is to learn how to balance a desire for constant entertainment with a personal code of ethics and integrity. It has to learn not to use its quick wit to take advantage of others. This internal advisor needs to learn when it's *not* OK to break the rules. The Jester helps us to stay in good humor. As one of my former colleagues used to say when the rest of us had worked ourselves into a frenzy to meet a deadline, "Is any of this going to matter in a hundred years?" (The answer to his question, of course, is "No.") This realization sometimes served to loosen the knots in our necks. We would then take a short break and come back invigorated. The Jester likes to shake things up, imagine clever ways to get around obstacles; it excels at brainstorming and creativity. It has a spontaneous, carefree manner. Sometimes the Jester even turns things upside-down for us, taking us completely outside our normal frameworks and belief systems. Workplaces vary dramatically in how much they reward, or punish, the Jester's gifts.

The Jester's difficulties in the workplace include its facility with charming manipulation. It sometimes makes us irresponsible, finding it pretty much impossible to take anything all that seriously. Sometimes the Jester is so unconventional as to be disruptive, ranging from mild annoyances, like interrupting conversations with jokes or irrelevancies, to the collapse of a business because no one's minding the store. This Core Type's tendency to be easily bored means it will create chaos if given the opportunity. The less mature Jester will play with whatever it has at hand — *nothing* is sacred or off-limits. (Imagine teenagers playing with a hydrogen bomb.)

Another difficulty our Jester can have in the workplace is if we playact so much that others do not know who we really are, and therefore find it impossible to trust us. One high-level state government official I've met keeps his staff off-balance by saying one thing to one, and then giving an ever-so-slightly different message to another. He enjoys wordplay and is adept at it. Not surprisingly, he also has managed to survive several changes of administration unscathed. In highly politicized organizations, this form of Jester can help you survive. But it also can prevent you from gaining the trust of your co-workers, boss, or staff. And if these kinds of political interactions become endemic in a culture, they can erode trust to the point that the whole system gets jammed up. Clearly, one of the major challenges for the Jester Core Type is to build trust with our colleagues by coming out behind our play-masks, taking responsibility for our actions, learning when to get serious and when deadlines need to be met, so that we do not unwittingly overburden colleagues.

When Working with the Jester in Others

- Lighten up, enjoy the fun.
- Try to see things through their eyes.
- Show you get the joke, enjoy the fun (or they will bedevil you).
- Remember that they get bored easily and like to play games; stay one step ahead of them to keep their work challenging and as much fun as possible.
- When they are being disruptive, let them know what is truly off-limits.
- Let them know you see their talents; encourage them to put these to work.
- Be clear about limits, when they have to settle down temporarily, that is, when deadlines are actually "drop-dead" lines.
- Allow them autonomy; find ways to let them be creative; and, if this not possible, let them know when the end is in sight for a dull project.
- Keep a free rein AND keep in touch so they don't create chaos.
- Have them run brainstorming sessions and get others involved in creative fun; use them to bolster corporate community spirit.

When in conflict with Jesters: Expect trickery, charming manipulation, and an unwillingness to go directly at the problem. Try to diffuse the apparent seriousness of the conflict. Present it as a challenge to be overcome, a temporary obstacle that you need to brainstorm together about, to tackle together as playmates. Make a game out of arriving at a mutually satisfactory solution. Try to find ways to channel the creative energy into more productive areas. You may also need to explain exactly where and when Jesters can and cannot play.

Power and empowerment: For the Jester, power is the ability to laugh out loud, to let problems roll off your back, rather than rule (and ruin) your life. Empowerment is when you're allowed to play at work, to be your most creative, to follow an idea wherever it goes; to determine your own work hours, deadlines, and projects.

If your boss is a Jester: You may sometimes have to pick up the details after his or her grand schemes, much as a parent has to clean up after a child. Jester leaders range from fun and irresponsible to boldly creative, unconventional, fun, highly energizing of their staff members. They tend to allow a lot of the autonomy they themselves so prize. In the best cases, this results in an explosion of creativity and productivity; in the worst cases, staff members never coordinate their activities, nor follow-through, nor meet deadlines.

Jesters You May Have Met in the Workplace

The key workplace issue for the Jester is *autonomy* — independence, freedom. The Jester becomes significantly stressed when it is not free to be creative, have fun with work, or whenever it feels trapped within a boring job or with boring colleagues. Sometimes the Jester can respond maturely to its workplace's stresses (lightening up dire circumstances, helping to expose other possibilities) and sometimes it reacts poorly (uses its cleverness to take advantage of the system or unsuspecting individuals, or to make fun of others).

The **Illusionist** is a form of Jester that exists not only on stage (where it pretends to be a magician) but also in the workplace (where it pretends to be all kinds of things, e.g., competent). The Illusionist is someone who can pull off the "Now you see it, now you don't" charade. For example, I knew one CEO who would say to his board members, "There's no problem here" (after he had ordered his accounting staff to juggle the books to make the problem disappear until the next quarter, when he would have more time to deal with it). The Illusionist is adept at imitating other Core Types — for the sheer fun of duping others, or to hide out in the corporate culture, pretending to be one of the gang.

Of course, the workplace has many **Con Artists.** This aspect of our Jester thinks it's smarter than others, and that therefore it is entitled to take advantage of the system or unsuspecting colleagues and customers. (It was about this type of Jester that the phrase was coined: "Let the buyer beware.") One of my friends just stepped in as an interim marketing director in a young firm where his predecessor "went AWOL — just disappeared." This Con Artist had completely manufactured his resume and was about to be found out.

A very common form of the Jester is the **Trickster**, revered as a God in many traditions. For example, the Coyote was a Trickster in Native American traditions. As the story goes, Coyote created humanity by molding them, then baking them in an oven. According to the Cheyenne version of this myth, the brown ones were perfect, but the white ones were a little underdone. The Jester Core Type tricks us to teach us, to move us along when we are stuck. It is especially helpful when it tricks our minds so that we look at workplace or other problems differently — finding ways into them and seeing connections we'd missed before. The Trickster can also be a cruel manipulator, playing political corporate games with considerable skill.

Other types of Jester include the **Clown**, **Comedian**, or **Joker**. The Joker is the "wild card" form of Jester that appears in card decks; it often is the one card to whom the rules don't apply. In the workplace, the Joker functions as a class clown, the part of us that likes to tell jokes, funny stories, or play pranks to entertain colleagues. Traditionally the clown is someone who wears (physical or other) masks to entertain. I have noticed that as a profession, clowns and comedians are often people who are not happy offstage. Similarly, when we play the organization's clown, we may be protecting ourselves by hiding what we really feel and think. Other of these Jesters are mature individuals who believe laughter is truly the best medicine. They lighten things up for others, taking on the burden of seriousness, then turning it around so others can get out from underneath the weight. In this way, the Jester functions similarly to performers who go into battle zones to entertain the troops.

Jesters can even be **Liberators**, those freedom-fighters who liberate others from oppression via guerrilla tactics, using cleverness to outwit, outflank, and trick larger, much better armed opponents. The Liberators of many nations used trickery, camouflage, sniping, humor, and illusion — "underground movements"— quite effectively against opponents' powerful tanks and big guns.

The Jester's version of **Truth-Teller** tells the truth with humor and lightness, thereby often managing to deliver bad news. For example, we can put a hard truth in a story or a larger perspective, thereby both blunting the pain and augmenting the effect of this learning. We've all had the experience that some people can get away with delivering a message that would ruin others' careers. It is typically the Jester who can handle such a delicate task with ease.

The classic form of Jester is the archetypal **Fool**, the part of us that makes us whole by tricking us into integrating our "foolish" (illogical, unconscious) minds with its rich reservoir of untapped intelligence. It is our internal Fool who takes on problems with delight, never breaking stride. To the serious-minded onlooker, this may look like a catastrophe about to happen. But after our internal Fool falls flat on its face and dusts itself off, we emerge unscathed and can meet the challenge with laughter. Although the *Fool* is a term most often used derogatively these days, the heritage of its meaning is quite different. It represents both "psychic wholeness" and "the void, the precreation state containing all possibilities."[4]

PERSONAL AND PROFESSIONAL ASSESSMENT

Your Core Type Profile Score for Jester: _____

Aspects of the Jester with which you identify:

_____

Aspects of the Jester with which you do not identify:

_____

Situations that bring out the Jester in you (and which form of Jester?):

_____

_____

_____

Work colleagues (or friends or family members) in whom you see the Jester:

Person   *Form of Jester*

_____   _____

_____   _____

_____   _____

THE CAREGIVER

Joan has been an RN for 20 years. She is exactly the kind of person you want in charge of your care when you are ill. She moves deliberately, thoughtfully, a bit slowly. She smiles when she checks your pulse, and her hand lingers when she touches your forehead and shoulder. When she asks how you are today, you feel she actually is listening to your answer. You know you can count on her. She seems to provide a kind of "glue" between you and the doctors, lab workers, technicians, and other hospital staff. You rely on her to help you navigate this completely incomprehensible system, and you look forward to her rounds, because she gives you the feeling that you're going to mend well.

But under that professional demeanor, Joan hides a heavy heart. She is no longer sure she wants to continue nursing. Her hospital merged last year with a more aggressively managed one. Her collective bargaining unit narrowly averted a strike six months ago. At the time, Joan was one of the thin majority who voted against walking. Her reason: the patients would suffer. "That's the bottom line," she voiced her opinion at the time. "No matter how difficult things are, we must always put our patients first."

But in the ensuing months things have gotten worse. She has many more patients to tend to now — too many to do the job right anymore, she feels. Her new supervisor emphasizes efficiency, and he's always after Joan to pick up the pace. Although she would like to cooperate, she doesn't know how to do so while still giving her patients good care. She has started to exhibit physical symptoms of stress.

This morning, at her collective bargain unit meeting, she was one of a substantial majority who did vote for walking out. Her reason: the patients are suffering. "I cannot take good care of them anymore," she says. "And, I am suffering, too. If things don't improve, I may have to quit." There is no joy in the room at this vote, only resolve. The other nurses, like Joan, are convinced that, when they take the long view, the strike is the best way they can take care of those who come to this hospital.

The Caregiver Core Type is the part of you that tries through care and giving to make the world a better place. The professions of nursing, teaching, counseling, and public safety (firefighters, government regulators, and police officers) are filled with Caregivers who join

THE CAREGIVER

these organizations that have been specifically designated to fill a caregiving function for society.

The Caregiver teaches you how to give and what you care about. It is the part of you that brings *love* and *kindness, gentleness, respect,* and *appreciation* into the workplace. The Caregiver encourages you to *act responsibly, work hard,* and fulfill your duties. Its qualities of *genuine selflessness, a service attitude, careful attention to the tasks in front of you,* and *personal generosity* provide an *invisible glue* that can hold a workplace together under extreme stress. This Core Type contributes to your Self-mastery by helping you discover what's really important to you, what you truly value, that is, for what or for whom you're willing to sacrifice.

Ironically, even though the Caregiver contributes so much to the workplace and world, this Core Type is often not appreciated. The Caregiver is the solid part of us who sticks with things and sees that they're completed, even if it means putting in extra hours. This internal advisor feels our work is truly *making a difference* in the world, that if we didn't show up for a day, it would really matter to those in our charge. The customers, clients, and staff members of the Caregiver come first (before our own needs). Therefore, this type tends to do its job thoroughly, well, and does not demand much attention from supervisors. However, when shown any amount of appreciation, warmth, or care, our Caregiver will blossom.

Unfortunately, the Caregiver's very strengths are often its undoing. Because the Caregiver is so "good," so steady, and can be relied on absolutely, supervisors tend to focus their attention instead on "problem employees" and ignore the Caregivers who are among their most solid workers. The result of this benign neglect is that our Caregiver is often taken advantage of by the very workplace to which we are so dedicated.

The Caregiver's Story

> Kindness is the golden thread that holds society together.
>
> — GOETHE

In much of mythology, the Caregiver is the loving parent who shelters, protects, and serves his or her children, or the kind soul who tends to someone in need. The Caregiver relationship is not one of equals. As these stories point out, these others would have a difficult time if not for the Caregiver. This could include anyone who is temporarily in trouble — wanderers who've lost their way, neighbors who are out of food, an animal who's broken a leg, even a nation of oppressed people.

The act of giving provides the Caregiver's life with meaning, a significant reason for being. Caregivers make a real difference — for our children, our customers, our nation, the world. It is not what is given, but the *intention of providing for another* in need, of giving of one's self in some way, that signals the emergence of this Core Type within ourselves. It could be hot soup the Caregiver provides, or knowledge, or counseling. It is not *what* is given but *how* it is given that marks the Caregiver within us. This giving of ourselves is so important to the welfare of humanity that it is said that, of the three great virtues of faith, hope, and charity, the greatest is charity.

The Caregiver is the internal advisor who is hardwired for species survival. It is the part of us that compels fathers to set off in the heavy morning commute so they'll make next month's mortgage and mothers to hold their children tenderly while reading a bedtime story. The Caregiver also compels us to nurture those in our care so they can eventually become stronger and survive on their own. As an analogy, when teaching children how to ride that bicycle, a good parent allows them to fall and skin their knees in the attempts, then covers their bruises with ointment and kisses, and encourages them with praise for their new skill. Something similar can be seen in good supervisors who watch attentively, but do not interfere, as employees learn new tasks.

The Caregiver will give and give to the brink of exhaustion, and often beyond. This part of us believes that it's important to go out of our way to make things easy for others, to send thank-you notes, to be a little more attentive, considerate, and courteous than is absolutely necessary. Consequently, it is easy for us to become invisible to others. I am reminded of the children's story of the "giving tree." As a young boy grows up, he repeatedly goes to his favorite tree and asks for progressively more and more of it until only a stump is left. The boy returns as an old man, sits on what remains of the tree, and the giving tree is so very happy that the boy has finally returned. What I emphasize about the Caregiver is that we *must* include ourselves in the loop of care if we are to avoid self-destruction. In order to be able to continue giving care, this is an absolute necessity. Otherwise, like the giving tree, we will have nothing left of ourselves to give.

As the Caregiver gains in Self-mastery, this Core Type does learn how to give without harming itself, to sacrifice only for what really matters, to balance giving with assertion, and not to do for others what they can do for themselves. That is, this type teaches us how to give, when to give, what to give, and whether or not to give. This latter point is critical to empowerment and good leadership. A very important lesson for the Caregiver is to learn how to step out of the way so that clients or employees are able to move gradually from dependence to self-sufficiency. Otherwise, both the Caregiver and recipient of care are trapped in a destructive cycle.

Recognizing the Caregiver in Yourself and Others

- *Eyes*: Focused outward, checking for others' needs: solicitous, comforting, kind.
- *Face*: Serious, concerned, kind, burdened.
- *Body*: Bends over and down to serve others. Motions are gentle and cautious. Seems to be carrying a heavy burden. Often solid, like a tree trunk. Sometimes heavy or out of shape.
- *Walk*: Slow, steady, aware of others, careful not to disturb or step on others. Walks as if burdened by weight on shoulders.
- *Talk*: Asks questions regarding others' needs. (Do you need, want something? How can I help? How are you?) Conversation is often parent to child, or servant to master. Can be solicitous, comforting, soothing, or patronizing (as when talking down to child).
- *Clothing*: Practical; sometimes frumpy, slightly out of fashion, as if the money went for the kids' clothes. Clothes are not so important because Caregivers have other priorities and concerns.

Contributions and Difficulties within the Workplace

The goals of the Caregiver in the workplace include wanting to do good work *and* wanting to do work that does good. The Caregiver is the part of us that is unselfish. However, it would also like to be seen and appreciated for the excellent work it does. This Core Type's worst fear — in itself or others — is selfishness, callousness, or indifference to the plight of others who need help.

The Caregiver's attitude towards work is that it provides a chance to serve a purpose. Caregivers contribute to the workplace by just digging in and doing whatever needs to be done. This part of us has a clear sense of duty, of priorities and responsibility and morality. Care can manifest in a thousand ways — in our voices, actions, attitudes towards customers and co-workers. Caregivers hold the workplace together in both tangible and intangible ways. Under stress, the Caregiver is the part of us that others can count on to come through, often no matter what the cost is to ourselves. When the Caregiver is active in us, we care so much that it hurts our insides when we're unable to deliver. The Caregiver is dedicated, self-sufficient, a "grown-up" employee who works long hours. Caregivers are kind to people whom we supervise and loyal to our supervisors. This Core Type also has a keen sense of social responsibility — both inside and outside the company walls. The Caregiver is the one who arranges for the annual picnic, and also the one who suggests ways for the corporation to help the larger community.

Caregivers also have many difficulties in the workplace. Because this internal advisor is so dedicated, because it mostly wants to be allowed to do its work, it will have us go out of our way to make no trouble for our boss or colleagues. This tendency, combined with its tenderheartedness, means the Caregiver wants to avoid confrontation. Caregivers tend to be overly passive, to give in on issues, to appease others (a bit like the mother who insists on eating the leftovers when everyone else has completed a meal). This makes our Caregiver a sitting duck for less scrupulous people in the workplace. The Caregiver will even allow ourselves to be walked on like a doormat, if that is what is needed to get the job done. By picking up after others who are not pulling their weight, or by allowing others to abuse this part of us, we can become "caretakers" — enablers of dysfunctional workplace behavior.

There is a significant caveat to the Caregiver's even-temperedness. If those in our care are threatened, Caregivers can turn into "mother bears" — lashing out suddenly and ferociously. In this state, we can effectively take on all comers and are not to be trifled with. And, in cases where the Caregiver really disagrees with something that is going on, we simply dig in stubbornly, and, "like a tree that's gathered by the river, we will not be moved."

The Caregiver can have an entirely different kind of workplace difficulty. We can use our giving to manipulate others; we can give only in order to receive. For example, the Caregiver can help us get our way by withholding or doling out special treatment, like the dragon-secretary who allows passage to the CEO only to those employees who behave as she wishes. Another example of manipulative behavior is "guilt-tripping" colleagues. Certainly you've heard people say things like: "Oh, that's no problem. I'll do it. (Deep sigh.) I always do it. No one else seems to notice." The Caregiver's lamenting can drive others away, creating a vicious cycle where we have to do more and more because people want to be around us less and less.

Sometimes the Caregiver's complaining is entirely justified and understandable, because it causes Caregivers real pain if co-workers or others are indifferent, lazy, or don't give fully of themselves. But this attitude too can cause alienation from co-workers if the Caregiver part of ourselves indulges in self-righteous pride that others are likely to find intolerable.

Sometimes Caregivers cause our own problems with overburdensome workloads because we are certain no one else can do the job as well, or cares as much as we do, or will pay enough attention to critical details. This attitude makes it impossible for us to delegate. And, even if we do manage to force ourselves to delegate, this attitude may soon resurface as a sort of fussing micromanagement (which is roughly the equivalent of, "Your room is still not clean enough. Try again." or "Let me help you do it right.").

When Working with the Caregiver in Others

- Be appreciative of all they do to help others.
- Say thank you. A lot.
- Appeal to their loyalty, altruism, and sense of responsibility.
- Let them know their cooperation will make a real difference to others.
- Realize that they require little external motivation.
- Recognize their limits, and don't allow them to exceed them.
- Make certain they include themselves in the caring loop; reinforce them for doing so.
- Pay close attention to how hard they are working.
- Have them model caring — towards each other, clients, and the work itself.

When in conflict with Caregivers: Be aware that Caregivers tend to fear and avoid conflict. They will sacrifice their own interests, but not those of the people in their care. (Remember the mother bear.) Elicit the Caregiver's concerns, issues, and difficulties. Show that you care about their wards and also about them. Thank them for what they've done, their loyalty to you and the organization, and their willingness to enter into solving this shared problem. If the Caregiver is enabling a dysfunctional individual, you may need to convince them that the best care is "tough love."

Power and empowerment: Power is the ability you have to give your customers the best possible service and products — what they need, when they need it. This includes both your external and internal customers. Empowerment is when you are given the authority and resources you need to respond appropriately and quickly at the point of others' requests.

If your boss is a Caregiver: He or she is likely to be attentive to you and other staff members. If a mature personality, your boss will be caring, empowering, self-sacrificing, hardworking. If significantly stressed or immature, s/he may be meddlesome, manipulative, or enabling of the dysfunctional behavior of favored staff members.

Caregivers You May Have Met in the Workplace

The key workplace issue for the Caregiver is *agency*, in this case, acting to make the world a better place. This desire can manifest in numerous ways, depending on the particular Caregiver's values about what is "good." It is therefore not uncommon to see different Caregivers with different values working at cross-purposes to create their idea of a better world.

Because the Caregiver in us lives to serve, its most stressful work situation is to be unable to help people in need, such as the clients we are supposed to serve. These situations could result, for example, from downsizing or budget cuts, or from new policies that define who is no longer a customer. When Caregivers are at our happiest and most successful, we serve others in ways that are both easy for us and truly helpful for the recipient of care. Mother Theresa, for example, is reported to have said that it is easy for her to serve the beggars because she sees only God in them. This perception transforms a burden into a joy with no weight whatsoever.

Like every other Core Type, stress causes our Caregiver to revert to its worst self. This means that, in trying to make things better, we tend to take all the burdens on ourselves, and give of ourselves until we collapse. And, if we're really in a bad state, we can manage to do all this while simultaneously making others feel that they are contributing nothing of value to the effort. Even under the best conditions it is a challenge for the Caregiver to (1) let others know when we need help and (2) graciously receive help when it is offered. (We tend instead to just hunker down and keep trying to accomplish the task by ourselves.)

The kinds of Caregivers who are the least easy to live and work with are the **Suffering Martyr** and **Guilt-Evoker**. Sometimes this behavior is the result of a stressful situation. The Caregiver really is being martyred, is really in tremendous pain, and the suffering is beyond our ability to endure.

The **Enabler** is the Caregiver who gives too much, at the wrong times, and for the wrong reasons to the wrong people. In Alcoholics Anonymous and similar organizations, this is called *caretaking* behavior. It is the part of us that, in the name of kindness, makes excuses for others. The unintended consequence of the Caregiver's enabling is that others remain dependent and continue with their self-destructive behaviors.

The **Workaholic**, Caregiver-style, works all the time because (in its mind) if it did not, the workplace (home, project, team, or world) would fall apart. What distinguishes a hard worker from the Workaholic is the quality of compulsion in the latter, the sense of not really having a life outside work, a quietly desperate air. When we are Workaholics, we take our self-definition almost entirely from our jobs.

The Caregiver is a strongly supportive Core Type for those people who function as **Bureaucrats**, especially those public servants who are in charge of guaranteeing our public safety (ranging from the efficacy of a new pharmaceutical product to the building of a nuclear reactor to the shelf life of canned tuna). It is interesting that in prior centuries such sacred societal trusts were performed by *clerks* (a title which has the same root as *clerics* and *clergy*). These were scholars who could read and write. Unfortunately, we still expect our bureaucrats to take care of society, but we use the term pejoratively.

Service Workers of all types are those of us who have chosen jobs with the designated function of caregiving. This does not necessarily mean that service workers are strong in the Caregiver Core Type, but it does mean that this internal advisor should function well for us and those in our care. But this is not always the case, I've discovered. I once presented a week-long intensive retreat for administrators of a hospital chain that was in significant transition. I was surprised to see that the Caregiver Core Type received the second *lowest* score in this group. I stopped the class so that together we could contemplate the repercussions of this management configuration for an organization whose stated mission was caregiving.

The secretary who guards the boss's schedule and the security guard at the front desk are both **Gatekeepers**. Indeed, we rely upon this part of us to know exactly when to open and close the gates. These kinds of jobs call upon us to be like dragons guarding our treasures, fierce to the uninvited and those whom we consider unworthy, but welcoming to those who come when called.

It is not uncommon for leaders to act (or for us to feel they are acting as) "parents" in workplace. Caregiver supervisors often take the form of the caring, helpful, attentive, **Benevolent Boss**. Whether or not workers thrive under this form of leadership depends on whether the benevolent boss empowers workers so that they learn how to manage on their own, or encourages dependency instead.

Caregivers can function in the workplace as the **Good Friend** or **Colleague** — the co-worker who is there for us, the people we can count on to come through, to help us out when we are in need. One of the best qualities of such Caregivers is that they are not overbearing, that is, they are able to distinguish when others need or want help.

PERSONAL AND PROFESSIONAL ASSESSMENT

Your Core Type Profile Score for Caregiver: _____

Aspects of the Caregiver with which you identify:

_____

Aspects of the Caregiver with which you do not identify:

_____

Situations that bring out the Caregiver in you (and which form of Caregiver?):

_____

_____

_____

Work colleagues (or friends or family members) in whom you see the Caregiver:

Person   *Form of Caregiver*

_____   _____

_____   _____

_____   _____

The **Charitable Person** comes in many forms because there are so many ways to bring the Caregiver aspect of ourselves into the world. Charity can take the form of physical assistance, giving of one's time, or donating money to a good cause (**Philanthropist**). Charity can also mean contributing a kind word or soft touch, contributing insights and knowledge, or writing an uplifting poem. Caregivers come in so many shapes and forms because we all have so many different talents, and therefore so many different ways to give to our work and our world

The **Transformative Martyr** is the Caregiver whose actions are more public. Their suffering is often dramatic in its impact. I have often thought that for people who give of themselves constantly, it is not so hard to make the ultimate sacrifice. Their whole lives have been the training ground. This high form of Caregiver also includes those steadfast workers who give daily of themselves, their time, and whose attention to mundane matters gradually bears the fruit of transformation.

THE WARRIOR

Mike is an officer on staff at the Pentagon. He is tall, rugged, smart as a whip, opinionated, dedicated, and has a great sense of humor. His job is to sift through complicated intelligence reports, then brief his executive officer. His specialty is the Middle East, a hotbed of international concern. He works very long hours and believes that what he does for a living matters greatly to every single one of us.

I first met Mike through a mutual friend. Over the years, we developed both a professional and personal relationship. As I did considerable work for various branches of the Department of Defense, Mike offered me "briefings" too — sometimes historical, sometimes political, at other times personal — which gave me more insight into the worldview of our society's professionally designated Warriors. I came to appreciate their love of country as a heartfelt emotion (rather than as a cliché), and their willingness to fight as a necessary response to evil (rather than as an evil in itself). I came to respect the rigors of training that prepare these people's minds to be steady and resourceful under real-life or corporate fire.

Mike has watched the military go through radical budget cuts and numerous phases of downsizing in the past decade. At such a high level, he has little to worry about personally. His concern, however, is that, as a nation, we are "cutting ourselves to the bone." He worries that if trends continue, pretty soon there will be no one left to turn out the lights.

He and I have, from our different vantage points, also watched the military establishment struggle with how to redefine its Warrior identity in this unprecedented time of peace and extraordinary transition. This is a time when many professional Warriors are asking themselves: "Who are we now that our great enemy, the Soviet Union, is gone?" He and his colleagues now turn their attention to monitor the numerous small hot spots around the globe, while they also try on "peace-keeping" and "humanitarian" missions to further stabilize the international scene.

The Warrior is the part of you that comes to your rescue when you need to be strong, confident, tough, and willing to take decisive action. It contributes to your Self-mastery by pushing you forward into the world whenever you are frightened, unsure, feeling small and inadequate. This Core Type is so highly valued in the workplace that most reward systems are designed to increase the Warrior's emergence in all workers. Indeed, most traditional management literature has addressed itself to this internal advisor.

Your internal Warrior is drawn to workplaces where you can strut your stuff, show your competence, compete, and excel. Its gifts for the workplace are numerous: it contributes *discipline, endurance,* and *hard work.* It is *assertive* (sometimes aggressive), it helps you *know what you really want,* and it gives you *the desire to win* that prize. Your Warrior generates *forward-moving, highly directed energy* to overcome obstacles, and helps you gather *courage* when you are in dangerous situations. It contributes *quick action, speed,* and *decisiveness* to work. It helps *focus your intent* and cuts like a laser through any "B.S." It uses *competition and internal drive* to sharpen everything about you — skills, intellect, will, and survival instincts. The Warrior is also valued in the workplace because it is *loyal* to the organization and a *team player,* willing to shoulder its share of the load. This Core Type, like the Caregiver (with whom it shares the key workplace issue of *agency*), can be counted on to *get the job done.*

Another important gift of the Warrior, so critical to your survival, is a sense of *personal boundaries* — what is yours, what is not. This includes not just material possessions or corporate territory, but also personal or physical boundaries, which if crossed, spell real danger. I am quick to remind anyone who says that the Warrior has dominated humanity much too long, that it's time to put it into retirement, that this Core Type helps us stay alive. Much as a cell dies if its membrane is broken, we too need to keep our psychological, professional, and physical boundaries intact. The truth is paradoxical. Yes, we are all profoundly connected, part of the whole. And, we are also all separate, distinct organisms. The Warrior is what protects your sense of separation, your personal boundaries. It helps contain your life force in your own distinct package.

The Warrior is attracted to workplaces where you will have challenges to overcome, chances to compete, achieve, and prove yourself. When the Warrior is strong in us, we are hungry for the kind of success that is visible to others. Therefore, we gravitate to places where there is a tangible way to keep score. For example, the Warrior fills Wall Street offices with analysts and brokers who are trying to make their mark on the world. Sales forces are also populated with workers eager to succeed, to earn big bonuses and make a great living. Any high-prestige professional school (such as medicine or law) teems with young Warriors who are eager to "do well" in life. Less mature, or highly stressed, Warriors are motivated by the desire to prevail over others, to win at any cost (to others, the organization, or ourselves). More mature Warriors take on responsibility for making the world a better place by getting rid of real enemies and defending our boundaries against the same.

The Warrior's Story

> Life is either a daring adventure or nothing.
>
> — HELEN KELLER

The standard Warrior story has three characters: the Warrior, the Villain, and the Victim to be rescued. As the classic stories go: the Warrior confronts the Villain — often a huge, fire-breathing dragon

— in order to rescue a hapless Victim (often a damsel in distress). It is important to recognize that there are three principal characters in this script: we have added another possibility — that of the Warrior/Hero — to the Orphan's story of Villain and Victim.

The Warrior's version of the Heroic Journey is so well known that it has overshadowed other aspects of our learning journey. (In fact, many people use *hero* and *warrior* interchangeably.) As a society, and particularly in the workplace, we need not to employ this Core Type inappropriately, for example, when other Core Types could do better work for us. Otherwise, the Warrior loses its richness and becomes a stereotype, a caricature. We wind up acting like Arnold Schwarzenegger's movie characters at work, mowing down the competition. We lose the real meaning of the Warrior archetype. This makes our actions empty, and we become like children pointing sticks at each other and saying, "Bang, Bang. You're dead." With such overuse, the Warrior loses its depth, its best gifts, its power.

The Warrior's story is really a story about having the courage, will, heart, and discipline to confront the enemy — *within and without*. This cannot be emphasized enough. The Warrior first notices the outer enemy, and in confronting this outer enemy, the Warrior teaches us about our own *internal* enemies, the ones that are actually keeping us from being able to overcome obstacles.

In the Warrior's story, if you are successful, you kill the dragon. If you are not successful, the dragon kills you. It is a dramatically clear either/or situation that the Warrior sees and acts upon. And, although this worldview has many times been quite limiting in its options-generation — let's face it, sometimes the dragon really does need killing.

Warriors know how to deal with real enemies in real time. Sometimes we don't have the time, resources, or access to provide bloody tyrants with the counseling they need to uncover the psychological cause of their aggression, see the error of their ways, and stop terrorizing the world. The same sometimes must be said of really bad supervisors who are similarly terrorizing their subordinates and refusing to move with organizational change. I encountered one MD, an emergency room director, who resigned in advance of a 360-

degree review by her own staff. She characterized her own management style as being like "Ghengis Khan." She thought she was quite effective, she liked having people jump when she told them to, and there was "no way," she told us, that she was going to change or wait around to be insulted by her subordinates.

What the Warrior part of ourselves needs to learn is to fight only for what really matters, to choose the timing of the fight, and also to learn alternate techniques of out-and-out warfare. The reason: too often "winning" becomes losing. For example, maybe you win today, but your opponent is going to come back tomorrow with new organizational alliances and wipe you out. Or, sometimes the costs of fighting may be too high, as when the battle is so feverish that no one is left with enough energy or desire to complete the project you were fighting over.

Recognizing the Warrior in Yourself and Others

- *Eyes*: Focused, intense. Meets you with direct gaze. Assertive look to check you out, to determine whether you are friend or foe, or whether you will pass muster.
- *Face*: Determined, square, jaw set, strong. Serious, no-nonsense expressions.
- *Body*: Often strong, solid, muscled, athletic, in shape. Confident motions. Uses hands to make a point (finger pointing at people or charts), makes fist to show intensity or determination.
- *Walk*: Strong stride, whole back slightly forward, energetic, fast, efficient, moves from "point a to b" in a straight line, with determination and no wasted effort. Confident; will not be sidetracked or deterred.
- *Talk*: Tough, no nonsense, serious, engages in difficult issues, addresses conflict quickly. Likes debate, can be brusque, verbally tests others (their competence and commitment). Enters competitive conversations without hesitation.
- *Clothing*: Workplace dress is a uniform — all business: clean lines, functional, pressed. Power suits, which often subtly display rank. Dress for competition, for battle, to show others that you have won in the past and intend to keep doing so.

Contributions and Difficulties within the Workplace

The Warrior is the internal advisor that teaches us how to fight, what's worth fighting for, and when or whether to fight at all. The Warrior's goal is to win, and to overcome fear and other obstacles by being strong and effective. This Core Type's worst fear, in ourselves or others, is weakness of any kind, cowardliness, ineffectiveness, losing, or vulnerability (which is why anything "touchy-feely" makes this Core Type run for cover). The Warrior tends to be stoic; it values toughness and team spirit in ourselves and in others.

Warriors have high standards that are often set via external competition, be it the GMAT scores needed to qualify for Wharton Business School or the Boston marathon's entrance requirements. For the Warrior, the issue is to live up to whatever standards we choose, and in this way to prove our worth. Because Warriors work so hard for our goals, we expect tangible and "commensurate" rewards. I remember learning this lesson from a physician I interviewed, who proclaimed indignantly that he had survived the rigors of medical school and the tortures of internship, and therefore deserved a much higher salary than we were offering at our group health plan. For someone who was interested in salary as a way to keep score, our HMO's other benefits (such as reasonable lifestyle and hours) just didn't measure up. It is not surprising, then, that some of the Warrior's major challenges include: seeing more than two sides to a problem, entertaining multiple options for solving these problems, having compassion for others, and respecting diversity and difference of opinion.

The Warrior contributes to the workplace primarily by being a "good soldier," a loyal worker and team player. The Warrior helps us to be disciplined, focused, assertive, and willing to act. This part of us is good at defining and eliminating discrete, tangible problems (and less adept at solving more complex and subtle systems problems). The Warrior demonstrates its courage by confronting challenges head on. While others back away, run, hide, or hesitate, our Warrior has already launched into pitched battle. And as we all know, sometimes this tendency is good, sometimes it is bad.

The Warrior in us also has many workplace difficulties, particularly when we are under stress. This internal advisor's dualistic, "either/or" approach to problems can be troublesome, considering the complexity of the work issues facing us today. The Warrior can cause us to compete with co-workers or supervisors, with whom we need to cooperate. This then throws up barriers and creates enemies where we had none before. The Warrior may create an artificial battlefield, just so we have an arena in which we can demonstrate our skills. The Warrior's drive to win can make us unnecessarily combative or cut-throat with anyone who stands in our way. After a while, its battle-readiness translates to a working or leadership style that is aggressive, quarrelsome, blustery, even belligerent. Over time, this makes us rigid in both mind and body; it is as if our armor becomes a part of our permanent identity, and we cannot take it off. We then lose the flexibility that is a necessary companion, along with strength, for victory. We can see this difficulty in the workplace, where the Warrior needs flexibility to adjust to changing workplace conditions and to entertain multiple options if we are to survive. The formerly helpful straight-line strategy of just working harder has lost much of its effectiveness in the age of chaos. Another significant challenge for this Core Type is to understand that, paradoxically, our strength lies in our vulnerability; we are actually stronger if we are not overly dependent upon our external armor for protection.

When Working with the Warrior in Others

- Be strong and assertive, or you won't be respected.
- Let them know if you're on their side; if not, let them know why.
- Under no circumstances be a "wimp" (or they will demolish you).
- Get cooperation by appealing to their team spirit and desire to win.
- Appeal to their discipline and focus to get things done.
- When they are experiencing obstacles, let them know they "can take it."
- Challenge them to experience and accept difference without being threatened.

- Have them help you focus the effort and energy of work teams.
- Show your competence and authority if you are in charge.

When in conflict with Warriors: In conflict, the Warrior takes no prisoners. You must project confidence and strength in your body and language. Be assertive, rather than either passive (they'll walk all over you) or aggressive (this will escalate into full-scale warfare). Demonstrate your readiness to enter the fray. This makes it possible for you to negotiate from a position of power, and can stave off combat. Be sure that you have the weapons, however, as bluffs are very risky. Try to show that you are on the same team against a shared enemy or problem. Find ways to join forces and redirect their attack.

Power and empowerment: Power is considered a scarce commodity: if you have more, that means I have less. Power is valuable (often it literally determines who lives and who dies). Therefore it is worth fighting for. Empowerment means giving someone a higher rank, more perks, more authority, and responsibility. The less mature Warrior will fight over every scrap of power and resist empowerment of others, because it does not believe that everyone can be empowered. More mature Warriors see everyone involved as being on the same team. Therefore, they believe that if you have more power as my teammate, we all will do better in fighting our competition.

If your boss is a Warrior: Warrior leaders tend to be strong, aggressive, challenging, and quite demanding of their employees. If you are productive and meet your work requirements, all will be well. However, expect to have your armor checked regularly for weaknesses; the boss may bat you about to see if you can pass muster, rather than send you out into "battle" if you are unprepared or too weak to succeed.

Warriors You May Have Met in the Workplace

Because our Warrior is so action oriented, one of the most stressful things we can experience is having our hands tied in some way so that we are forced to be inactive. Our blood rises almost to stroke level under such conditions. Warriors tend to respond to high stress by becoming more combative and competitive. Interestingly, many Warriors I have met cannot imagine working under conditions other than high stress. They feel it helps them "keep their edge." In fact, it's kind of a kick for our Warrior to see how far we can go on adrenaline alone. This is like survival training, when soldiers are dropped in the middle of a wilderness with only a knife, their wits, and a map to make it back to camp. When this Core Type is at its best, we pace ourselves (like long-distance runners), use our strength wisely, and focus our intention so as to get a lot accomplished.

The least pleasant Warrior co-worker, supervisor, or subordinate is probably the **Pugilist** or **KneeJerk Fighter**. This part of us is overly aggressive, unthinkingly compulsive in our combativeness. Everything's a fight. Every decision is contested. No one is trusted.

The **Workaholic**, Warrior-style, thinks that stress is a good thing. In fact, we sometimes set up conditions that create stress in order to keep pressure on ourselves to produce. This part of us seems to live on its own adrenaline, little food and lots of coffee. We push ourselves, test the levels of our endurance, and usually succeed at making our goals. Workaholics are productive workers, and the workplace usually rewards them well for their efforts. This part of us laughs at the wimps who take stress-management classes, until our doctors order us to attend because our blood pressure is so high.

The **Disciplinarian** enforces workplace policies regarding right versus wrong behavior. We tend to see things in a somewhat dualistic way. Not only do we live by the rules, we make sure *others* do so as well. Disciplinarians are the "hall monitors" of the workplace — policy makers who set and enforce standards, or the financial managers who keep departments in line so that the organization works within agreed-upon limits.

Although the **Athlete** has little formal standing in the workplace (except in the big business of sports franchises, where they are the commodity), it is an ideal prized in management for its discipline and competitiveness. The adulation of the Warrior-Athlete is reflected in the many sports metaphors that are used in business conversation and literature.

We see the **Debater** frequently in corporations. This part of us uses language as a sharp weapon to persuade others and win conflicts. The Debater often overlaps with another type of workplace Warrior, the **Politician**. The Politician is a Warrior who keeps score with votes, who goes into battle against a political opponent. No one of us would deny that the workplace is filled with politics, nor that it is pretty serious stuff. We all have a lot at stake in the political battles that go on daily in our workplaces. And, although this term is generally used pejoratively, in large bureaucracies a certain amount of political savvy is a requirement for survival.

One of the Warrior's most respected qualities is that of being a **Team Player**. As in the real battlefield, Warriors use the strengths of our team members, with their differing gifts, to make our com-

---

PERSONAL AND PROFESSIONAL ASSESSMENT

Your Core Type Profile Score for Warrior: _____

Aspects of the Warrior with which you identify:

_____

Aspects of the Warrior with which you do not identify:

_____

Situations that bring out the Warrior in you (and which form of Warrior?):

_____

_____

_____

Work colleagues (or friends or family members) in whom you see the Warrior:

Person   *Form of Warrior*

_____   _____

_____   _____

_____   _____

bined efforts stronger and more effective than that of our opponents. As a team player, the Warrior Core Type plays the role of the "good soldier," who puts our team or organization first and does exactly what we are commanded to do.

The **Assertive Person** is a Warrior who clearly states what we want or need, and where and by when. This part of us differs from aggressive Pugilist in many ways. When we are assertive, we make "I" statements, and stand our ground rather than take over someone else's. This doesn't assure that we will get what we want or need, but it does increase the odds.

The **Crusader** is a Warrior who is fighting for some noble cause. The Crusader is convinced that God is on our side. This provides intensity to our fighting. It can also provide a self-righteousness that blinds us to the underlying political nuances of the fight or to the suffering of those who are in our way. There are a surprising number of such Crusaders in the workplace, for example, workers who believe that our product is better than that of our competitors, prosecutors who want to see repeat criminals put away, or the public defenders who want to make certain that every citizen is given a fair shake in the judicial system.

We even see the **Spiritual Warrior** in the workplace. These are high-level Warriors who are reluctant to fight, but are awfully good at it, nonetheless. Many are experienced executives who have taken our personal journeys, looked deeply within ourselves, examined our failings, and become stronger as a result. Great leaders and writers have exposed their own heroes' journeys to us (see Joseph Jaworski's *Synchonicity: The Inner Path of Leadership* and Michael Ray's *Heroes in Everyday Living*). Such stories show us how the Warrior can, through its vulnerability, contribute mightily to our shared future.

THE MAGICIAN

Marianne is a management consultant whose specialty is helping organizations through difficult transitions. When she teaches in the workplace, her seminars make the subject come alive. Her face and hands are extremely expressive, in motion, causing the normally dead air in conference rooms to

THE MAGICIAN

practically swirl around the room. She specializes in experiential adult learning. As a result, no one can sit back and relax during her time with them. Moreover, she is extremely attentive to those she teaches, the executives she coaches, and the teams she facilitates. She also is often called upon to act as a mediator and general troubleshooter, where she relies upon her excellent intuition to lead her to solutions. More often than not, she acts as a catalyst — a critical ingredient whose function is to open up her clients to discover for themselves how to solve their own problems.

Marianne is particularly good at helping teams develop the processes that support their work. She describes herself as always "reading between the lines" about what's really going on underneath the words and posturing of corporate life. She sees herself as serving a healing function — more midwife than physician — for those who call upon her and her colleagues. She feels that her job is to provide very short-term interventions. Wherever she is invited she tries to transfer skills so that her clients quickly gain sufficient competence to proceed independently. As a result, she receives enthusiastic recommendations and is almost always invited back for further work.

Marianne is the principal of her own small firm. She prizes the flexibility of her position, the ability to say yes or no to clients (usually depending upon whether or not she believes they are capable of the changes she is likely to propose). Marianne and her colleagues are an intense, bright, forward-thinking group. On the rare occasions when all of them are gathered in the same room, their combined energy practically crackles. She has selected like-minded colleagues who have complementary, yet differing talents and work styles. Together they can handle the tasks that come their way.

The Magician opens your mind and heart to reveal possibilities and solutions — options — you would not otherwise consider. The Magician expands your understanding, and in so doing works through you to *transform* the situations and people with whom you deal. The Magician helps you achieve *balance* — in your work and among the diverse, sometimes fragmented, parts of your life. It makes you *whole, healthy, integrated.* It heals you from the inside out.

One of the Magician's greatest gifts is how it helps us *reframe problems* as challenges and lessons to be learned. With the Magician, the whole world and everything in it serves as a lesson plan, a book of wisdom for you to read. Magic was originally defined as *the study of Nature*. Ancient Magicians wanted to know Nature's laws so that they could cooperate with them. This Core Type's strength is due to its *flexibility and focused intent*; these qualities keep it alert and open to possibilities. The Magician is often a good *visionary or prophet*. Indeed, it is sometimes so enamored of the future that it lives somewhere between the worlds of present and future. Because the Magician Core Type believes that we are all a thread in the fabric of life, it is compelled to look for *win/win solutions* to all problems. Anything less is a loss.

What the Magician wants from the workplace is the opportunity for you to be as creative and authentic as you can be, to do work that fits who you are, in your essence, and to bring the dreams you envision to life. This internal advisor's gift to Self-mastery is a desire for *integrity* that compels you to become "saturated" with who you truly are, so that eventually you develop the same congruent, unifying identity all the way through your mind, body, and soul. This congruence gives the Magician considerable *energy* with which it moves us into the world and affects change. This kind of integrity and energy also gives us the *personal power* that the Magician seeks.

Magicians are attracted to work as change-agents, mediators, inventors, artists, writers, teachers, consultants, scientists, researchers, futurists; indeed, any field where we can express ourselves fully and/or delve into an aspect of nature that particularly interests us. This Core Type is also strongly represented in the alternate (holistic) healing professions, which have seen a worldwide resurgence in recent decades. Indeed, the Magician is the ancient archetype of the Healer or Shaman, who approaches health with a whole-system framework.

The Magician's Story

> Mystery is truth's dancing partner.
> — GOETHE

In the Magician's story, the hero travels through a maze or deep woods. En route we receive gifts, guidance, direction, and assistance at critical junctures. These gifts are often magical in nature. Eventually we come upon the same dragon who bedeviled the Warrior, and who guards a great treasure. Often, this monster presents us with a complex riddle or impossible task. The Magician must solve the problem to win the treasure, but the stakes are high: if we fail, we forfeit our life. (The "grace" — the magical gifts the Magician received as we traveled — winds up being the key to our success.)

What is also important in the Magician's story is how this internal advisor responds to the dragon. The Magician transforms, rather than kills, it. One of my favorite examples of the difference between the Warrior and Magician is the children's story of Jerome, a little frog who succeeded where all before him had failed. His town was besieged by a fire-breathing dragon. When Jerome set out, no one expected to see him again. However, Jerome discovered, by talking with the dragon, that it was the dragon's *Nature* to breathe fire. It was what he did, who he was. After some thought, Jerome came up with a brilliant compromise — the dragon was to come to the town twice weekly and burn all the town's garbage.[5]

The Magician's primary gifts for us include this ability to reframe old problems, to turn them around completely, to change a difficulty into an asset, a challenge into a learning. Another way to say this is that the Magician excels at making lemonade out of lemons. The Magician is an Alchemist who transforms lesser realities (symbolized by lead) into better realities (symbolized by gold). The internal power of our Magician is the power of mind over matter. The Magician changes reality by the power of our intentions, that is, by having us act today in ways that are consistent with our vision of tomorrow.

This Core Type also may intervene in organizations as catalysts who, by introducing a third element (an action, idea, feedback) into a situation, transform it without apparent effort. Indeed, the Magician in us is always searching for such "points of leverage," which create change easily, almost as if we had waved a magic wand. The Magician also can create what has never been before by opening us up to inspiration and then "grounding" these new ideas, turning them into concrete reality.

The Magician enjoys change so much that it often needs to learn the value of order and stability, of rest periods, of time out, of enjoying life and work as they are right now. Because of the Magician's considerable power, it also often needs to learn humility. If we use our personal power to "play God," we are likely to have a lightning bolt–equivalent hit us so hard our world falls apart. The Magician also needs to learn how to emotionally let go of outcomes once we have set things in motion, to practice what we preach, and to let Nature take its own course.

Recognizing the Magician in Yourself and Others

- *Eyes*: Alert, focused, intense. Watches energy within and between people.
- *Face*: Attentive; inquisitive; always trying to understand and learn.
- *Body*: Usually flexible and strong. Tends to be in shape, more lithe than muscled. Hands and body move fluidly. Seems to move energy with hands.
- *Walk*: Easy, fluid but strong, determined. Energy and power are inside moving out. Quietly attentive to what is happening around it; will alter pace and direction accordingly.
- *Talk*: Matches language of those with whom speaking. Asks questions. Trying to learn, even if teaching or in charge of others. Inquisitive.
- *Clothing*: May mask self so as to identify with and not disturb others, a shape-shifter. Will try to honor others' customs to make them comfortable, to "pass." *Or,* wears extremely comfortable clothes that move fluidly with the body.

Contributions and Difficulties within the Workplace

The goal of the Magician Core Type is to bring our vision of the future into reality as soon as possible, to be empowered in the fullest sense of that word, and to always find "win/win" solutions to problems. Its worst fear is that we will inadvertently do harm with our power, that we will unwittingly hurt others as we exercise our will and/or move into the future.

Magicians see work as a vocation, its own reward, an opportunity to grow and learn. Of particular value to the workplace are the Magician's (1) attitude toward change (that it is the real nature of the world) and (2) creativity (that inspiration must be wedded to action). The Magician often provides new (usually systemic, holistic) approaches to old problems. The Magician helps colleagues with its talent for mediation and conflict resolution. This internal advisor is compassionate and seemingly tireless in its (often optimistic) "win/win" approach to problem solving. A great help is also the Magician's reframing attitude towards problems and mistakes — that these are challenges and opportunities for learning. The Magician is a master at generating multiple options and "holographic" rather than linear solutions. This part of us is very flexible and helps us to cope well with transitions. It is an excellent advisor to the Rulers of organizations, helping them to better see and move into the future.

The Magician's interest in the diversity of nature encourages in us a respect for the differences between ourselves and others. In this way, the Magician helps us walk between the worlds — or departments — increasing the likelihood of effective, direct, honest communication. Moreover, the Magician is an androgynous Core Type, balancing the male and female within each of us. This is the part of us that helps capture the gifts of both genders for ourselves and the workplace. In these many ways, the Magician functions in corporate settings as its ancient healing counterpart, the Shaman.

The Magician Core Type can also get us into considerable trouble in the workplace. For example, some managers at the top of corporations resist the Magician's suggestions because, quite frankly, we like things just the way they are. In fact, especially if we have set things up this way, we are likely to be offended by the Magician's audacity. If our Magician persists in the face of such resistance, we will be punished. Oftentimes, organizational leaders resist the change Magicians suggest because the Magician tends to create change when it is not absolutely necessary. Its desire for knowledge, for understanding, means that this Core Type can easily become bored with sameness. The Magician urges us to approach life and work as great experiments. This makes us crave diversity of experience. This same quality exhausts our co-workers, because we are always out front, on the cutting edge. The Magician is easily frustrated if we can't carry out our ideas. We may even evidence contempt, impatience, and intolerance for the "small minds" who oppose our transformative efforts. Indeed, it is a major challenge for the Magician to be understanding about colleagues' resistance to change, "limited" imagination or aspiration. If the rest of the organization is moving too slowly for us, the Magician may "check out," that is, we may be present in body only while our mind explores the future we so clearly envision.

When Working with the Magician in Others

- Place them in a position where they can be creative and carry ideas to completion.
- Give them as much "room" as possible.
- Encourage them to brainstorm and do team-building activities.
- Put them in a position to affect change.
- Use them to increase more effective communication, including real dialogue.
- Use them as mediators and conflict resolvers.
- Control their attempts to make too much change too fast.
- Keep them "grounded" in today's realities without crushing their dreams of tomorrow.
- Find a community of like-minded individuals who can support each other in change efforts.

When in conflict with Magicians: State your linkages to each other and your intent to work side-by-side for win-win solutions. Clearly define visions of the future each of you is attempting to create. See what these have in common and note specific differences. Also, clearly define what you both believe to be the current reality (sometimes Magicians live in the future). Where there are differences, research facts and come back to the table. Use a mediator. Use the conflict as a teaching tool to pinpoint underlying root cause of the problems, and to heal the system in which you both work.

Power and empowerment: The Magician believes that real power comes from within, and that therefore, power is NOT a scarce commodity. In fact, you can *increase* your power by sharing it, that is, by empowering others. Power is not directly related to your position within the organization, but rather to who you are as a human being (internal power). Your power and effectiveness can be multiplied by mutual sharing of resources, skills, knowledge, and ideas. Then when you have more power, so do I (and vice versa).

If your boss is a Magician: He or she is likely to be an unusual person, charismatic, persuasive. Your boss is also likely to empower subordinates, build work teams, make certain people receive all the training and retraining they need. Magician bosses encourage self-management, promote high self-esteem, and provide a powerful vision. Sometimes, however, they burn out their subordinates by expecting them to work miracles on a regular basis or by trying to make the future happen right now.

Magicians You May Have Met in the Workplace

The key workplace issue for the Magician Core Type is *power*. This is not your power *over* others, but rather (1) power *with* others, and (2) the personal power to grow, change, and learn, that is, to increase your own *internal* power.

The Magician often has a gift for seeing the future that we intend to create. Therefore, one of the principal stressors for this Core Type is being able to clearly see the future, but being restricted in some way from moving towards it. This makes us feel powerless, extremely frustrated, even angry. When the Magician is at its best, we feel balanced and full, as if energy is moving freely through our entire mind/body/spirit (which the Magician sees as an indivisible whole). When we are under extreme stress, the Magician can become dangerously manipulative, for example, by skillfully "persuading" people to give their own time, energy, decision-making authority, or other sources of personal power away to us.

Perhaps the least likable Magician co-worker, colleague, or boss is the **Manipulator**, Magician-style. In legend such Manipulators come in many forms: the evil sorcerer, the wicked witch, the vampire, or the illusionist. In the workplace, I have seen manipulation honed into a perverse art form. Sometimes this is a conscious, deliberate strategy to get others to pull our weight, to do our work. At other times, the manipulation is rooted in an unconscious neediness, a cloying, an attachment in which we siphon off others' energy before they know what's happened. A great many people go to work every day who are (temporarily or more seriously) disturbed emotionally or mentally, or who are physically ill. The only way we can get through the work day is by hooking into others' energy. If you ever feel drained for no reason, look around you. Experiment by removing yourself from anyone whom you suspect of draining you in this way.

The **Change Agent** ranges from those skilled individuals who can see what needs to be done, and who know how to help others achieve success with minimum effort, to those bored individuals who make change where none is needed (the equivalent of just moving the furniture around). If the wrong kind of change happens at the wrong time in an organization, things can quite suddenly become a great deal worse. In the medical field there is a term for physician-created illness, *iatrogenic disease* (e.g., taking out the wrong organ in surgery). Similarly, leaders and change agents alike need to guard against "iatrogenic" change efforts. It actually is quite common to "operate" on an organization, to make dramatic changes where smaller ones, or none at all, might have been much more advisable.

The **Innovator** is a form of change agent who has ideas and makes them happen. Many innovators see ourselves as a channel for inspiration. We don't sit around waiting for angels to whisper the solution to us, but we have learned how to stay open to our Core's gifts of intuition. Many famous inventors and other creators describe receiving such sudden insights that "just come through" them. The magical Change Agent can also act as a **Transformer**, much like an energy generator, in which energy and power move through us and out into the world. If we understand that we do not own this energy, and do not become ego-inflated, we can work miracles in the workplace.

The **Visionary** or **Prophet** is a valued workplace function for the Magician. Even if leaders don't want to change, we'd sure like to know what's coming down the pike. Because many Magicians have a foot in both worlds, the present and the future, this part of us is a bit more attuned to what is likely to happen. The Magician's interest in and focus on the future makes us excellent advisors to receptive leaders, as was Merlin to King Arthur.

PERSONAL AND PROFESSIONAL ASSESSMENT

Your Core Type Profile Score for Magician: _____

Aspects of the Magician with which you identify:

_____

Aspects of the Magician with which you do not identify:

_____

Situations that bring out the Magician in you (and which form of Magician?):

_____

_____

_____

Work colleagues (or friends or family members) in whom you see the Magician:

Person   *Form of Magician*

_____   _____

_____   _____

_____   _____

Not only is the Magician capable of moving between times, it can, in its role as **Shape-Shifter**, walk between worlds, taking on characteristics of others in order to understand and communicate better with them. Some workplace shape-shifters are people who have little shape of our own — "yes men" who are extremely pliable and who agree with whomever spoke to us last. The Magician's skill comes in staying who you are, while fully (with the focus of your whole mind and heart) listening and speaking with others. Not necessarily agreeing, mind you, but immersing yourself in others' opinions, trying them on for size. This highly tuned empathetic ability allows Magicians to more easily play the role of **Mediator** or **Peace-Maker** by focusing on what people have in common so that we can help them bridge and transform their conflict. The more skillful among these mediators can move people out of debate and help them enter the process of dialogue (from the Greek, *dia-logos*, passing through spirit). In such mediation processes, the Magician also employs its ability to generate options until we find a creative solution that is satisfactory to all.

The **Healer** or **Shaman** is a traditional role for Magicians. The Magician in us is now being called upon to heal troubled workplaces. The older healing arts were holistic, which is why many of us trying to heal today's workplaces are **Systems Integrators** whose worldview is that organizations function like living organisms and must be healed in holistic, comprehensive, integrated ways. Magicians flock to systems thinking, quantum physics, and other new sciences (many of which are referenced in this book and in other "transformative" business literature). Shamans believe that we cannot heal just one part of any living system. Just as your foot is connected to your blood system, the finance department is connected to human resources, and the health of one always affects the health of the other. Going even a step further, many workplace Magicians have come to the conclusion that if our workplaces are ever to become all they can be, they must be healed in their entireties, including their spirit, mind, and body.

THE RULER

Elizabeth is an entrepreneur who launched a clothing design company fifteen years ago. As a businesswoman, Elizabeth became impatient with the clothes available to her "off the rack." In frustration one day, she called together a number of other female friends who, she suspected, had similar complaints. Among the group she gathered for an elegant dinner, one woman had some retail buying experience and another was an artist with a flair for color and style. The other guests provided encouragement that grew as the evening wore on.

The core threesome spent the next several months determining whether they had the resources and desire to set up a small business. They consulted with friends and a business advisor, who drew up a formal plan, outlining the capital they would need. At a second meeting, the original group grew to include other women and men who potentially had the interest and money to contribute to their friends' ideas. Elizabeth and her new partners presented the line they were proposing — classic business clothes for working women, with beautiful lines and fabric, that were feminine, comfortable, and attractive.

Because Elizabeth's family comes from old money, she did not hesitate to become the primary investor. Due to her confidence, other investors soon followed. The threesome rented a storefront, worked part-time for the first year, gradually turning the new work into their careers. Very soon business was booming.

Elizabeth functions as the principal of this enterprise, and her two partners are thrilled that she is willing to take on that responsibility. She is a personable, slightly reserved, but eminently fair employer. Her employees are paid well and have options to buy into the still-growing company.

The Ruler is the internal advisor who contributes to Self-mastery by having you "own" whatever responsibilities you have. It also helps you find or recognize the order in chaos, and enforce order where there is anarchy and despair. Because the key workplace issue for the Ruler is *power* (*control* of the externals of your life and work), this Core Type wants a position of authority in the workplace, a clearly defined, and significant, area of responsibility.

The Ruler tends to gather in high-prestige professions, to own its own businesses, or to reign in the upper echelons of corporations or government bureaucracies. It is very present in boardrooms, particularly those of powerful corporations or large public agencies. Some Rulers function as political power brokers on the international, national, social, or corporate level. The common thread is that the Ruler tends to create or enforce its own "aristocracy," its own ruling class, wherever it gathers with others of its kind.

Your internal Ruler helps you maintain stability and order in your life and work, even in matters as small as being able to put your hands easily on a file you're looking for. The Ruler is the guide who helps you take responsibility for your life. It is the inner steward of your finances, your career choices. It helps create order in the office or at the dinner table. It enables you to make tough decisions in a deliberate, thoughtful way, and then see that these decisions are carried through. It helps prioritize your own, and your organization's, goals and resources. It believes in the utilitarian good, which is why it keeps in mind the benefit of all.

The Ruler's Story

Responsibility is the navel-strong of creation.

— MARTIN BUBER

In mythology, the Ruler is the Core Type who takes the kingdom from chaos to order, and who does so by finding a positive use for everything and everyone. The Ruler is the part of you who helps bring your gifts into the world by carefully managing whatever resources are at your command. This is the internal advisor who, regardless of your circumstances, knows your real value. Like Ludwig van Beethoven, it believes that "The only true nobility is that of the soul."

The Ruler is the Core Type who establishes, then maintains, order by taking diverse elements and making them into a harmonious whole. In the worst cases, the Ruler acts as a despot who creates order through a self-serving tyranny, by subjugating and terrorizing

THE RULER

the very people we are to serve, or by excluding or enslaving the less powerful members of the kingdom. At best, the Ruler is a compassionate leader who has the desire and the wisdom to steward all the kingdom's resources (including the talents of its members) so that everyone flourishes. This form of Ruler can be found in servant-leaders who use their positions to serve the kingdom and those within it (rather than the other way around).

It is said in much of lore that the Ruler enjoys a magical relationship with the kingdom, which literally mirrors the health and well-being — or lack of same — of its king or queen. (The most famous example of this in western mythology can be seen in the contrast between the neighboring territories of Camelot and the Wasteland Kingdom, whose rulers were, respectively, the great Arthur and the ailing Fisher King.) In some ancient traditions, the Rulers and their land were thought to be so intertwined that Rulers were expected to give their lives for the welfare of the kingdom, that is, every few years the reigning monarch would be killed as a way to "replenish" the soil. (Similarly, many organizations seem to find it necessary to "kill the king" when they are in trouble. Especially if you're the designated Ruler, it helps to understand this tendency as archetypal rather than personal. Do not, however, underestimate this deeply rooted human tendency.)

In our own individual lives, it is the Ruler within us who understands that we are responsible for both our internal and external realities. Another way to say this is that our outer world and inner world are reflections of each other, and that to change your work life, you will first need to get your inner house in order.

So, how did the mythical monarchs get their inner houses in order? By taking their heroic journeys. Legends from across the world chart the course that we should be requiring of workplace leaders. The prospective Rulers of yore were sent out into the woods (their inner selves) in order to gain some sense of Self, to find out who they were. Those who proved worthy of becoming Rulers were the ones who faced their inner dragons, rescued the damsel-in-distress (i.e., claimed their hidden selves), and returned to the kingdom with the treasures they had discovered (their wisdom).

One of the things that intrigues me about the Ruler Core Type is how few of our designated workplace leaders have its strengths. This is not surprising, because organizations tend to throw people into management positions for all the wrong reasons. Workplaces often select as leaders those of us who are professionally accomplished in a particular field, or politically savvy, or who have been around longer than others. Then we are promoted to our "level of incompetence." When designated leaders have not learned the lessons of the Ruler Core Type, we wind up managing our subordinates with the same fear or anger that is driving us. Leaders need to develop sufficient inner resources so that a healthy workplace will be mirrored from our internal state; otherwise, all the workers — and the work — under our sway will suffer. As psychiatrist Douglas La Bier described in *Modern Madness*, when he was called into organizations to treat "disturbed employees," he quickly discovered that the employees' bosses were the truly crazy ones. As often happens in dysfunctional families, it was the *healthier* people who first exhibited symptoms that were visible to the outside world.

Recognizing the Ruler in Yourself and Others

- *Eyes*: Acknowledge you; watching and managing all that's around; often looks down on others or looks over them. Not a direct gaze, unless giving a command.
- *Face*: Well-controlled, small, contained motions that others have to pay attention to in order to interpret, for example, slight nods of agreement or disagreement.
- *Body*: Commanding, takes up space. Sits or stands above others. Hands used to direct or acknowledge others. Others come to them. Conscious of indications of position and power of self and others, for example, sits at appropriate power spot at meetings.
- *Walk*: Regal, confident, sets the pace of the group. Often walks with others who are in attendance or following them.
- *Talk*: Sure of self, gives orders and opinions, commanding style can range from quiet to dominant. Well-spoken; well-bred; gracious.

- *Clothing*: Indicates trappings of power. For example, expensive suits, monogrammed shirts, rich fabrics, a prosperous look. A cut above the rest. External trappings also include expensive cars, the corner office, a reserved parking space, office size and furnishings.

Contributions and Difficulties within the Workplace

The primary objective of the Ruler is to create a stable, orderly kingdom. This part of us acts as a steward for the wealth in our trust. It helps us design systems in which everyone has a role, everyone contributes, and the resources available are allocated properly, then optimized in their usage. The Ruler balances the need for stability versus innovation, and helps us "harmonize" the diverse components of our organizations. What it fears most is chaos, losing control. This, we are certain, will result in the dissipation, loss, or complete destruction of valuable resources, people, or the traditions that have successfully held things together for so long.

The Ruler part of ourselves is very responsible. This Core Type tends to think of the organization as a whole, and therefore keeps the good of the entire group in mind. It also makes certain that tasks are seen through from beginning to end, because the Ruler is the one left holding the bag if there are any missing links in the chain. Harry Truman expressed the Ruler's motto when he stated, "The buck stops here." The good Ruler does not shy away from, but rather fully claims, the mantle of responsibility that is ours to bear. The kingdom relies on its Ruler to be a stabilizing force, to keep things balanced; and when we get thrown out of balance, to bring us back into some semblance of order. Employees respond with loyalty and respect when their Ruler is fair, judicial, and even-handed. This Core Type rests easily with external power, assumes it, and carries its weight or more no matter what position we hold in the organization.

The Ruler finds sudden or rapid change completely disorienting. This trait frequently puts the Ruler Core Type in a dilemma nowadays. Rulers can become overly controlling, dominating our employees and micromanaging them by watching their every move.

This part of us tends towards inflexibility and has been heard to utter words similar to: "It's my way or the highway." It is also not uncommon for Rulers to be out of touch with "the people," to be unfeeling for others, in part due to the insulation provided by a position of authority. This sometimes causes us to evidence contempt for our "underlings." Another difficulty Rulers have is limiting ourselves to our own area of authority (this type contributes significantly to turf fights in organizations). We may also find ourselves chafing at following the leadership of others, especially if we do not respect their abilities or power base, or when they give us orders that conflict with our own judgment.

When Working with the Ruler in Others

- Explain needed activities and changes with reference to the good of the whole organization.
- Clearly define areas of, or limits to, responsibility and authority.
- Use their sense of responsibility for the whole to keep things coordinated.
- Call upon them to provide a stabilizing influence during change.
- Elicit their cooperation during change efforts, demonstrate what is being preserved versus changed (and how, and why).
- Provide reasonable autonomy with their area of responsibility.
- Encourage them to act more as coach than micromanager of their subordinates.
- Offer leadership development that helps them claim their inner wealth and deal with their less noble aspects.

When in conflict with Rulers: Conflicts are likely to be over disputed lines of authority. Take care to respect theirs, and make it clear when Rulers are outside their own territory. Rulers challenge those whose competence or authority they do not acknowledge; be prepared to prove, justify, and defend yours. Rulers also resist rapid change or apparent disorder, and will not be flexible in chaotic circumstances. Look at the resources available to both of you, and how changes can be made in an orderly way. Let the Ruler know you too are interested in the long-term stability of the system.

Power and empowerment: Power and prestige are the natural inheritance of the Ruler. Power is absolute, unchallenged control over the kingdom's resources and people. For the less mature Ruler, this results in tyranny; for the high-level Ruler, a peaceful, orderly kingdom results. Empowerment is the power the Ruler either gives or takes away from others as and when needed. Empowerment must be done slowly, incrementally, and only to the degree that subordinates prove themselves worthy, loyal, and able to handle the increased authority/responsibility. Empowerment is NOT a right. It is a perk, an indication of your increased prestige. It is conferred, like knighthood, by the Ruler only on the worthy and able.

If your Boss is a Ruler: He or she is decisive, authoritative, sees the overview, is concerned with and responsible for whole departmental or organizational goals and outcome. Ruler bosses assume responsibility without hesitation, and they may expect you to follow orders without questioning.

Rulers You May Have Met in the Workplace

The key workplace issue for the Ruler is *power* — in this case, external power, control over your particular piece of the world. Clearly, then, one of the most stressful possible workplace situations for Rulers is to lose the trappings of power, rank, and prestige (because these reflect or contribute to real-life power loss). It is quite understandable, then, when the Ruler Core Type is under excessive stress, that we do whatever we can to protect our advantages so these are not eroded. This often takes the form of digging in, of becoming more controlling and dominating. We also tend to become more rigid under stress. This inflexibility reflects our fear that if we give, even a little bit, our whole world will fall apart. When this part of ourselves is at its best, it helps coordinate and balance the many diverse aspects of our life and circumstances. In short, it makes us feel somewhat more sane and in control of our own destinies.

Probably the worst kind of Ruler is the **Despot** or **Tyrant**. Unfortunately, in the workplace we have many petty despots who graduated from the ruling-by-fear school of management, for example, bosses in sweatshops. This variation of the Ruler Core Type often hangs out in corners of our bureaucracies, or in small family-owned businesses, where it can get away with mismanagement because others don't see what's going on. In some of the worst cases, such despots are so powerful than no one can stop them. As one mogul reportedly said of the workplace conditions of his diamond mines, "You can't run a mine without machine guns." The Despot tends to be highly territorial about its fiefdom and often Machiavellian about getting more turf. Much as modern media has exposed and helped depose international tyrants, 360-degree supervisory feedback in the workplace can help pull the veil off some of these people. (This is not a guarantee, because some employees are so frightened that they will not risk the retaliation that would be certain and swift if the boss knew who gave that honest feedback.)

Aristocrats are those people in the world or the workplace who, in reality, are heirs to the throne (inheriting the family business or having a very wealthy family who sets you up in business). Aristocrats are also those of us who, by virtue of our personality or personal circumstances, seem destined to rule. Thomas Wolfe, in *Bonfire of the Vanities*, called such Wall Street stars the "Masters of the Universe." My maternal grandmother, Winifred McLaughlin, knew this form of the Ruler Core Type. Whenever she was in a room all the activity and people in it would soon be revolving around her.

Most of the people who work in the workplace also work at home as **Parents** and **Householders**. Whether our homesteads are small apartments or real palaces, whether we have one small child or several teenagers, a great deal of our time and effort needs to be stewarded by our internal Ruler if we are to manage this aspect of our lives while we simultaneously earn our livelihood. Indeed, sometimes we need the skill of a corporate leader to juggle our time and resources properly.

We also have **Power Brokers**, a.k.a. **King-Makers**, in organizations and politics. Rulers who are very powerful are often most comfortable exercising power from hidden places, "behind the throne," as it were. In the workplace, power brokers are not necessarily even designated leaders, but those of us who have the ears of other leaders and the cooperation of diverse factions of the system. Power Brokers may also be people who exert power due to the resources at our command — be it cash flow (investors), reputation (lending a well-known name to a product), talent (a needed expertise), or spiritual leadership (someone who has the trust and respect of a large portion of the staff).

The **Judge** is expected to be fair, to carefully weigh right and wrong, and to determine what is best for all concerned — the individual, group, and society. These judicial qualities are highly valued traits in workplace leaders. Indeed, even-handedness, such as not

---

PERSONAL AND PROFESSIONAL ASSESSMENT

Your Core Type Profile Score for Ruler: _____

Aspects of the Ruler with which you identify:

_____

Aspects of the Ruler with which you do not identify:

_____

Situations that bring out the Ruler in you (and which form of Ruler?):

_____

_____

_____

Work colleagues (or friends or family members) in whom you see the Ruler:

Person   *Form of Ruler*

_____   _____

_____   _____

_____   _____

playing favorites among staff members, is sure to engender the respect and loyalty of our employees.

The **Manager/Steward** is a facet of leadership that is supported by the Ruler Core Type. It is a requirement for those who have a position of authority that includes managing any of the resources of organization. Such stewarding is critical to keeping things together — the last stand against chaos. Much of what is taught in business schools relates to this aspect of the Ruler Core Type. An intriguing reframing of the Manager was described by David Fearon and Ivan Blanco in *Managing in Organizations that Learn*. They describe the new **Managerial Mind** in "undisclosed" managers, that is, frontline workers who understand their work processes, know how to improve them, and speak up.[6] Such a level of ownership requires your internal Ruler to have the attitude that, no matter where you are in the organization, you don't "just work there"; you too are responsible for the good of the whole.

Total Quality Management supports an attitude shift regarding the nature of management from both directions — supervisors and employees. It suggests that leaders see themselves more as **Coaches** than as police officers who make sure people put in a good day's work. The new managerial minds described by Fearon and Blanco will flourish where we are given coaching and support. The Coach is an empowering Ruler who helps others give their best in their own way. The techniques used to accomplish this may range from hands-off leadership style, to coaxing, to teaching, to querying, to cajoling. All of this effort is directed at producing the best effort from the team and the individuals on it.

Management author Peter Drucker wrote about the comparison between workplace leaders and musical **Conductors**. This kind of Ruler must stay completely in control of this extremely "dynamic" situation. Conductors need to keep every individual in mind, to keep the whole in mind, to adjust what's happening in the moment, and also to stay mindful of what's just ahead. Business leaders resonated deeply with this comparison, which so colorfully describes a truth about the work of being a manager. John Clarkeson, Chairman of the Boston Consulting Group, goes even further.

He compares managers with **Leaders of Jazz Ensembles** rather than of orchestras, and he has hit upon an important truth here. We don't ever have a score in front of us to run our businesses. Like jazz improvisers, we too have to make things up as we go along.

Perhaps the very best boss one could ever have — or be — is the **Servant Leader**, whom Robert K. Greenleaf described in *Servant Leadership: A Journey into the Nature of Legitimate Power and Greatness*. The Servant Leader sees our positions of leadership as being of *service to those we lead*. In this model of leadership, the lines are blurred between those who lead and those who serve, much as the lines of authority in our shifting organizational structures are also becoming increasingly blurred. The Servant Leader knows the truth: that work is woven of relationships in which we all serve each other, and the whole. The goal of the Servant Leader, then, is "to find the wisdom and the power to serve others."[7] And, in so doing, the Ruler Core Type helps us augment the whole of which we are a part.

THE LOVER

Robert is a history professor at a large university. His classes are always the first to be signed up for in his department. The word is out that this is one professor who can really make history come alive. Robert is a somewhat unusual faculty member — colorful, flamboyant, charismatic. Not only are his classes filled to overflowing, but every year a new crop of young women sit up front, dreaming of projects they can do for extra credit. Fortunately his personal and professional boundaries are solid. He deflects their admiration for him into admiration for the subject in which he is so absorbed.

Robert speaks passionately about the lessons the past has for our present and future. How can we not see what we've done before, he asks? If we do not, we are doomed to repeat our mistakes. He spices up lectures with a multimedia, multisensory approach. Not only do his students read about the period, but they also listen to its music, learn the dances, read the poetry, produce plays, and deliver political speeches. Many of these exciting projects are delivered by teams of students in period costume, to the delight of all. Robert's goal is to have his students immerse themselves in the five senses of a given period, so they learn — at a body level — what this time was about.

Although his colleagues at first found his teaching style to be unorthodox, his results (scores and accolades) have influenced some of them to follow suit in their own way. Besides, he is such a congenial person, they agree, and so energetic. Lord knows the department could use a bit of that. Truth be told, his superiors had some idea of what they were in for when they hired him. After all, he had burst into a song during his interview in order to illustrate a point he was making!

The Lover is the part of you that feels it cannot hold the world close enough, and that life is too short. It truly believes it is better to have loved and lost than never to have loved at all. This Core Type is your internal poet and minstrel, causing you to burn with desire, or to swoon at beauty: as Blake said, "to see heaven in a grain of sand." Typically the *flamboyance, passion,* and *emotional intensity* that this Core Type projects are considered "over the top" in workplace settings: not safe, too hot to handle, too touchy-feely, blatantly sexual, a loose cannon, dynamite.

However, I have noticed that as men and women become more comfortable with each other in workplace settings, we are better able to tap the extraordinary energy of this Core Type. In *Business and the Feminine Principle: The Untapped Resource,* Carol Frenier says, "The feminine is only fully *conscious* at work when one experiences the deepest kind of satisfaction from simultaneously knowing oneself as lover and valuing one's work for that reason."[8]

The goal of the Lover is *transcendence* — going beyond our normal limits to become extraordinary. The Lover tries to accomplish transcendence through *attachment*, the Sage through detachment. In the workplace, this part of us wants to be something very special, to surpass what has been done before. The Lover urges you to pour your heart and soul into your work, to burn the candle at both ends, not out of self-sacrifice or duty, but because you absolutely *love* what you're doing.

The Lover is the part of us that suffers significantly in many workplaces. It wants to do work we love and to love the work we do. For many of us, this is far from easy. Fortunately, this Core Type can *show us the dignity in and the need for any kind of work,* so that we can transcend and transform it by infusing it with our best selves.

THE LOVER

Considering the soul-grinding, dispiriting work available in most workplaces, this particular gift of the Lover provides a salvation for those of us who do not want to turn into robots. Instead of the work dragging us down, the Lover helps us simultaneously uplift the work and ourselves.

The Lover also contributes mightily to an exciting, stimulating, and caring workplace environment. No other of our internal advisors is more dedicated to achieving the vision, mission, or tasks with which it agrees. This is the Core Type that tells us to *follow our bliss*, to stop and smell the roses, to find and pursue our vocational passion. Otherwise, it warns, we will go through our lives saddened and burdened by regrets. We will always wonder what it might have been like if we had just tried a little harder, just taken this job rather than that one. Or, like Willy in *Death of a Salesman*, we would always regret that we hadn't taken that trip to the world's fair. Indeed, with the Lover as our advisor, our daily work can become an adventure in itself.

The Lover teaches us *passion* and *commitment,* makes us feel alive in the moment. It refreshes us deeply by *showing us the beauty* all around us. It *connects us emotionally to others,* allowing us to *dialogue* with our colleagues. It gives us enough powerful *energy* to sustain long efforts (by allowing us to harness erotic energy for more generalized use). The Lover helps us *notice and appreciate the diversity* in our colleagues and customers.

The Lover's Story

> Work is love made visible.
>
> — KAHLIL GIBRAN

The Lover is that part of us that falls in love with something or someone we consider to be beautiful, extraordinary, beyond comparison, desirable, and worthy of great love. We are completely fascinated; we are infatuated. The "other" is idolized and can do no wrong. Another version of the Lover's story is that we fall in love and are somehow separated from our loved one. We then overcome obstacles in order to attain, or be reunited with, this wonderful person or goal. We dedicate ourselves completely to this difficult task — body and soul — in order to overcome the many obstacles in our way. We do whatever it takes to get us there. Once Lovers are united with our transcendent goal (as mythology promises), we "live happily ever after."

The Lover tends to accept and appreciate the reality that the Warrior, the Caregiver, and the Magician parts of us try to change. It delights in the senses. It is beauty personified. The way of the Lover is the way of Eros, the god of passion and love. As this Core Type increases in its understanding, we learn how to move from loving only a few people or things to feeling ecstatically connected with everything that exists. The Lover also gives us the capacity to commit to one person or one job in an exciting and complex world with many options. It teaches us how to be intimate, honest, emotionally true, and also how to "open up" at appropriate times to appropriate others. One of the most difficult tasks for this Core Type is to learn how to be more inclusive, to widen the circle of what we love, because it tends to hate just as fiercely as it loves. Moreover, this Core Type can move very quickly from love to hate if we are betrayed or abandoned by the "other." At the highest level, the Lover Core Type helps us understand that we have projected our love of the Self onto the world and people around it.

Recognizing the Lover in Yourself and Others

- *Eyes*: Looking for personal connection, intimate, open; notices beauty; attention focused on what it loves.
- *Face*: Expressive, reveals whatever feeling — from love to hatred; soft/receptive *or* intense and passionate, *or* glaring with dislike.
- *Body/Gestures*: Alive, attractive, open, expressive. If culture allows, will physically touch or embrace others. Hugs colleagues; moves towards others, uninhibited, sometimes erotic.
- *Walk*: Uninhibited, free; effortlessly sexy; sweeping motion that draws attention, focused on going wherever attention is focused.

- *Talk*: Intimate, emotional, dramatic, personally disclosive, open. Use of exclamation points and superlatives. Exaggerates to make a point.
- *Clothing*: Attractive, attention-getting, artistic. Colorful, makes a dramatic personal statement. Personal fashion versus mainstream fashion. *Or,* so focused on mission that inattentive to personal attire.

Contributions and Difficulties within the Workplace

The goal of the Lover Core Type is to love the work you do, and to be in a loving relationship with yourself and others. This part of you fears coldness, emptiness, soul loss, indifference, and being separated from the object you love. For the Lover, work is meant to be a great pleasure of life. We are often challenged in the workplace by having to complete tasks we are not fond of, or being forced to work with people we don't like. The Lover Core Type contributes to the workplace in many ways. When we are in the right place, with the right people, we are happily committed and seem to have limitless reserves of energy. We will go out of our way to inspire others to join the "cause." Others seem to feed off the fuel we so freely provide. This Core Type infuses the workplace with intimacy, empathy, and understanding. It is charismatic, caring, and warm. Its appreciation of diversity and genuine interest in others helps people and projects to bloom. The Lover takes us into deeper waters than many workplaces are used to, or would allow. However, if the workplace does permit the Lover's energy, the organization can achieve real dialogue and connection among its members.

Other Lover's contributions to the workplace include its sense of beauty, its appreciation of the senses, and its artistic flair. These qualities can often humanize drab, grey, and depressing workplaces. Another joy the Lover brings the workplace is a sense of celebration. Any excuse will do — the completion of a project, a birthday, the end of the week.

Traditionally, the Lover Core Type has had many difficulties in the workplace. It tends to be dismissed as irrational. This means we have to beat our heads against a wall on a regular basis. This frustration increases our likelihood of burning out, because we will tend to respond by just trying harder to prove our point. The Lover's intolerance of particular tasks or co-workers gets us into a lot of trouble. It can also nurse grudges, or become vengeful, when affection and admiration have turned to anger and contempt. Moreover the Lover easily becomes overattached, sometimes even symbiotic and cloying.

One of the greatest difficulties this Core Type has in the workplace is our misreading of erotic energy. I believe that much of the confusion over sexual harassment in the workplace is due to our repression of the Lover energy and our lack of understanding about how much good it can do. Unfortunately, instead of using the Lover's energy to form democratic, egalitarian bonds, we try to control this power by dominating others.

When Working with the Lover in Others

- Express your commitment to the task and the relationship.
- Respect the intensity and passion of the Lover's attitude.
- Don't misread the erotic energy that surrounds such passion.
- Remember that the quality of personal relationships often sustains them through the boring work that has to be done.
- Appeal to their hearts.
- Give them extra support when they need to detach from people or tasks they love.
- Help them widen the circle of who and what they appreciate.
- Use their sense of beauty to humanize the workplace setting.
- Have them help you establish a more democratic work environment.

When in Conflict with Lovers: Although Lovers will go to great lengths to avoid conflict, once engaged they tend to be fierce, with love quickly turning to hatred. To defuse a potentially explosive situation, try to show how much you care for them. Be respectful. Work to resolve the underlying problem in order to remove barriers to the long-term health of the relationship. Deal with the disagreement in a straightforward manner. Whenever emotions run too high, take a break until you both cool off. Use a trusted mediator. Air feelings. Keep focused on the issues that need resolution. Do not allow blaming or name-calling. Constantly remind each other of your shared affection and the goal you both seek.

Power and empowerment: Power is the ability to do what you love doing, to work with those you love and respect, and to have an attractive work environment. It is also the ability to NOT have to do things you dislike or work with people you abhor. Power, like love and the magic penny, multiplies when you give it away. Sometimes, however, the Lover empowers only those people we like. The more mature Lover believes all people, organizations, and the world itself will thrive and prosper if all people are empowered to do the work they love.

PERSONAL AND PROFESSIONAL ASSESSMENT

Your Core Type Profile Score for Lover: _____

Aspects of the Lover with which you identify:

_____

Aspects of the Lover with which you do not identify:

_____

Situations that bring out the Lover in you (and which form of Lover?):

_____

_____

_____

Work colleagues (or friends or family members) in whom you see the Lover:

Person   *Form of Lover*

_____   _____

_____   _____

_____   _____

If your boss is a Lover: He or she will tend to be charismatic, intense, and very hardworking. The Lover leads by going out in front, inspiring others, and infusing them with his or her passionate commitment. Lover bosses tend to bring others along in the wake of their energy. The danger here is that workers can become like "cult followers" who do not think or act for themselves.

Lovers You May Have Met in the Workplace

The key workplace issue for the Lover is *transcendence* — becoming extraordinary, going beyond accepted limits. The most significant stressor for the Lover Core Type is being forced to work on a project or with people we dislike. When the Lover is at its best, we feel passionately alive. Moreover, we enliven everything and everyone around us with that passion. When we are under too much stress, we will lash out at anyone who criticizes us or the object of our affections.

One of the worst forms of the Lover Core Type is the **Don Juan** or **Juanita**. This part of us uses our erotic powers inappropriately in the workplace. This would include male bosses who sexually harass their subordinates, or executive women who flaunt their sexuality in order to gain political advantage. Predatory actions, lascivious language, or inappropriate sexual behavior are typical of this lower form of Lover.

Another form of Lover you may have come across is the **Symbiotic** or **Cloying Person**. The level of attachment is so strong that we become disabled by our mutual dependency. Symbiosis is a form of narcissism where we see our reflection in the other person and can no longer clearly distinguish who is who. The personal boundaries so necessary to survival become too permeable and eventually dissolve. The difficulty is that, like Siamese twins, both people are hobbled. Although not as common in the workplace as in personal lives, this "infatuated" form of Lover occurs in work relationships where one person excessively admires the other, and the other fosters that adulation.

Connoisseurs in the workplace are those of us who so love our work that we have formed a passionate expertise. If anyone asks, we can tell them anything they want to know about the subject, and will if they give us a moment (which sometimes turns into hours). With a willing subject, we will wax eloquent, eyes glowing, becoming more animated as the conversation, or rather monologue, continues.

The Lover also serves as a **Team-Builder**, and is particularly adept at "maintenance" issues. These include communication skills, facilitation, mediation between members, and managing conflict. When teams have sufficient Lover energy present, they tend to be highly energized and can withstand all kinds of stresses. One organization I worked with had a management team that was extremely successful and felt passionately dedicated to its mission. When the larger system instituted a reorganization effort, this team was informed that because they had done so well, they were to be broken up so members could be assigned to different parts of the organization. The team had attracted attention, and supervisors wanted to take that Lover energy and disperse it throughout the organization. However, the members of the team thought it over, then refused, saying that if one of them went, they all would go. As a result, the organizational leaders backed off and the team was kept together in order to fulfill its stated mission.

The Lover appears in organizations anytime we are **ecstatic** about our work or colleagues. This translates to friendship, collegiality, and community building (within and without the organization). This ecstatic energy is available in each of us to help us transcend the mundane aspects of our work lives. In fact, one of the Lover's highest realizations is to make us understand that the love we feel for others is the same love we carry inside ourselves all the time. It's just that it is often easier for us to see that love when we project it onto other individuals or noble causes.

THE SAGE

Fred and I met through a colleague who asked us to write an article together. I liked Fred immediately, and found him most pleasant to work with. He was cerebral, with a dry and sometimes elusive sense of humor that I found delightful.

When Fred is in a meeting, he is quiet for long periods of time. More vocal participants sometimes forget he's even there. I have discovered, however, that he is silently absorbing the comments of everyone around. Really listening. Processing. Putting things together. When Fred does speak, his comments are insightful, synthesizing what has been said up to that point. Because he has sometimes fast-forwarded to significantly greater understandings while the rest of us were chatting, Fred occasionally needs to go to the board, draw the model he's come up with, and move into a teaching role so that the rest of us can catch up. As another of my colleagues repeatedly comments, "This guy is so bright, it scares me."

Fred now spends his days building an "autognome," a self-referencing, autonomous machine that he is, among other things, teaching to read. When Fred gives the autognome something new to read — the children's story "Peter Rabbit" for instance — it ponders away, trying to make sense of how language is being used and what it means. If Fred is successful, the autognome will ultimately rival the capability of the fictional HAL from 2001. My sense is that if anyone could produce this breakthrough invention, it would be Fred. Interestingly, despite his native genius and depth of understanding in this newly developing field, Fred is extremely humble, refusing to allow anyone to describe him as an expert.

The Sage is the part of you that seeks to transcend your daily limitations through *detachment*, versus the Lover's path of attachment. This Core Type contributes to your Self-mastery by getting you to pause, quiet your mind, and contemplate the issues before you. The goal of the Sage is to realize the Self, to understand the Truth, or to gain specific knowledge through study, experimentation, and quiet contemplation.

The Sage is drawn to workplaces where we can teach ideas or increase our knowledge. It prefers "laboratories," think tanks, or research centers where we will be left alone. This Core Type most fears becoming overly attached to others, or having people become dependent upon us. It also fears illusions, the confusing and obscuring of the truth, and in workplaces, the politics that obscure or dismantle efficient work processes or systemic solutions. This Core Type, consequently, has to balance its desire to remain "above the fray" with its goal of optimizing the system in which we work.

THE SAGE

The Sage in you keeps calm when everyone around you is going crazy. Its detached perspective helps to minimize stress and prevent you from launching into a fight-or-flight reaction. The Sage knows how to keep things in perspective. The Sage is also helpful in getting us to detach emotionally from outdated concepts, ways of doing things, and dysfunctional colleagues or workplaces. The Sage part of us makes us step back from ego involvement or becoming embroiled in conflict. When it is at its best, the Sage sees everything and everyone as equal, perfect in its own way. The Sage urges us to listen to ourselves, think, and thereby access our own inner wisdom, rather than mindlessly adopting someone else's ideas.

The Sage's Story

> In knowing yourself you will know the universe.
> — KRISHNAMURTI

At the end of the Sage's journey, knowledge and wisdom are the rewards. The Sage part of us is willing to travel all of our lives to reach this destination. The Sage's journey is primarily inward, and it requires the ability to let go, to rid our self of attachment to people, things, ideas. At the lowest level, the Sage may have a global perspective but little ability to empathize with ordinary people. This kind of Sage loves humanity but despises people. At the highest level, however, the Sage appreciates both, but without ego attachment.

Having a historical, philosophical, or spiritual perspective allows our internal Sage to identify with a global outlook rather than with either the problems or triumphs of the day. In the workplace, the Sage may have us take on an explicit teaching function, act as an elder statesperson, mentor, or general advisor, or may make us retreat to some variety of "ivory tower" for contemplation. The Sage Core Type may seek specific intellectual knowledge, or the highest truths known to humanity, that is, spiritual knowledge, Wisdom. The former requires us to look outward, and through research, sort out what is and is not true. The latter requires us to explore our vast inner landscape. With its demands for extroverted activity, the traditional workplace is not particularly amenable to either Sage activity.

Recognizing the Sage in Yourself and Others

- *Eyes*: Looking inward for answers, or off into distance, vague — looking at forest versus trees. Looks for understanding of listener (as teacher to student).
- *Face*: Calm, wise looks; unperturbed, has seen it all; serene.
- *Body*: Minimal motion; still. Sometimes doesn't seem to be "at home"; is elsewhere mentally.
- *Walk*: Unhurried; thinking as walking; calm.
- *Talk*: Little of it, unless delivering a lecture; then can talk indefinitely on topic in which an expert. Looks at big picture, tries to put everything in context. Often is quiet during meeting, then says the last thing that sums up meeting perfectly.
- *Clothing*: Professor clothes. Practical, does not pay a lot of attention to them. Can be disheveled and unfashionable; looks distracted, e.g., forgets glasses or where left the file. Similarly, office often messy, a jumble of papers.

Contributions to and Difficulties in the Workplace

The Sage is the internal advisor who teaches you how to think for yourself and to value your own personal understanding of the truth. In this way, it makes a significant contribution to your Self-mastery. This Core Type's contributions to the workplace include our ability to see the overview, to keep the whole system in mind, and to maintain a global perspective. It is constantly seeking out information, doing planning, and "scanning the environment" for any kind of change that could affect our organization. The Sage's objectivity and fairness lend a sense of sanity to workplace interactions. Its ability to be detached makes people trust that we will arrive at even-handed decisions. The Sage makes significant contributions to systems thinking. It approaches problems with the philosophy that no one is personally to blame. Rather, the Sage encourages us to first look for the flaws in the system. Total quality management and other improvement methodologies are employed by our Sage to keep the whole system running smoothly. This approach removes fear; we feel able to accomplish our work without the threat of reprisal, should we make a mistake.

Due to its global perspective, the Sage can serve simultaneously as both a visionary and a historian for the organization. This ability to keep past, present, and future in mind is how the Sage keeps the organization from repeating its errors. This part of ourselves is an astute observer of events and people, sometimes critically so. Workplaces use the Sage's gifts to properly orient new employees, by giving them the "big picture" of the organization.

This Core Type can get into difficulties in the workplace when we become so focused on the big picture that we can't see the "trees for the forest." The Sage's tendency to immerse itself in ponderous, weighty issues sometimes prevents us from having the time we need to get smaller, yet important, tasks completed. Its preference for working in isolation and its tendency towards critical commentary does not foster connection with co-workers. In fact, the Sage sometimes is experienced by co-workers as looking down on them. The Sage also make us extremely irritable when distractions disrupt our work.

When Working with the Sage in Others

- Provide them with working environment that gives them time and opportunities for reflection.
- Involve them in long-range planning.
- Allow them to provide an overview perspective.
- Use their calm to save sanity, to help de-stress the work environment.
- Remind them of detail work to be completed.
- Do not expect closeness or emotional demonstrativeness.
- Coach them on how to give criticism in a way people can receive it.
- Continue to invite them to social activities despite their reluctance or shyness.

When in Conflict with Sages: Don't let your anger escalate when they ignore you or others. Point out that this conflict will not go away. Paint it as a problem to be solved, a puzzle that requires their input and would benefit from their experience, wisdom, intelligence. Be cool and rational when addressing the issues. Look at problems within the context of the big picture. Put your heads together to find the root cause of the problem. Don't settle for anything less than systemic, comprehensive, detached solutions. Bring all the evidence, data, and facts you have to the table.

Power and empowerment: The Sage believes that knowledge is power. Empowerment is sharing knowledge so as to multiply it. Low-level Sages hoard knowledge for ourselves, believing that others are not worthy, or would misuse or dilute the inherent power of this knowledge through "popularization." High-level Sages are mentors and teachers to others, empowering them through education and the sharing of our learning experiences. Sages also consider power to include the ability to be left alone to do our work without interruptions.

If your boss is a Sage: He or she is likely to be fair, even-handed, and to play no favorites. You will likely have candid performance evaluations on a regular basis. You will be expected to justify your opinions and prove your theories. Sage bosses may appear uncaring and hypercritical. If so, ask them to also let you know exactly what it is you're doing *right.*

Sages You May Have Met in the Workplace

The key workplace issue for the Sage is to transcend our limitations by mentally detaching from them. One of the worst things that can happen to the Sage in the workplace is to have so many distractions, or so much busy work, that we are no longer able to think. This puts the Sage Core Type under so much pressure that its worst traits emerge. When it is at its best, our Sage is calm, cool, collected, at peace. Clearly, this is a perspective most workplaces desperately need. However, when we are under too much pressure, the Sage detaches emotionally and removes itself from the stressful situation: nice house, nobody home.

The least helpful form of Sage co-worker, supervisor, or subordinate is the **Critic**. Excessive criticism thwarts creativity and reduces morale. It also fosters antagonisms and "one-upmanship," as we try to best each other intellectually. This form of Sage is blaming and does not take a systems perspective to problems. There are positive forms of the Critic, who are thoughtful, thought-provoking, and who challenge anything that borders on the trite. One gentle Sage I know cringes when he hears what he calls "blinking words." These are words that have lost their meaning because of their excessive and/or improper use. One of these, for him is *deep*, a New Age term that he thinks is used indiscriminately.

Hermits and **Ascetics** exist not only on mountaintops, but also in workplaces. This part of us finds it necessary to stay isolated in order to get our work done. When this kind of Sage is active in us, we are quite content to go days without interacting with other staff members. If we have office doors, these tend to remain shut. If not, our body language clearly signals that there is no welcome mat here.

PERSONAL AND PROFESSIONAL ASSESSMENT

Your Core Type Profile Score for Sage: _____

Aspects of the Sage with which you identify:

_____

Aspects of the Sage with which you do not identify:

_____

Situations that bring out the Sage in you (and which form of Sage?):

_____

_____

_____

Work colleagues (or friends or family members) in whom you see the Sage:

Person   *Form of Sage*

_____   _____

_____   _____

_____   _____

The Sage also appears as the **Scholar, Researcher**, and **Expert** who contributes a sound intellectual knowledge base to the organization's activities. These forms of Sage verify facts and make certain that the organization is on course. However, we can also become so absorbed in minutia that we sometimes know more and more about less and less.

Sages also serve as reasonable, judicial **Mediators** when conflict erupts. Because the Sage tends to play no favorites, other staff trust this part of us to help them arrive at the solution that is most fair for all concerned.

The Sage Core Type can also serve the organization as **Oracle, Futurist**, and candid **Prophet**, studying, then predicting, where trends will lead. The Sage's mindfulness of history as part of the big picture gives its predictions some perspective and, therefore, credibility.

Sages sometimes take on the role of **Detective** for the organization. This part of us enjoys sleuthing throughout the organizational systems to uncover its flaws. We then study the case until we arrive at solutions that will increase our likelihood of success.

Other forms of workplace Sage include not only the **Mentor** and **Teacher**, but also the **Philosopher**. As Deming once said, what the workplace most needed was a "philosophy of management." Otherwise, he said, what leaders did was too much like driving down the road by looking in our rearview mirrors.

The highest form of the Sage is the **Spiritual Teacher**, who serves organizations by raising the morale of individuals and increasing the cohesion of the whole system. The spiritual teacher does not shy away from the issue of soul or spirit in the workplace. This is the part of us that helps us remain centered and calm so we are better able to work from our Core. This form of Sage believes that perfection is our real inner nature *and* acknowledges our full humanity. Referring to an ancient sculptor who was chided for sculpting in the round when only the fronts of his statues could be seen, Peter Drucker confessed: "I have done many things which I hope the Gods will not notice, but I have always known that one has to strive for perfection even if only the Gods notice."[9]

TRANSFORMING YOURSELF

One way to transform yourself is to fully appreciate, learn the lessons, and then receive the gifts that each of the Core Types has for you. When we do this, according to mythology, we become the Transfigured Hero, that is, we achieve Self-mastery. I have noticed that the people I consider to be giants walking among us appear to have the highest attributes of all the Core Types.

Transformation begins at home. We cannot change the world for good until and unless we have first changed ourselves. As we become more complete, more fully human, we can have a transformative influence on our colleagues and workplaces.

We become richer as we take our personal journeys and learn the lessons of each Core Type. Not only we, but those around us — and the world as a whole — are benefited by every step we take towards the development of our full Self.

NOTES

1. Joel Barker, "The Business of Paradigms: Discovering the Future," Charthouse Video, Minneapolis, MN.
2. Joseph Campbell with Bill Moyers, *The Power of Myth*, Doubleday, New York, 1988, p. 151.
3. Tom Robbins, *Even Cowgirls Get the Blues*, Houghton Mifflin, Boston, 1976, p. 43.
4. Vicki Noble, *Motherpeace: A Way to the Goddess through Myth, Art, and Tarot*, Harper and Row, San Francisco, 1983, p. 23.
5. Philip Ressner, "Jerome the Frog," *Parent's Magazine*, New York, 1967.
6. David S. Fearon and R. Ivan Blanco, The Prism of the New Managerial Mind. In *Managing in Organizations That Learn*, Steven Cavaleri and David Fearon, eds., pp. 37–65.
7. Joseph Jaworski, *Synchronicity: The Inner Path of Leadership*, Berrett-Koehler, San Francisco, 1996, p. 118.
8. Carol Frenier, In *Business and the Feminine Principle: The Untapped Resource*, Butterworth-Heinemann, Boston, MA, 1997, p. 176.
9. Peter Drucker and Isao Nakauchi, *Drucker on Asia: A Dialogue Between Peter Drucker and Isao Nakauchi*, Butterworth-Heinemann, Oxford, 1997, p. 104.

PART III

Ten Forms of Organizational Culture

4

Defining Your Workplace's Core

> At the heart of every organization is a self reaching out to new possibilities . . . the expression of a self that has realized it cannot succeed alone.
> — MARGARET WHEATLEY AND MYRON KELLNER-ROGERS

This chapter is designed to help you understand your organization's dominant cultural influences. The Organizational Culture Profile (OCP) provides a way for your organization to reflect upon itself, to examine issues of underlying, and unifying, identity. Cultural influences consciously or unconsciously shape the way your organization does business, including its values, beliefs, policies, structure, mission, vision, management style, accepted behaviors, "unwritten rules," and typical employee interactions.

You may complete the OCP with an eye to your entire organization, or your division, or just your department. Be consistent. Even though the self-scoring version of the OCP reflects just *your* opinion of your organization or department, it will give you valuable insights into some of its underlying patterns.

This information will provide you with a significant advantage: by illuminating much of what is now hidden from your view, it can give you a vital, fresh paradigm for first understanding, then solving, workplace problems. It will help you make certain that whatever you do takes into account the cultural identity, the *real* strengths and weaknesses of your organization. In other words, it will help you work from your organization's Core.

If you are able to pool data from the OCP with others, you will get a better sense of the cultural cohesion of your organization. Unfortunately, not all organizations have strong Cores. Indeed, many organizations are unclear about their identities. As a result, they do not hold together well. They do not move together in a coordinated fashion, nor in any one direction at any one time. This results in a workplace schizophrenia in which the total system's cultural identity is not strong enough to contain the subcultures of its departments. Some workplaces are so poorly integrated that they are organizations in name only.

If other of your colleagues read this book and share their scores with you, you can put together a reasonable composite picture of your system's cultural core. Moreover, if you have the computerized version of the OCP administered for your workplace, you will gain a much stronger foundation for future organizational change efforts. Here is an instance where there truly is strength in numbers. When people in an organization pool their various perspectives, a clearer picture of the truth will inevitably emerge.

Unfortunately, most of us are oblivious to the organizational culture within which we work. We think this is the way the world is, the way work must be done. We are like fish in water — we live in our workplace cultures, but don't realize how this environment determines and sustains, or obstructs, the life force of our work. One of the gifts of *Working from Your Core* is that it can help you step back and see things more clearly. By reviewing both your own Core Types and your workplace's Core Culture, you will better understand your special gifts for (and the likely difficulties within) this workplace. This knowledge will help you increase your effectiveness because organizational cultures not only differ significantly from each other, they also affect each of us differently (depending, in large part, upon our own individual Core Type preferences.)

Working from Your Core presents a rich, archetypal methodology for viewing organizational culture. It assumes that organizations have a self-determining identity, that they are dynamic organisms, "alive," and able to change, as we do, over time. The Organizational Culture Profile helps you access some of the invisible forces that influence your workplace, and therefore your day-to-day work. The Core Cultures methodology is a form of cultural analysis referred to as *organizational symbolism*. In *Psyche at Work*, organizational symbolism is described as the way "individuals attach meanings to their working environments . . . [which] then help them predict or explain workforce performance." Such rich cultural symbolism, some argue, allows us to "serve the Self and awaken consciousness."[1]

THE ORGANIZATIONAL CULTURE PROFILE

The OCP is a powerful tool for understanding and discussing organizational culture. It is particularly helpful in tailoring strategies for that culture when systemic changes need to be made. The OCP is designed to help you better understand the organization within which you work by identifying which of ten different cultural patterns most influence the way it does its work. These are common archetypal patterns that occur both in individual human beings and in the human systems we create. Each of these cultural models has an important contribution to make to the workplace. None is better or worse than another. Therefore, there are no right or wrong answers in the OCP.

The OCP has two sections. The first addresses the *dominant* cultural influences within your organization. The second section helps you determine the *health* of each of those influences.

Directions for Section I

First, complete each of the following sentences by checking ALL the answers that are true of your organization. Then, from those checked answers, *circle* the ONE answer that is most like your organization.

A. This organization's strength is that it:

___ 1. provides good job security.

___ 2. has survived despite tough times.

___ 3. provides enough freedom for people to get their work done.

___ 4. is a lively, fun place to work.

___ 5. emphasizes providing excellent service.

___ 6. is results oriented and goal directed.

___ 7. transforms its innovative ideas into reality.

___ 8. is widely accepted as being at the top of this industry.

___ 9. inspires fierce commitment to its mission.

___ 10. thinks all issues through objectively.

B. The organization's weakness is that:

___ 11. it is so comfortable that people don't move on when they should.

___ 12. there is a lack of trust and honest communication.

___ 13. the "right and left hand" often don't know what the other is doing.

___ 14. it tends to jump unpredictably from one idea or strategy to another.

___ 15. people burn out taking care of an unending supply of needy clients.

___ 16. its internal rivalry and action orientation impede teamwork.

___ 17. it expects people to be so empowered that they can work miracles.

___ 18. it is too rigid, satisfied with current standing, slow to change.

___ 19. decision-making is often overly emotional, irrational.

___ 20. it has a tendency to analyze problems to death.

C. This organization highly values:

___ 21. tradition.

___ 22. street-smarts.

___ 23. autonomy.

___ 24. playfulness.

___ 25. kind actions.

___ 26. winning.

___ 27. vision.

___ 28. reputation.

___ 29. passion.

___ 30. logic.

D. This organization discourages people from:

___ 31. being negative about authority or the way things are traditionally done.

___ 32. being naive or taken advantage of by others.
___ 33. meddling in others' areas (especially if they have less knowledge).
___ 34. being dull, conventional, or a spoil-sport.
___ 35. selfishness.
___ 36. not measuring up or proving ones self.
___ 37. not fully using all their abilities or their personal power.
___ 38. being insubordinate or ignoring (written or unwritten) rules.
___ 39. indifference/apathy.
___ 40. offering solutions that are too simple, quick, or easy.

E. In this organization, "quality" means:
___ 41. doing what we've always done (or, doing that even better).
___ 42. doing the best we can with the resources available.
___ 43. delivering a product/service that is uniquely ours.
___ 44. having the most cutting-edge ideas and products.
___ 45. providing complete satisfaction to those we serve.
___ 46. delivering a better product/service than anyone else in the market.
___ 47. inventing what the customer hasn't even thought of yet.
___ 48. producing top-of-the-line products or services.
___ 49. providing a product/service that we completely believe in.
___ 50. consistently meeting the standards we set for ourselves.

F. Decisions here are usually made:
___ 51. by the boss (who keeps the employees' interests in mind).
___ 52. with little input from the employees who will implement the decision.
___ 53. by the person or group whose purview includes that subject area.
___ 54. by whomever notices and is faced with the (often last-minute) deadline.
___ 55. with the best interests of the clients foremost in mind.
___ 56. as expediently as possible, in order to maintain a competitive edge.
___ 57. after consulting with all who might be affected or have good insights.
___ 58. via an orderly procedure appropriate to the importance of the decision.
___ 59. by a process of group dialogue, until we arrive at consensus.
___ 60. after the matter has been carefully researched, discussed, thought through.

G. The structure of this organization is:

____ 61. a family-style, stable hierarchy.

____ 62. not always clear or stable; it shifts with power struggles.

____ 63. decentralized, with autonomous areas of activity.

____ 64. constantly changing due to innovations and new projects.

____ 65. built to ensure complete satisfaction with our services/products.

____ 66. an efficiently functioning machine.

____ 67. evolving, mutable, adaptive, "organic"; often an unorthodox structure.

____ 68. a pyramid with well-delineated authority and clear political lines.

____ 69. flat, egalitarian; form changes to best fulfill mission.

____ 70. rationally determined and adjusted to optimize the organization's work.

H. Conflict here is usually handled in the following way:

____ 71. conflict rarely happens because people do what they're told to do.

____ 72. whoever is weaker temporarily submits; however, conflict often returns.

____ 73. people go off to own corners, leave each other alone, dissociate, or leave.

____ 74. not taken too seriously; humor is used to diffuse conflict or to try to outwit opponent .

____ 75. people avoid conflict by sacrificing their own self-interest for the greater good.

____ 76. frank discussions of disagreements; open challenges.

____ 77. mediate win/win resolutions by looking below surface of conflict.

____ 78. the subordinate person usually defers immediately, or tries persuasion.

____ 79. people avoid confrontations with colleagues they're fond of.

____ 80. conflict is considered petty and is settled by fact-finding and analysis.

I. The most characteristic interactions here are:

____ 81. getting/giving orders; making sure things are done the way the boss wants.

____ 82. discussion of shared difficulties.

____ 83. requesting information from or sharing expertise with colleagues.

____ 84. brainstorming/tossing around new ideas.

____ 85. discussions of client problems and needs.

____ 86. lively discussion and debate of the issues on their merits.

___ 87. dialogue (to problem-solve, share insights, and create synergy).
___ 88. clarification of prescribed procedures and lines of authority.
___ 89. sharing feelings about work, colleagues, or any obstacles to mission.
___ 90. thinking out loud, determining facts, or discussing interesting concepts.

J. In addition to a paycheck, employees are rewarded with:
___ 91. acknowledgment and attention from those in charge.
___ 92. the chance to keep their jobs.
___ 93. freedom to pursue their unique interests and use their special skills.
___ 94. a highly stimulating, fun, irreverent, informal, and relaxed workplace.
___ 95. the opportunity to help those who most need that help.
___ 96. a chance to test and hone abilities in challenging situations.
___ 97. doing meaningful work that is compatible with personal talents.
___ 98. being part of a highly respected, prestigious organization.
___ 99. the opportunity to work with colleagues they like and value.
___ 100. a calm workplace where you can hear yourself think.

K. When sudden, unexpected change happens here:
___ 101. people tend first to avoid or deny, then they freeze or panic.
___ 102. self-protecting alliances are quickly built up.
___ 103. people determine separately how to respond; there is no central control.
___ 104. change considered stimulating; often is embraced enthusiastically.
___ 105. issue addressed first is how this will affect customers.
___ 106. change not welcomed, but will adjust if it can improve performance.
___ 107. try to learn from it; adjust quickly, and where possible, be proactive.
___ 108. responded to slowly, carefully; try to maintain status quo where possible.
___ 109. either embrace or fight it; depends on how it affects colleagues and mission.
___ 110. change is studied for potential impact, so response is not piecemeal.

L. The following would be most likely to cause a crisis here:
___ 111. loss of current trusted management.
___ 112. prevailing fears or rumors come true.
___ 113. any threat to worker independence.
___ 114. imposing new rules that limit spontaneity and inventiveness.

___ 115. being unable to provide for those for whom we're responsible.
___ 116. being beat out by the competition.
___ 117. workers feeling unable to bring creative ideas to fruition.
___ 118. any threat to current internal order or standing in industry.
___ 119. hard feelings that cause a serious division in staff.
___ 120. discovering that facts are wrong or theoretical underpinnings are flawed.

M. Mistakes are usually handled in the following way:

___ 121. the guilty parties fess-up, are suitably penitent, and then are forgiven.
___ 122. considerable effort is expended in finding out who's to blame.
___ 123. people defend mistake, or consult with each other to find answer.
___ 124. mistakes are accepted as part of the fast-moving creative process.
___ 125. try to correct error before it gets to customer; otherwise, apologize.
___ 126. whoever made mistake admits it, then shoulders responsibility to correct the situation.
___ 127. no blame; treated as early warning signals that point to real problems.
___ 128. position/power reassessed if mistakes are significant and/or recurrent.
___ 129. people quickly apologize, are forgiven, work together to set things right.
___ 130. analyze why error happened, then plan and execute systemic correction.

N. When employees here burn out, it tends to be because:

___ 131. they try so hard to please management that they overwork themselves.
___ 132. they are convinced that things are never going to get better.
___ 133. supervisors start to micromanage independent employees.
___ 134. people have gotten serious; it's no fun to work here anymore.
___ 135. recipients of our services (or coworkers) are not being treated well.
___ 136. we don't have resources or leadership to win; it's an uphill battle.
___ 137. we're trying to move into the future too fast by changing too much at a time.
___ 138. the organization's status in the industry is being eroded.
___ 139. exhaustion from trying to save cause or project that is under fire.
___ 140. too many petty distractions; don't have quiet time to think or do real work.

O. The motto of this organization could be:

___ 141. "Doing business the old-fashioned way."
___ 142. "It's a dog-eat-dog world."
___ 143. "Don't fence me in."
___ 144. "Work and play do mix."
___ 145. "Do unto others as you would have them do unto you."
___ 146. "Where there's a will, there's a way."
___ 147. "The future is now."
___ 148. "Born to rule."
___ 149. "When love and skill combine, expect a masterpiece."
___ 150. "Planning before action."

P. This organization learns and makes its own changes by:

___ 151. our own firsthand experience.
___ 152. staying vigilant for threats to survival and moving out of their way.
___ 153. getting cross-fertilization of ideas from competent people.
___ 154. rapidly trying out one thing, then another, until something works.
___ 155. asking our clients how to improve what we do.
___ 156. doing market analysis to determine where we're excelling or failing.
___ 157. treating every event as a potential opportunity for improvement.
___ 158. consulting advisors who are widely regarded as experts in their fields.
___ 159. immersing in a topic area until it becomes an integral part of us.
___ 160. observation, introspection, and quiet reflection.

Q. Working here is most like:

___ 161. being home for a pleasant family gathering.
___ 162. gossiping with neighbors.
___ 163. traveling with non-intrusive companions.
___ 164. playing games at summer camp.
___ 165. serving in a soup kitchen.
___ 166. working out on a sports team.
___ 167. seeing the world through a totally new lens.
___ 168. attending a black-tie social or political event.
___ 169. taking up a noble crusade.
___ 170. studying in a library.*

Directions for Section II

In the next three questions (R, S, and T), please check ALL the words or phrases in both columns A and B which describe your organization. *You may check as many, or as few, items as you consider to be true of your workplace.*

R. Check all the phrases that describe your *workplace*:

Column A

I.
__ takes good care of employees
__ stable
__ many long-time employees
__ protected market niche
__ mutual loyalty between
   organization and employees

II.
__ tough, resilient
__ allows room for human error
__ always meets bottom line
__ difficulties not minimized
__ survived despite great odds

III.
__ rewards autonomous work
__ has many people with high
   expertise
__ continued accomplishment
   expected
__ constant search for knowledge
__ decentralized control/power

IV.
__ minimum rules/maximum
   freedom
__ inventive, stimulating
__ hotbed of creativity
__ little pressure to "produce"
__ much laughter and levity

Column B

I.
__ low innovation
__ behind the times
__ problems ignored or denied
__ any change is threatening
__ not in touch with hard reality

II.
__ lack of trust
__ gossip is major communication
__ little job security
__ "every man for himself"
__ continually in crisis

III.
__ poor coordination of parts
__ departments pull in different
   directions
__ weak center
__ sense of whole organization
   lacking
__ new or dependent employees lost

IV.
__ chaotic
__ nothing ever stays the same
__ no accountability
__ deadlines met at last minute
__ many ideas never followed up

V.
__ a caring community
__ safeguards client satisfaction
__ harmonious work conditions
__ people courteous and kind
__ socially responsible

V.
__ inadequate pay scale
__ overly bureaucratic
__ many people needed to OK
    decisions
__ employees not respected/cared for
__ precautions slow work

VI.
__ excellent teamwork
__ focused on beating competition
__ expects toughness and hard
    work
__ rewards tied to performance
__ a precision operation

VI.
__ demands constantly prove
    yourself
__ won't "coddle" employees
__ weeds out weakness (dangerous)
__ like being at boot camp
__ stressful internal competition

VII.
__ problems treated as challenges
__ adaptable, constantly evolving
__ ahead of time/on cutting edge
__ accomplishes "miracles"
__ paradigm-vigilant

VII.
__ too far out for its time
__ exhaustion from being on cutting
    edge
__ too many simultaneous projects
__ overextends, over-reaches
__ expects miracles if in trouble

VIII.
__ orderly; everything in place
__ considerable wealth, resources
__ well-considered protocol/rules
__ reputation helps keep success
__ civilized work environment

VIII.
__ resists change — already on top
__ doesn't easily see client discontent
__ slow to recognize problems
__ protocol burdensome/inflexible
__ favoritism determines success

IX.
__ emphasizes consensus
__ embodies a noble cause
__ devotion is all-consuming
__ accepting/intimate
__ displays of affection common

IX.
__ consensus overshadows service
__ blurring professional/personal lines
__ repressed feelings explode
__ so intense, people collapse
__ relations swing (love/hate)

X.
__ pleasant, quiet workplace
__ rational, fair, even-handed
__ work processes logical
__ good feedback/data gathering
__ optimizes the whole system

X.
__ no "glue" between people
__ cold, uncaring environment
__ policies overly detached
__ an ivory tower; irrelevant
__ conflict repressed as "petty"

S. Check all the phrases that describe the leadership/management style in this organization:

I.
__ trustworthy
__ benevolent
__ optimistic about future

I.
__ overbearing, meddlesome
__ treat employees like children
__ intolerant of "backtalk"

II.
__ compassionate
__ streetwise/savvy
__ treat employees as human/fallible

II.
__ cynical
__ can trust as far as can throw
__ Machiavellian; unscrupulous

III.
__ democratic
__ hands-off; allows autonomy
__ trusts competence of workers

III.
__ preoccupied with own tasks
__ promoted by expertise
__ unaware outside own domain

IV.
__ excel at overcoming obstacles
__ enjoy being mavericks
__ unworried, free-wheeling

IV.
__ distracted by management fads
__ erratic; unpredictable
__ take nothing seriously

V.
__ dedicated, thorough
__ work long hours for little pay
__ champion to customer and staff

V.
__ plodding; slow to decisions
__ a soft touch
__ careful to a fault

VI.
__ priorities clear; focused
__ no-nonsense, no excuses
__ action oriented

VI.
__ act before think
__ competitive within leadership
__ tactics, strategy inflexible

VII.
__ practical visionaries
__ empowering
__ transforms problem to learning

VII.
__ manipulatively charismatic
__ "live" in future reality
__ has weird, New-Age ideas

VIII.
__ aristocratic manner
__ best credentials; tops in field
__ good stewards of resources

VIII.
__ stuffy, status-conscious
__ rigid re: territory and rules
__ demand perks/prestige symbols

IX.
__ intensely committed to cause
__ egalitarian
__ inspires devotion in employees

IX.
__ irrational decision-making
__ uncompromising
__ fanatical about beliefs

X.
__ calm, even in crisis
__ big picture always in mind
__ captivated by ideas, models

X.
__ overly detached, uncaring
__ head in the clouds
__ absent-minded, forgetful

T. Check all items that describe most of the employees here.

I.
__ content
__ feel secure

I.
__ overly dependent
__ naive

II.
__ proud of survival capacity
__ realistic ("life is tough")

II.
__ anxious, nontrusting
__ feel abandoned/betrayed by
   management

III.
__ self-reliant
__ competent

III.
__ don't see overlapping activities
__ no sense of whole organization

IV.
__ creative
__ fun-loving

IV.
__ irresponsible
__ unreliable

V.
__ conscientious
__ glad to do work that does good

V.
__ burnout from self-sacrifice
__ feel taken for granted

VI.
__ disciplined self-starters
__ highly motivated to produce

VI.
__ competitive with each other
__ quick to conflict

VII.
__ empowered
__ integrate work with whole life

VII.
__ don't acknowledge limitations
__ get stretched beyond abilities

VIII.
__ respectful, well mannered
__ behave according to position

IX.
__ strong, affectionate bonds
__ tireless for cause

X.
__ intellectually alert
__ detached from specific
   outcomes

VIII.
__ prone to put on airs
__ jockey for position, favors

IX.
__ overly emotional
__ very demanding of each other

X.
__ emotionally uninvolved
__ robotic

Now turn to Table 4–1, Figure 4–1, Table 4–2, and Table 4–3 to self-score your answers.

Table 4–1 Assessment of Your Workplace's Core Culture

Please transfer your scores in items A through Q to this grid. Each checked answer is worth one point. The circled answer is worth three more (+3) points.

Categories #1s	In #2s	Or #3s	Sk #4s	Js #5s	Cg #6s	Wr #7s	Mg #8s	Rl #9s	Lv #10s	Sg
A. Strengths										
B. Weaknesses										
C. Values										
D. Taboos										
E. Quality										
F. Decisions										
G. Structure										
H. Conflict										
I. Communication										
J. Reward										
K. Change										
L. Crises										
M. Mistakes										
N. Stress										
O. Motto										
P. Learning										
Q. Atmosphere										
Total Influence:										

Summary: Dominant Cultural Models

IN	OR	SK	JS	CG	WR	MG	RL	LV	SG	
TOTAL:										

Figure 4–1   Bar Graph Representation of Your Organization's Core Culture

For a visual representation of your organization's culture, you may transfer your scores to the bar graph below. Mark in each column below your TOTAL score (from the preceding page) for that cultural model in your organization. Feel free to use different colors to represent the different Core Cultures.

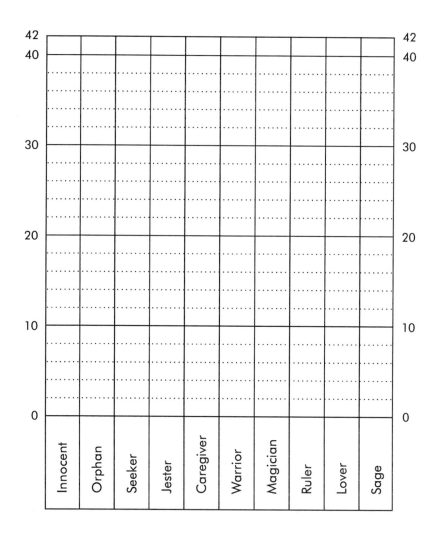

Table 4–2 *Assessment of Your Workplace's Health*

Please note in the appropriate boxes below the number of checks you marked for questions R, S, and T. The numbers are to be added separately for each Core Culture (see roman numeral) under either column A (healthy) or column B (unhealthy).

R. Workplace

	I IN	II OR	III SK	IV JS	V CG	VI WR	VII MG	VIII RL	IX L	X SG	TOTAL
TOTAL A:											
TOTAL B:											

S. Management

	I IN	II OR	III SK	IV JS	V CG	VI WR	VII MG	VIII RL	IX L	X SG	TOTAL
TOTAL A:											
TOTAL B:											

T. Employees

	I IN	II OR	III SK	IV JS	V CG	VI WR	VII MG	VIII RL	IX L	X SG	TOTAL
TOTAL A:											
TOTAL B:											

Summary of R, S, and T

	I IN	II OR	III SK	IV JS	V CG	VI WR	VII MG	VIII RL	IX L	X SG	TOTAL
TOTAL A: Healthy											
TOTAL B: Unhealthy											

Table 4–3 **Graphic Representation of the Cultural Health of Your Organization**

Transfer your scores from the "Summary of R, S, and T," that is, the totals for both Column A and Column B, to this chart. For example, if you checked a total of five column A items for all of Roman numeral I, then shade in column A up to the top of the "A, Five" space. If you checked three items in column B of Roman numeral I, then shade in column B down to the bottom line "B, three." When you are done, you will have a picture of your opinion of your organization's cultural "health." The healthier you consider your organization, the more section A will be shaded in, whereas the less healthy you consider it, the more section B will be shaded in.

	Innocent	Orphan	Seeker	Jester	Caregiver	Warrior	Magician	Ruler	Lover	Sage
A. Ten										
A. Nine										
A. Eight										
A. Seven										
A. Six										
A. Five										
A. Four										
A. Three										
A. Two										
A. One										
Zero	I	II	III	IV	V	VI	VII	VIII	IX	X
B. One										
B. Two										
B. Three										
B. Four										
B. Five										
B. Six										
B. Seven										
B. Eight										
B. Nine										
B. Ten										
	Innocent	Orphan	Seeker	Jester	Caregiver	Warrior	Magician	Ruler	Lover	Sage

QUESTIONS FOR DISCUSSION & PERSONAL REFLECTION

1. The dominant Culture in your Organization: _____

2. In which categories: (e.g., "strengths," "weaknesses," etc.)

   _____

   _____

   _____

3. Next two prominent cultures:

   _____   _____

   Categories:

   _____   _____

4. The lowest scoring culture(s):

   _____   _____

1. Review the description of the ten organizational cultures. How well does your assessment of your organization's dominant cultures describe your organization, its values and beliefs?

2. To what degree is your organization's mission and vision supported by its dominant culture(s)?

3. Do you consider your organization to represent the more — or less — well-developed aspects of its primary cultural influences?

4. What core cultures are most noticeably absent in your culture? How does this absence affect your workplace?

5. How can these cultural models help you design changes that are needed in your workplace?

6. Note any thoughts you have for follow-up action.

Please look to Tables 4–2 and 4–3 to answer the questions on page 160.

QUESTIONS FOR PERSONAL REFLECTION

1. What is your assessment of the total balance of healthy and unhealthy traits in your workplace, the organization's managers, and its employees?

   _____

   _____

2. Which Core Cultural aspects are most healthy and which are least healthy?

   _____

   _____

3. What is already working well in your organization, and what needs to be improved? How can the current difficulties be addressed? What might be their root cause, the underlying issues that cause these symptoms to occur?

   _____

   _____

4. How can thinking of the Core Cultures help you design and implement the changes that are needed?

   _____

   _____

5. Which aspects of each of the ten different cultures would benefit your workplace?

   _____

   _____

6. Note your primary insights overall.

   _____

   _____

7. Note your recommendations for action.

   _____

   _____

THE TEN FORMS OF ORGANIZATIONAL CULTURE

The OCP tests for ten distinct forms of organizational culture. As is true for individuals, no workplace culture is just one pure type. The summary descriptions below are of "pure" Core Cultures. As you've just seen in your analysis of your own culture, no workplace is any one type. Each has its own unique identity. Moreover, the influences on your culture can shift over time — unconsciously, in response to outside stressors, or as part of deliberate change efforts to make your organization more healthy and successful.

Each of these Core Cultures feels different, responds to change differently, and learns in different ways. In order to effectively make lasting improvements, organizational culture must first be properly understood so that it can be managed successfully. Here, then, is a summary of the ten Core Cultures.

Innocent. Highly hierarchical and centralized organizations in which management functions like parents and employees like well-behaved offspring. It also usually provides employees with considerable job security. A well-developed Innocent organization is a pleasant place to work — the environment is full of hope, optimism, and contentment. The least successful are so steeped in tradition and convention that they avoid changes that should be made and may have a tendency toward denial of reality.

Orphan. The Orphan organization may be the most common kind of organizational culture. It includes many organizations that have experienced some wound or serious disruption. The most successful Orphan organization is aware of its wound and functions as a "wounded healer" (such as Alcoholics Anonymous or Solidarity). Less well-developed Orphan cultures are those in which BOTH management and employees feel fearful and powerless; this results in a milieu that is dispirited, cynical, and distrustful.

Seeker. Highly decentralized organizations that place a primary value on the autonomy of individual workers. Professional associations in which colleagues work together, but separately, are typical of this cultural type. The most successful Seeker organizations are peer groups with enough interest in each other's work to keep in regular contact, and thereby develop some level of organizational cohesion. The least successful Seeker organizations have such weak centers that they are organizations in name only.

Jester. Highly creative, fun organizational environments that value spontaneity and innovation, and that have little tolerance for forms, policies, or bureaucratic procedures. The best Jester organizations are characterized by lightness, having fun even in difficult situations, brainstorming, and maximum creativity. Less well-developed Jester cultures can take shortcuts that result in inferior products, not complete their work by deadline, or use "flim-flam" techniques to sell their products.

Caregiver. Organizations whose purpose is to make life better for, or to care for, other people, particularly the less fortunate; they are characterized by selflessness and service. In a well-developed Caregiver organization, the service performed is its own reward, AND the employees themselves are also well taken care of. In a less well-developed Caregiver culture, employees are not paid well and work long hours; this contributes to burnout, low self-esteem, little mutual respect, and high staff turnover.

Warrior. Highly competitive organizations that are focused, results oriented, and goal directed. The well-developed Warrior organization expects its employees to function as a winning team, and rewards are commensurate with work results. Values include loyalty, discipline, hard work, and constantly proving oneself. A less well-developed Warrior organization may be inflexible, have too much activity just for activity's sake, and also encourage internal competition that undercuts work as a team.

Magician. Organizations that are highly energized, focused, flexible, innovative, and quick to respond to change. This makes them able to "thrive on chaos" (such as rapidly changing market conditions). A successful Magician organization uses its energy, will, and focus to do its work in the easiest, most efficient ways possible, and it always looks for win/win solutions to problems. A less successful Magician organization may change too much too fast, burn out its workers, or be too "far out" for its time.

Ruler. Organizations that are stable, orderly, and function smoothly with timely procedures and policies. They are usually hierarchical and often bureaucratic. Their "currency" is power and prestige. The best Ruler organizations use their power judiciously, treat their staff fairly, and actively seek talent and diversity of all types. The worst Ruler organizations are authoritarian, elitist, intolerant, inflexible, slow to adapt to changing conditions, and clogged by their own bureaucracy.

Lover. The Lover organization is intense, highly energized, and seemingly tireless in its attempts to fulfill its mission. Consensus and harmony are major values. In a well-developed Lover organization, there is a shared passion for both the mission and one's coworkers, and the atmosphere tingles with positive energy and enjoyment. In a less well-developed Lover organization, there can be slow decision-making and a de-emphasis on the product while staff focus on consensus and personal relationships.

Sage. The Sage organization values quality, competence, planning, analysis, intellectually interesting models, and clear, logical thinking. Its structure will be determined by the organization's mission. It emphasizes fairness, equanimity, and respect, and is intolerant of petty conflicts. A successful Sage organization is pleasant, calm, easygoing, productive, and seems unflappable, even during times of crisis. The least successful Sage cultures are so emotionally detached and analytical that they feel inhuman and are cold, uncaring places to work.

* * * * *

In Chapter 5, each of these Core Cultures is described in detail. Also included in each of these cultural descriptions are suggestions for how *you* can best work within it.

NOTE

1. John Hollwitz, "Individuation at Work: Considerations for Prediction and Evaluation." In *Psyche at Work: Workplace Applications of Jungian Analytical Psychology*, Murray Stein and John Hollwitz, Ed., Chiron Publications, Wilmette, Illinois, 1992, p. 24.

5

The Ten Forms of Organizational Culture

INTRODUCTION:
THE CULTURAL CORE OF ORGANIZATIONS

You now have a snapshot of your organization's cultural core. Since our workplaces are reflective of the larger human systems within which they exist, they are influenced, to a greater or lesser degree, by all the organizational archetypes. Much as all the Core Types are facets of human nature, the Core Cultures can be thought of as *possibilities* in the nature of human systems.

Now that you have a clearer picture of your workplace, your subsequent organizational change efforts are likely to be much more effective. Each Core Culture has its distinctive qualities, its strengths and weaknesses. Because some cultures may be more facilitative of your organization's mission, you may want to significantly increase the influence of that type upon your system. Organizations also benefit greatly from increasing the health of any of the dominant cultural influences. As you read this chapter, you will not only understand your organization better, you may also come across many ideas for strengthening that system at its Core.

I have long been intrigued by the ramifications of organizational culture. For many years I worked within the health care industry. What I have observed going on there was a pitched archetypal battle, reminiscent of the old horror movie in which King Kong and Godzilla fought each other to the death. The history and mission of health care organizations are typically Caregiver. However, many of these organizations have "given away the store" — been so charitable or inattentive to the bottom line that they've gotten into serious financial trouble. In recent years, the Warrior has come "to the rescue" — in the form of hospital management firms who insist on efficiency, strong boundaries around the institution's resources, and competing fiercely against other hospitals for dwindling healthcare dollars. The Caregiver has reacted with horror, complaining that patients are no longer receiving adequate care. High staff turnover, passive-aggressive activity, or unionization are frequent reactions to this cultural divide.

Clearly both of these Core Cultures have part of the answer to the health care system's difficulties. For the best organizational results, the strengths of these and other cultural archetypes need to be developed. For example, most health care systems would benefit by infusing their cultures with more influence from the Magician, who is after all, the traditional Healer or Shaman. This might take the form of studying the efficacy of alternate healing modalities, experimenting with innovative ways to deliver health care, and asking basic questions such as: "What is health?" Indeed, without a fundamental cultural examination and shift, I believe the health care industry's problems will worsen.

Each Core Cultural description that follows includes the distinctive aspects of this kind of work environment: what it values, what's taboo, its typical structure, how it tries to achieve quality, likely staff interactions, more and less well-developed forms of this culture, etc. Each organizational description also includes a summary chart of the contributions and difficulties of individuals within that system: how each Core Type views this culture and how each, in turn, is perceived within it. Also listed are "survival tips" for that culture. You can use these charts to help you determine where you fit within your culture and what you can do to thrive within it.

THE INNOCENT ORGANIZATION

In a midsized Midwestern town there is a manufacturing company that was founded in the early 1900s and is still thriving today. It has always employed a significant percentage of the people in the surrounding community, and has a reputation for taking good care of its employees, some of whose families have been working there for generations. As I walk around the halls, I notice that people seem happy and productive. They also are friendly, quickly recognizing and welcoming the stranger in their midst. One of my childhood friends has just become a manager here, and we are planning to have lunch together — after the complete tour he insists upon.

My friend is proud of his new company. Although not a native of the area, he fits in well with the management style favored here. This is still a family-owned business. In past years it has rejected several buyout offers, never trusting that the interested bidders — despite all assurances — would honor the traditions that they felt made their company so special.

As my friend introduces me to the company president, he includes the information that I am a consultant and writer of management books. Our lunch date is delayed as I am queried at length by this congenial man. I find myself thinking as we chat informally, "This guy reminds me of my own Dad. Is this why I feel so comfortable, almost at home?"

The president cites the company's record of quality in its somewhat-niche market, the pride everyone shares in the company's products, its strong sense of community, and how people look out for each other. "Truth be told, don't you think things were better in the old days?" he states, more than asks. "I think we've managed to hold on here to some of the best qualities of the workplace, even as we've moved into the future."

I had to agree. Not only because it was the only way I could ever get out the door to lunch, but also because — in this particular case, from all I'd seen and heard — this company had not only created, but had also managed to maintain, something quite enviable. Perhaps it wasn't paradise, but it was close.

Innocent organizations tend to be benevolent, highly hierarchial and centralized organizations in which management functions like caring parents or good kings, and employees like well-behaved offspring or willing subjects. Unfortunately, this type of organizational culture is constantly under siege today. This is a shame because the

Innocent culture has a great deal to offer. In past decades of regional and local markets, it was easier for organizations to carve out relatively protected niches (at least by today's standards). Now, however, many industries are shifting to global markets. Clearly, with change happening so quickly throughout the world, with so much corporate reengineering, downsizing, and merging, many Innocent organizations are having difficulty maintaining their cultural identity.

If you work in an Innocent system, you are likely to find that it provides considerable job security — an increasingly rare workplace commodity. I once analyzed the cultures of several hospitals that had formed a consortium. One of the hospitals had a healthy Innocent culture in place; these workers simply could not understand why their peers in the other hospitals were complaining so much. It is certainly understandable why employees are hesitant to leave the Innocent organization, as they believe that they would never be so well cared for anywhere else, which is probably true. The work atmosphere can be quite harmonious and comfortable in an Innocent environment, making it a bit like a pleasant family gathering that no one wants to leave.

The Innocent organization highly values tradition, that is, *its own* values and traditions. (Often these are the founding father's personal values and traditions.) These are clearly spelled out for all leaders and workers. Indeed, you may feel that adhering to said values is almost a badge required for membership, a litmus test for who fits in and who does not. And, because many such organizations are major employers in their communities, you may rightly interpret these as standards to which you need to either shape up or ship out.

Often not only the workers and leaders, but also their families, friends, and neighbors have pride in the company's product and reputation. Indeed, Innocent organizations and their leaders tend to be quite active in supporting the surrounding community, often functioning as "pillars of the community." Especially in one-company towns, the community and Innocent organization have an acknowledged interdependent relationship, and they go to considerable lengths to make sure the other prospers.

The Innocent work environment often has a product or service that has been successful for generations of workers. When the word *quality* is used in the Innocent organization, it generally means doing what it has always done (or sometimes: doing what it has always done, but even better). In fact, the motto of such cultures could be: "Doing business the old-fashioned way."

The structure of an Innocent organization tends to be a family-style, stable hierarchy. Indeed, many family-owned (especially multigenerational) businesses fall into this category. In Innocent systems, management almost universally makes the decisions and takes responsibility for outcomes. Employees are rarely consulted in decision-making, but their interests are always kept in mind by their (often) benevolent leaders. Whether you are a manager or secretary, you are expected to be conscientious, put in your time doing a fair day's work, show up for the company picnic, not make waves, and follow orders and company rules.

Because stability and tradition are so highly prized, everyone in the Innocent culture is discouraged from rocking the boat. You will certainly notice that this is not a place that encourages questioning, dissent, empowerment, risk-taking, and inventiveness. Conflict rarely surfaces in Innocent organizations because people tend to do what they're told and not question authority. If you do disagree with your bosses, you are likely to keep it to yourself. Or, if your supervisor is also a neighbor or personal friend, you can bring the issue up in a nonchallenging side conversation at work or after hours.

The most characteristic interactions in these kinds of workplaces are getting orders from the boss, and sometimes asking questions to clarify the specifics of how those orders are to be carried out. When you do make a mistake, you are expected to fess-up, be suitably penitent, and then be forgiven by an understanding manager.

The Innocent culture offers its workers much more than a paycheck: you are likely to be rewarded with acknowledgment and attention from those in charge, and also with pride in the products you make or services you deliver. However, it is not uncommon for workers to internalize the Innocent's corporate values as their own.

If the organization encounters difficulties, they can become so stressed by trying to please management that they burn out.

If management in an Innocent organization becomes distant and ignores workers, some employees may begin to act out, much as children do when a normally attentive parent is on the phone for too long. The organization's culture will then start to erode, as it is highly dependent upon a close-knit, family feel, a trusting relationship between workers and leaders. This strong positive management–labor relationship and a sense of worker security are so significant in the Innocent organization, that the factor most likely to cause a crisis is losing managers whom workers like and trust.

If you are a leader in an Innocent organization, remember that you need to approach change slowly. When sudden, unexpected change happens here, people (managers and employees alike) tend to panic, dig in their heels, freeze, or avoid responding altogether. The best way for an Innocent system to learn and make changes proactively is by (1) fully processing its own first-hand experience, and (2) combining those insights with objective feedback received from advisors it has come to trust over time.

The Experience of All Core Types in the Innocent Culture

Table 5–1 summarizes the contributions and difficulties of each Core Type within the Innocent Culture. Also listed are how all the Core Types view this culture and how they, in turn, are perceived within it. Clearly, neither you nor your organization is any one pure type. However, these charts can give you some ideas about how to maximize your assets and minimize your liabilities, so that you can better survive — even thrive — within your organization.

The More and Less Well-Developed Innocent Organization

If you are lucky enough to work in a well-developed Innocent organization, you will find it very pleasant — the environment is full of hope, optimism, and contentment. Most employees have a sense of stability that permeates their work and the rest of their lives. The most successful Innocent work environments use this positive outlook and enthusiasm to maintain productivity, keep costs down, and move right past barriers that would stop other cultures in their tracks. The higher level Innocent organization's actions can puzzle outsiders who are often baffled by the lack of apparent logic or market wisdom in their strategies. However, such Innocent organizations are often able to survive where other systems fear to tread.

A high-level Innocent organization is financially stable and enjoys the loyalty of many long-time employees, who in turn benefit from the loyalty of the organization to its workers. The work environment is cooperative and harmonious. Leaders and workers alike take pride in their work and in the products they produce. Managers tend to be trustworthy, benevolent, reliable, and optimistic. All these conditions, of course, justify the over-riding sense of security that everyone shares.

In sharp contrast, you would find working in the least successful Innocent workplaces (which are often those under significant stress) to be both quite unpleasant and inherently unstable. Such organizations are so steeped in convention that they avoid changes that need to be made, thereby weakening themselves further. Their motto could be "don't fix what ain't broken." Leadership declares again and again that things are fine just the way they are. Or, they deny publicly that things are amiss. Under enough stress, even good Innocent organizations can become paralyzed, standing dead still, much like a deer whose eyes are locked on the approaching headlights.

Problems that face highly stressed or poorly developed Innocent organizations are often ignored, not noticed, or simply not taken very seriously. Difficulties can persist or recur because the organization has a tendency toward denial of external competition, internal financial or personnel problems, or other harsh realities. As a result of low innovation and risk taking, employees' lack of decision-making authority, and managers' ignoring or denying of problems, the less well-developed forms of the Innocent organization can quickly fall so far behind the times that they are unable to catch up.

Table 5–1 **The Experience of All Core Types in the Innocent Culture**

Core Type	Contributions	Difficulties
INNOCENT	Enthusiasm, positive energy A cooperative, willing worker Contributes to trusting management/labor relations	Contributes to culture's tendency to denial, avoidance of problems, and conventionality
ORPHAN	Names limits and constraints Punctures denial	Chronic complaining Doesn't understand optimism
SEEKER	Avoids "group-think" Confrontational truth-telling	Disconnected, "absent," too much angst
JESTER	Uses playfulness to trick others into seeing real problems Humorous truth-telling	Manipulates system Doesn't follow rules Creates chaos
CAREGIVER	Takes care of organization, shields from some realities, protects idealism	Burns out from giving too much Enables denial of problems by carrying too much of workload
WARRIOR	Challenges, confronts If shares mission will fight to protect organization	Bull in china shop. Preference for action and competition Doesn't feel need to "be nice"
MAGICIAN	Innovative, creates new realities Paradigm-vigilant	Wants change in organization that wants stability/sameness
RULER	Responsible guardian Helps organization fit into outside world	Domination of easily controllable group
LOVER	Passion for work Helps release joy and energy Focused commitment	Stability is boring. Conflict results if wants to fix problems organization denies having
SAGE	Objectivity, overview Helps detach from old ways/concepts	Wants to focus on big picture, long-range vision and planning versus organization's tendency toward denial/optimism

How Perceived	How See Organization	Survival Tips
As a good, steady, reliable worker	As a good place to work, a good fit	Be respectful and hardworking, but not docile and unthinking.
Pessimistic, paranoid, cynical, unpleasant	Unrealistic Dangerously naive	Give bad news in a way others can hear it — don't whine. Be compassionate with colleagues.
Misfit, loner, nonconformist	Too confining Demands conformity	Show respect for the culture; stand apart without putting down; give expertise.
Unpredictable Irresponsible Fun to be around and/or disruptive	Too rigid and fixed in its ways, or as potential dupe	Resist impulse to play tricks on unsuspecting people or system. Engage others in playing at innovation — brainstorming, etc.
A nurturer: mommy or daddy Does job well Conscientious	As full of good children who need a parent to help them get by in the world	Be careful not to overburden self by taking care of or enabling others
Combative, aggressive; disciplined, good soldier, loyal team player	Dangerously naive Lacking initiative Slow to action	Temper assertion, be firm, but not heavy-handed in dealings
As visionary, but often too far out for organization	Too set in ways Limited outlook	Explain why change is necessary to move the culture to greater security
Decisive Stabilizing force As father or mother	As children who need a wise, good leader/protector	Your desire for order is shared in this culture. If you have a position to rule, OK; if not, back down
Intense; threatening if demands intimacy or too flamboyant	Loves optimism, harmony, and hope Feels things could improve	Tone down conversation, don't gush. Be careful to not confuse others with "wrong message" (sexual)
Cool, distant Odd, eccentric Good mentor/teacher	Overly attached to what have always done; lacking in analysis	Teaching role helpful. Overview is important to give, as culture doesn't always look outside itself.

The combination of pretending that it is in paradise and not being in touch with harsh reality is deadly for the Innocent culture, as it makes any potentially adaptive change appear as a threat.

In the low-level Innocent organization, the boss can be highly paternalistic, overbearing, and meddlesome, treating employees as if they were learning-disabled children. Here you will find that differences of opinion, management style, or values are simply not allowed. Indeed, such differences are treated almost as if they were "back-talk." Even necessary feedback is discouraged because there is so little allowance for disagreeing with "Dad" or "Mom." A vicious cycle is created in which employees become overly dependent, then cannot help the system learn what it needs to know in order to make lifesaving course corrections.

Summary of Innocent Organizations

Strengths: Excellent job security. Shared traditions, values, and pride in product. Harmonious and cooperative work atmosphere. Stable, often with protected market niche.

Weaknesses: Little innovation, tendency to denial, reinforcement of dependency, easily absorbed or "taken over" by other Core Cultures. So comfortable that people don't move on when they should.

ANALYZING YOUR ORGANIZATION

1. List the Innocent scores you gave your organization:

   _____

   Specific areas:

   _____

2. What strengths or weaknesses of the Innocent Organization are similar to your organization?

   +s: _____

   − s: _____

THE ORPHAN ORGANIZATION

The ABC biotechnology firm has sustained a few serious hits in the last few years of its ten-year existence. After a mercurial rise, it almost crashed during the last recession. It has proven a tough competitor in a highly competitive market — a survivor when similar firms have collapsed. To do so, however, has required one major layoff, another minor one, and some belt-tightening by those left behind.

However, most workers continue to slug it out, even though payday is sometimes delayed. People complain about the difficulties, but they stick together and help each other out. The CEO had the foresight in the early heyday to set up a decent employee assistance program, which has turned out to be a lifesaver for those who were laid off. He is appreciated for his candor, tough-mindedness, kindness, and ability to help the organization rebound from the blows it has received as a small player in a big market.

When the second layoff seemed inevitable, the organization called everyone together for a retreat and several follow-up work sessions facilitated by a colleague of mine. Although the heads of the departments at first scrambled to cover themselves and protect their own turf, when thrown together in the same room, they eventually all put their cards on the table. People began to talk about their shared problems as if they were on the same sinking boat with only so many life rafts among them.

Executives and frontline workers alike took a look at the whole system. What was causing the difficulty? Where could things be improved? What was needed to help the organiztion survive? What, and who, was expendable, at least temporarily? The CEO credits this up-front, holistic approach with minimizing the second layoff, and the group's increasing success since that time. He hopes eventually to retrieve some of his former employees when things improve sufficiently.

Chances are you've worked in an Orphan organization at some time or other because it is a prevalent organizational culture, particularly during difficult financial times. This kind of workplace includes many systems that have experienced some serious shakeup — an economic setback, layoffs, or market entry of a competitor who has pulled the rug out from underneath them. The Orphan organization's trump card is that it is tough, with excellent survival instincts.

Because of its resilience, it can manage to scrape by during times when even bigger organizations fall by the wayside. It has a strong emphasis on the bottom line, and (in its higher forms) also has compassionate employee policies.

Many organizations that tend to be other cultural types may go through a highly stressed, low-level Orphan stage when they experience massive downsizing, a hostile takeover, a negative shift in market conditions, or when workers are subjected to inept or otherwise poor leadership. In such cases, they will exhibit the worst aspects of the Orphan culture: low morale, an increase in finger pointing and blaming, outbursts of territorial disputes, generalized anxiety/insecurity, and lack of trust and honest communication. As a trouble-shooting consultant, I have seen many organizations who by nature are, for instance, Caregiver systems (government agencies who safeguard public health) or Warriors (branches of the Department of Defense), shift their culture uncharacteristically to highly stressed Orphan as a shock reaction to the decimation of their workforce.

For very good reasons, the Orphan organization highly values street-smarts in its employees. After all, survival is the name of the economic game. In this kind of organization, you would be strongly discouraged from being naive or in any way allowing yourself to be taken advantage of by others. In the Orphan workplace, *quality* is defined as doing the best you can with the resources you have available. Decisions are usually made by whomever currently has power over that area, with little input from the employees who will implement the decision. This is due in large part to expediency: after all, who knows who is going to be around tomorrow?

The structure of the Orphan organization is not always clear or particularly stable; it changes with shifts in leadership. Sometimes people are let go, sometimes they leave for a more secure workplace, and at other times there are power struggles from which employees receive conflicting messages about who actually is in charge. During such power struggles, and other conflicts, whoever is weaker temporarily submits. However, the conflict is often returned to later with new political alliances. Hence the sense of continually shifting sands.

The most characteristic interactions in Orphan organizations are discussion of shared difficulties, the problems we all face and need to solve together if we are to survive as a whole. Indeed, working here is a bit like talking over the fence post with neighbors (about other neighbors, politics, or whose turn it is to drive the carpool tomorrow).

When sudden, unexpected change happens in this kind of organization, people are expected to absorb this last blow and just keep going on. What tends to cause a crisis is when the prevailing fears or rumors come true. Obviously, in the stressed Orphan system, employees are rewarded less by the amount of the paycheck itself than by the chance to keep their jobs. ("Yea! We're still in business.") Over time, the employees who stay get used to living in this state of constant stress. However, workers eventually burn out if they become convinced that things are never going to settle down or get better.

Interestingly, an Orphan culture can easily become a "learning organization" in the autognomic sense, that is, it makes changes by first staying vigilant for any threats to organizational survival, then adapts by moving out of the way. Unfortunately, fear is often a constant companion and a survival incentive in the Orphan organization. Mistakes usually result in expending considerable effort to find out who is to blame (or, in some cases, to find someone to use as a scapegoat so as to shift blame away from oneself). These tendencies can divert an Orphan culture from learning what it needs to learn in order to survive.

The More and Less Well-Developed Orphan Organizations

The most pleasant and successful kinds of Orphan cultures are those that are aware of their wounds and that function as *wounded healers* for their people. As a worker here, you would find that the Orphan archetype's underlying sense of powerlessness and fear is consciously addressed — *acknowledged* rather than ignored or covered up. This releases energy that can be used for organizational good, for example, to empower workers to address both systemic and their

Table 5–2   The Experience of All Core Types in the Orphan Culture

Core Type	Contributions	Difficulties
INNOCENT	Teaches how to trust, gives hope and optimism Challenges cynicism Sees possibilities	Use of denial to remain "Innocent" Dependency Enables addictive behavior
ORPHAN	Realistic approach; names and anticipates problems Empathic	Blames others Complains
SEEKER	Encourages organization to define purpose, meaning, and ethics	Often punished for independence/telling truth; if so, will detach and distance self
JESTER	Encourages others to lighten up and see positive side of things Finds new ways out of difficulties	Plays the game; assumes role in order to stay out of harm's way or to win; can lose self along the way
CAREGIVER	Care, love, warmth Selfless sacrifice Kindness, even during tough times	Taken advantage of Enables addictive or other dysfunctional behavior
WARRIOR	Models discipline, focus, and how to overcome fear. Teaches real teamwork	Lack of trust and underlying fear makes teamwork difficult Can get hooked into rescuing
MAGICIAN	Concept of win/win solutions to problems Empowers others—shows people how to help themselves	Frustrated by organization's view of "reality" (scarcity, negativity)
RULER	Stability and order Acts for good of all Responsible	Either overly relied upon or revolted against
LOVER	Appreciation; passion for being alive; joy and commitment	Effort and energy "goes down the drain"
SAGE	Helps eliminate egos, good mediator for conflicts	Intolerance for pettiness, distractions, or infighting

How Perceived	How See Organization	Survival Tips
Unrealistic Naive Stupid, foolish	Hellish Depressing	Avoid cheerleading; don't minimize or sugar-coat problems — others will only dismiss you
Realistic, tough	Resilient; able to survive despite difficulties	Don't overdo problem spotting and complaining; this causes others to lose heart.
Not a "team player" Does not see real world	As confusing, dangerous, amoral	Balance good and bad news; help others stay mindful of integrity issues, so they don't cut corners to survive.
A "loose cannon" or a "go-to" trouble-shooter	As worriers, complaining, dangerous If game is played their way, will be OK	Use humor to lighten situations and brainstorm solutions. Don't make fun of others; they may retaliate and/or be more vulnerable than they appear.
Soft touch Willing victim	As wounded, full of victims Unappreciative; uncaring or careless	Be aware that your good work may not be noticed or appreciated. Don't take on more than you can handle or enable bad behavior.
Stupid for willingness to fight over a principle or cause. Potential rescuer/captor	Undisciplined belly-achers; untrustworthy	Use personal discipline to help direct complaining into action. Don't take offense; deflect fights. Watch out for passive-aggressiveness.
As if Innocent (or if power perceived, as dangerous)	Fearful, wounded, energy blocked	Use mediation to resolve conflicts. Help clarify options, tease out creativity and hope. Show how win/win could actually work.
As savior or the cause of all problems; bossy; paper pusher; bean counter	Unruly, self-destructive, not harmonious	Stability will be helpful in crises. Help others think of good of whole — how they're all going to sink or swim together.
As Innocent, air head, someone can use up Uncontrollable	Full of pain and fear Hurtful, indifferent	Use charisma, energy, and passion to propel others toward solutions. Be careful not to burn out by taking on all problems at once.
Irrelevant, harmless odd egghead	Infighting squanders talent, energy, and time	Overview will help with perspective. Take the long view rather than focus on each problem. Look for root cause and enduring solutions.

own individual work problems. Instead of thinking that they are crazy, people are allowed to admit the difficulties they have to endure. Compassion and empathy for similarly suffering individuals is the driving force in such high-level Orphan organizations that honor and teach the hard lessons of how to ask for and receive help, where to find safety and hope, and the universality of human and organizational problems. (Alcoholics Anonymous is a prototype.)

The high-level Orphan culture is tough, resilient, and allows room for human error. Because it protects its strong bottom line, it is likely to survive. It does not minimize its difficulties, but rather faces them head on, with no sugar coating. This allows the Orphan organization to survive against all odds. Leadership in a good Orphan work environment is compassionate, treating employees with respect, recognizing and honoring what they've endured. Because leaders understand that workers are fallible and under considerable stress, they will not pin the tail on the donkey, but rather will shoulder the blame and get to fixing the problem. Leaders in Orphan organizations often come from the ranks. They tend to be no-nonsense, streetwise, proud, and savvy survivors with long experience and their own share of scars. They consider themselves realistic: not only is life tough, but they are tough enough to meet it on its own terms.

ANALYZING YOUR ORGANIZATION

1. List the Orphan scores you gave your organization:

   _____

   Specific areas:

   _____

2. What strengths or weaknesses of the Orphan Organization are similar to your organization?

   +s: _____

   − s: _____

You would find the less well-developed, or highly stressed, Orphan organization more likely to be highly centralized, primarily because management does not trust employees to share in decision making. Interestingly, *both* management and employees feel unappreciated, fearful, and powerless. This results in a work environment that is cynical, dispirited, distrustful, with little feeling of job security. Under these circumstances, people have a tendency to become territorial, suspicious, to withhold information, and to be discourteous to customers and each other.

A key belief in many less well-developed Orphan cultures is that this is "a dog-eat-dog world" and anyone who says anything different is either self-deluded or conning you. Here, the attitude towards problems is: "That's life." Obviously, this problem solving approach can actually contribute to and perpetuate difficulties when it becomes an excuse for inaction. Another version of a lower level Orphan workplace is one where leadership is benign but weak and ineffective (for example, always second guessing what it should do).

In the worst Orphan organizations, there is a feeling of constant crisis. "Every man for himself" becomes the rule. Villains and Victims abound. Gossip becomes a major source of information and communication. Leaders become cynical. Workers are anxious because they feel betrayed by their superiors, whom they consider to be Machiavellian and unscrupulous. Both feel about the other that they can be trusted as far as they can be thrown. I once had a doctor describe it to me this way: "In similar kinds of stressful circumstances, rats eat their young." Behaviors here include constant power struggles, turf fights, politicizing, strangle-control of information, convoluted communication, and decision making that benefits the leadership first, the organization second, if at all. In these work environments, it is almost impossible to know what is really going on, which leaves people feeling a bit crazy.

What is perhaps most intriguing — and frightening — about the really bad Orphan cultures is that they often do so well financially. Their problems are masked by good bottom lines, which management uses to keep up its image, hide difficulties, and justify abusive policies. I believe that the bottom line in such organizations is fed (almost literally) by the life blood of its employees. What I have often witnessed is that people are seduced into staying (usually with excellent salaries), sucked dry, then tossed aside as empty husks. Even those who stay on as leaders in such systems feel emptied. For some time I was the consultant to probably the worst such organization I'd ever stepped into. Even the CEO felt the sting. "If only," he once confessed to a colleague, "I could become disabled — just enough to retire. Not enough to be permanently bedridden. Maybe lose a limb. Then I could finally get out of here."

Summary of Orphan Organizations

Strengths: Ability to survive despite difficult times. Toughness, strong survival instinct, resilience, emphasis on bottom line, acknowledgment of problems, and compassion.

Weaknesses: Lack of trust and open communication. Cynicism. Low morale, dishonesty, fear, blaming, territoriality; lack of job security.

THE SEEKER ORGANIZATION

I was conversing with a dean of an East Coast university. He and I had been colleagues in the HMO field, and I was curious about his new work. He described his organization in classic Seeker terms. He and his colleagues operate almost entirely independently, he said, each in his or her own specialty. They are among the most respected academicians in their fields. They tend to respect each other greatly, but cross paths infrequently. They gather, somewhat reluctantly, for staff meetings. He works hard to emphasize their common purpose, which tends to be more apparent when budget cuts loom and they need to defend their share of the university's resources against other departments.

Although these professors are mostly cordial to each other, there are a few long-standing rivalries that occasionally cause bristling at department meetings. Historically these people have had little reason for interaction. The dean is trying to strengthen the group's sense of cohesion by encouraging shared research projects and regular reporting out of individual projects — so that the left and right hand know what the other is doing, and also so that opportunities for collaboration are not lost. Although some grumble, several professors have begun to discuss exciting projects in which their individual expertise could augment each other. A couple of creative, synergistic ventures are now in the works as a result of this more systemic management approach.

If you work for a consulting firm, medical office, university, professional association, publishing firm, or research institution, you are likely to be familiar with the Seeker culture, because it tends to thrive in any place where peers work together but separately, sharing facilities but doing independent work. Seeker organizations tend to be highly decentralized. They place a primary value on the autonomy of individual workers. If you work in a Seeker system you were likely hired or requested to affiliate for your special expertise. Once on board, you expected (and were expected by those who hired you) to go your own way. Often employees have the freedom to set their own hours and determine the specifics of their workload. Workers tend to interact as equals in Seeker cultures. If formal evaluation procedures exist, they are often peer evaluations. Administrative workload, including leadership responsibility, is shared and/or rotated.

Other types of Core Cultures can go through a Seeker phase when they are in significant transition. This is because, during organizational transition, the issues to be addressed are those of meaning: "Who are we now?" "What do we want to become?" During such times of institutional turmoil, you are likely to be given greater autonomy by default, that is, management is too busy orchestrating the transition to oversee employees. At some point, every healthy, growing organization has such passages. These can be as awkward as adolescence, and are best dealt with by fully involving everyone within the whole system to shape its future. This accesses all possible expertise from all organizational levels.

The Seeker culture relies upon the competence of its employees to establish its place in the market. Employees tend to have considerable freedom, often commensurate with their recognized expertise

THE SEEKER ORGANIZTION

and value. In this kind of workplace there typically is much tolerance for diversity of opinion. However, there can be a great divide between the haves and have-nots in Seeker organizations. For example, in many academic departments, I have seen a wide gulf of respect and autonomy, as defined by layers of expertise — the tenured professors versus the nontenured versus the research assistants versus the secretaries. In medical offices, I see the same kind of chasms between, for example, physicians, nurses, and medical transcribers. Seeker cultures tend to encourage individual initiative and achievement. Overall, you are likely to have few demands on you other than getting your primary tasks done (e.g., unnecessary paperwork is minimized in good Seeker workplaces).

The Seeker culture can run into problems with its decentralization, that is, everyone works so independently that the "right and left hand" often do not know what the other is doing. Fragmentation can occur without anyone noticing. Because everyone is doing his or her own thing, there is likely to be little system-wide planning or coordination of efforts that would benefit the whole organization. The fact that there is little accountability is (at worst) a potential for chaos. At a minimum, it can lead to inadequate records and inattention to employees' needs or problems.

The Seeker workplace discourages people from meddling in each others' areas especially if they have less knowledge about the topic. Unfortunately, this approach does not lend itself to cross-fertilization of ideas or systemic solutions to problems. Indeed, people in Seeker organizations are unlikely to notice that their colleagues are having the same or similar problems!

Quality in Seeker cultures means delivering a product or service that is judged to be excellent by the standards of that industry, and also distinguishable, unique. Decisions in Seeker organizations are usually made by the person, group, or department whose purview includes that subject area, and who has the most credentials in it or is most respected by his/her peers.

Because Seeker structures are more decentralized than most other cultures, work tends to be organized into relatively self-sufficient areas of activity. Partially due to that decentralization, conflict is usually handled differently from other cultures in which people are thrown together more; that is, you may be able to avoid conflict by going off to your own corner and leaving each other alone. If, however, colleagues are put in the unpleasant position of having to see each other regularly, they are likely to respond by formally dissociating, refusing to work together, or even leaving the institution. In one of the worst cases I've ever witnessed, colleagues at an academic institution stopped speaking to each other despite the fact that their offices were practically adjacent. Instead they fired searing e-mail messages at each other until, finally, one of them found a job elsewhere.

In Seeker workplaces, the most characteristic interactions are requesting information from and/or sharing expertise with a colleague. You probably were drawn to this organization because you felt it would afford you the freedom you wanted to pursue your interests, and that it would allow you to fully use your talents or special expertise with little hassle or extraneous demands on your time. People tend to do their own thing in Seeker cultures, each going his or her own way. Indeed, working in a Seeker organization is a bit like traveling with non-intrusive companions. Pretty much everyone here feels that it is pleasant, sometimes helpful, but not absolutely necessary, to have others along for the ride.

When sudden, unexpected change happens in Seeker organizations, the tendency is for people to determine *separately* how they each will respond. Due to the lack of central controls, it is difficult to coordinate change evenly throughout the organization. A number of influences can cause Seeker systems a lot of stress, but what would be most likely to send a shock wave throughout this kind of organization is any threat to worker independence. Indeed, nothing can cause more stress here than if supervisors start to micromanage. (The motto here could be: "Don't fence me in.") In response to any such attempts, productivity will pummel, people will dig in their heels or speak out, and many will leave (either physically or emotionally) if there is no relief. If you work in a Seeker culture you have probably noticed that mistakes are often handled by your colleagues defending themselves, that is, arguing that it is really not a mistake at all. Indeed, they may come back at the accuser: "You're the one making the mistake by saying I made a mistake." This can launch a vicious cycle.

In less ego-filled or stressed scenarios, people in Seeker organizations go after mistakes by consulting with each other, collaborating to search out the correct answer. This is a necessary route if a Seeker system is to become a *learning organization*. This kind of Core Culture tends to learn and make proactive changes by bringing together well-qualified individuals from different sections of the organization, airing opinions, and getting some cross-fertilization of ideas.

The More and Less Well-Developed Seeker Organizations

The most successful Seeker organizations are peer groups with considerable respect for each other, high tolerance for diversity of opinion and skill, and enough interest in each other's work to keep in regular contact. This results in a sense of cohesion — a feeling that this is really an "organization" as opposed to a random assortment of workers who've been thrown together at some task. In higher level Seeker organizations, once a problem is noticed, the responsible individual is identified (by some coordinator) to address it. And, others in the organization are called upon as needed.

As a worker here, you would be expected to be both competent and self-reliant. Indeed, rewards are built into the system for independent work. In a system as highly decentralized as this one, dependency of any type is discouraged. As a new employee, you would be welcomed, given a comprehensive orientation, and then a bit of time (under the wing of a colleague) to get on your feet. In this work environment there is considerable institutional and peer pressure to continue to seek, which would be reflected tangibly as research, writing, or other accomplishments in your field. Leaders in good Seeker organizations tend to be simultaneously attentive to and trusting of their workers. They hire well, looking for complementary and supportive competencies within their staffs. Seeker organizations favor democratic, hands-off managers and employees who tend to do well with such an empowering approach.

The least successful Seeker cultures have such weak centers that they are organizations in name only. They are virtual offices, convenient storefronts, or organizational fictions. Many have inattentive or token leadership. Since they are so loosely wrapped, weak Seeker workplaces easily come apart under any external or internal strain. Because no one is really minding the store, system-wide problems are rarely noticed until they are too big to ignore any longer.

In less well-developed or highly stressed Seeker organizations, there is little sense of the whole, and consequently, poor coordination of its parts. Not only is there a weak center of gravity, but departments often pull in different directions, causing great — sometimes fatal — strain on the whole system. (If you're in such an organization, it may at times feel a bit like the ancient torture of "flaying," in which ropes were tied to the limbs of an unfortunate soul, and several large beasts were driven in different directions.)

New employees or dependent individuals find themselves quickly lost here; sometimes they never get their bearings. Leaders tend to be preoccupied with their own tasks, unaware of what's happening outside their own domain, and rather neglectful of their staff members. Indeed, they probably became leaders not because they wanted to manage a department or its people, but rather because they were experts in their particular fields. Here is where Murphy's Law of promoting people to their level of incompetence is rampant. I have seen terrific research scientists promoted to division or branch chiefs when all they wanted to do was continue their research. Their staff quickly became as miserable as they were. Seeker organizations often act as if leadership and other expertise were interchangeable, as if great doctors or editors could step into management positions and easily become great leaders.

Consequently, leadership and management are often sorely lacking in less well-developed or highly stressed Seeker organizations. Turf battles here can be petty, vicious and Byzantine to the extreme, as experts protect their particular fiefdoms as if their life-

Table 5–3 **The Experience of All Core Types In the Seeker Culture**

Core Types	Contributions	Difficulties
INNOCENT	Enthusiasm, positive energy Lightens up angst	Dependency Does not feel taken care of
ORPHAN	Draws attention to problems—acts as "squeaky wheel"	Lack of supervision can result in acting out feelings of powerlessness
SEEKER	Truth-telling; willing to bring own issues to the table	Lack of team-playing exacerbates cultural tendency
JESTER	Lightens up "angst" Playfulness and creativity	May not get any work done Could contribute to disintegration of already loose structure
CAREGIVER	Care and attention are stabilizing, cohesive forces for organization	Lack of acknowledgment May burn out trying to give organization cohesion
WARRIOR	Focus, teamwork, discipline Challenges what colleagues are doing	Frustrated by lack of action and teamwork
MAGICIAN	Encourages interdependence and synergy versus independence/separation	Lack of "chemistry," interaction and interplay is frustrating; however, allowed to do innovative work and take risks
RULER	Develops policies/procedures Brings diverse talent together, helps people work harmoniously	Bewildered by resistance to policies, procedures, planning, organizational cohesion
LOVER	Teaches commitment Energy and focus are cohesive forces	Dislikes lack of interaction and attention to employees
SAGE	Provides overview and planning Detachment from "angst" in search for meaning	Can "wander" off on own and never be heard from again, as prefers to work in isolation

How Perceived	How See Organization	Survival Tips
Needs too much supervision	Too many unnecessary changes; fragmented	May need to take care of yourself and work independently.
A complainer Not trustworthy	Abandoning Little security	OK to tell truth as you see it. Be able to justify opinion with backing of data or competent others.
As a colleague in charge of own area; to be left alone unless assistance asked	As ideal, because autonomy allows own work, little meddling	Look for areas of connectedness with colleagues to help hold organization together. Check for others having similar difficulties system-wide.
Charming, good humored Not responsible Irreverent	Too self-serious. May mistake at first for Jester organization	Be careful to not appear dilettantish or flighty. Use humor, but tread lightly around ideals, credentials, and other "sacred cows."
Hardworking, loyal Nice person but tries to interfere with other's independence	Lacking "glue" needed to hold together. Does not care about employees	You can provide some of the "heart" necessary to keep the organization together. Self-absorption is rewarded here; don't expect a love-in.
Hard worker Rigid about opinions, combative, controlling	Efforts are unfocused, dissipated	Help to develop cross-functional teams as way of getting teamwork, shared action, cross-fertilization of information throughout organization.
Creative, energetic, gets things done. Too pushy, intrusive	Open to change and diversity; needs grounding, focus, coordination	Help others to see the unifying, underlying forces that "organize" the organization. Help move energy through organization
Authoritarian, meddlesome. Inflexible	Like team of horses pulling in different directions; no clear lines of authority	Provide some order by letting people know what colleagues are doing. Don't expect others to want to work together.
Emotional Go-getter	No real "heart," center of focus, or shared mission	Show appreciation for diversity here. Provide energy and passion for shared cause/mission/goals.
A seeker who has found some "truth," an elder statesman	Insufficient attention to staff development, overview, and planning; loves autonomy	Help all find threads of Truth in individual "truths." Remind of context for why working together, what people share.

work (and life-blood) were at stake. Because systemic approaches to problems are almost nonexistent. These institutions and their people suffer needlessly. Neither leaders nor their workers see the potential for coordination within or among departments. There is no sense of the whole. As a result, when significant stressors occur, often no organization is left at all.

Summary of Seeker Organizations

Strengths: High expertise, great freedom, tolerance for diversity of opinion, encouragement of individual initiative and achievement, minimal paperwork. High productivity due to worker independence and empowerment.

Weaknesses: Uncoordinated efforts; little planning or accountability; inadequate records; inattention to employees. Everyone works so independently that the "right and left hand" don't know what the other is doing.

ANALYZING YOUR ORGANIZATION

1. List the Seeker scores you gave your organization:

   _____

   Specific areas:

   _____

2. What strengths or weaknesses of the Seeker Organization are similar to your organization?

   +s: _____

   − s: _____

THE JESTER ORGANIZATION

I was teaching a TQM team-building course that was being attended by members of several organizations. I decided to maximize the impact of their learning by putting as many of the participants as possible together into intact work teams. This way they could tackle real-life issues from their work place. The participants sorted out into two intact teams and one mixed team. As it turns out, I wound up learning as much as the participants did.

Towards the end of the course, in order to lighten up the group from their intensive labors — and to give participants another avenue of learning — a simulation exercise is included in the design: in this case, the building of a model bridge. Each of the teams was given a full assortment of bridge-building tools, a blueprint, and a time frame within which the bridge needed to be constructed. Then the several groups were left to their own devices.

I am always fascinated by how differently teams work, but what caught my attention this time was the dramatic difference between the two intact work groups. In the first team (definitely NOT from a Jester culture), the participants first divided themselves into "committees," which were in charge of distinct bridge-building tasks. They lined the pieces up and counted them. They compared them to the blueprint. They worked seriously and VERY slowly, talking little to each other. Clearly they believed in the old adage: "Measure twice, cut once." When it was agreed that everything was in its place, they actually began to build the bridge.

In the meantime, the second intact work group had gone into fast-forward. They began by dumping all the pieces into a heap in the middle of their circle. Then each person grabbed pieces from the pile and started fastening things together. All the time, they chattered about just about everything but the bridge. They also burst into laughter when they made mistakes. I was transfixed. They worked more quickly than any group I'd ever seen. In a matter of moments they had constructed a bridge. And, as they quickly noticed, it was much too short.

They held it up and laughed and laughed, pointing to all the pieces still unused, laying about. They disassembled their bridge immediately, apparently with no regrets and began again, with no more close attention than before. In no time at all they had built a second bridge. But pieces of it were quite out of whack. It didn't match the blueprint at all. Laughing harder still, and now attracting the whole room's attention to their antics, they somewhat dramatically tore down this second bridge, again tossing all the pieces unceremoniously into the center.

Still chatting up a storm, they started anew. In no time at all, they had constructed a third bridge. This time it met specifications. They glad-handed each other, then looked around at the other teams, wondering what to do next. Because they were starting to offer "help" to the other teams, I sent the whole pack off to an early lunch. They did not hesitate a moment for me to reconsider.

I turned my attention back to the other groups. One was nearing completion, but the extra-careful group wound up working into the lunch hour. It was pleased with itself, however, because it had completed the bridge, without error and on its first try.

If you work in a Jester organization, you probably have a lot more fun than most workers. These Core Cultures tend to have highly creative working environments that value spontaneity and innovation. You will find that this kind of workplace also has little tolerance for forms, policies, or bureaucratic procedures. Even leadership here tends to be nontraditional, unconventional, irreverent, and energetic.

The Jester system is very different from traditional workplaces. One distinguishing factor is that it loves change; it is not uncommon for staff members to shake things up just to entertain themselves. Jester structures also tend to be "loose" — even more decentralized, and certainly more freewheeling than Seeker organizations. In a Jester work environment, there may be rules, but they are viewed somewhat skeptically and are changed as needed (frequently) to accommodate changing circumstances. Clearly, the underlying attitude here is that "rules are made to be broken." To outsiders, the Jester culture appears unpredictable, eccentric — truly a wild card.

These organizations tend to be so lively that working at one is almost like attending summer camp, where your "job" is playing games. Because these cultures prize creativity so much, they allow their workers great flexibility — in hours, work styles, even reward structures. A friend once gave me a tour of his Jester workplace, an inventive research laboratory at a nearby university. As I walked through, I was struck by the high-pitched buzz of activity, the almost carnival atmosphere, and the state-of-the-art computer toys. Everywhere my eyes lit, there was something delightful to spark my curiosity. Workers dressed like students, and several looked rumpled and unshaven, almost as if they'd been cramming for exams. Fortunately this place has been so successful that it has outside sources of revenue to continue churning out its inventions — for not everyone at the university appreciates its nontraditional work style. As one dean complained bitterly to my friend, "I don't know why you people get so much money. All you do over there is play around!" People *are* encouraged to *play* at what they do in Jester organizations, because a core belief is that mixing work and play is the secret of success.

Consequently, mistakes are not a big deal; they are even *encouraged* as a necessary byproduct of fast innovation. These organizations take to heart the advice of management consultant Tom Peters, who said that the future belongs to those organizations who were not afraid to "make fast failures." Jester organizations tend to do well at finding ways around obstacles — these detours are often paradigm shattering, sometimes rule-breaking, and not always "proper."

The downside in Jester organizations is that work frequently does not get done on time. Sometimes projects are abandoned midstream when people are distracted by something more interesting. Activities tend to be somewhat unpredictable, as leaders and workers jump from one idea or strategy to another. Record keeping tends to be nonexistent or shoddy, and there are other evidences of systemic irresponsibility, including little or no planning for the future. As was described in the famous Aesop's fable, these are "grasshopper" rather than "ant" cultures. However, in this age of discontinuous and rapid change, the Jester work environment may now have gotten a real edge over other forms of organizational culture.

The Jester culture values playfulness, inventiveness, and good humor in its employees. It abhors workers who are dull, conventional or spoilsports. (In fact, it will probably torment such people until they lighten up or flee.) You will find that people here tend to be quite relaxed; generally they get on famously. The most characteristic interactions are brainstorming, tossing around new ideas. In fact, left to their own devices, people would do nothing else. This kind of organization considers *quality* to be rapidly generating the most new ideas and innovative, cutting-edge products. Even the organizational reward systems tend to be built around generating great ideas, rather than completing them.

Decision-making authority in a Jester culture is not as prized as it tends to be elsewhere. In fact, decisions are usually made by whomever notices and is faced with the (often last-minute) deadline. The structure of this organization is driven by individual activities and innovation, so its form is constantly changing. Work groups are thrown together and disbanded to handle new tasks almost as rapidly and as happily as the bridge-building team put together and dismantled its several bridge attempts. Conflict is not common, as people tend to be relatively carefree. However, when it occurs, the situation is downplayed and humor is used to diffuse emotions. If the conflict is "serious," people try to outwit their opponents rather than have head-to-head confrontations. In the worst cases, people trade clever barbs until someone "draws blood." After that, flailing begins and people may need to be separated, as it were, sent to their separate rooms until they cool down enough to come out again and play.

Although Jester systems tend to be fun, atypical, and relaxed workplaces, they too can become stressed. Under such circumstances, they can respond in a number of ways. They can become so manic and frayed that they spin out of control, like a top. They can sink into trickery, finding improper or illegal avenues out of their problems. However, if leadership is strong, the culture will fall back on its primary strengths and find an innovative way out of the temporarily difficult situation. If stress continues too long, however, especially if things stop being fun, people are likely to throw their hands up in despair and find another playground.

Typically, however, Jester organizations manage sudden, unexpected change rather well by quickly trying out one thing then another until something works. Indeed, change is considered stimulating, the spice of life. It is especially embraced if it involves trying out new technology ("toys"), new ideas, or new ways of doing old work. What is *not* embraced in this culture is the imposition of any limitations on worker spontaneity and inventiveness. If, for example, a new leader came into this culture and decided that it needed to be "shaped up," he or she would be subjected to all sorts of clever, seemingly absent-minded, perhaps cruel sabotage.

The More and Less Well-Developed Jester Organizations

The best Jester organizational cultures make work a joy. They are characterized by lightness, having fun even in difficult situations, brainstorming, and maximum creativity. Extremely inventive and energized entrepreneurial organizations, and "intrapreneurial" work groups within corporations, are often Jester cultures. The most successful Jester work environments find ways to address their biggest weakness; that is, getting work done as needed and on time.

If you don't work in a Jester organization, you may find it stimulating to visit one. In this kind of culture, people do as a matter of course what is usually forbidden in others, that is, they are encouraged to think and work and "color" outside the lines. Laughter echoes in the halls. Here there are minimum rules and maximum freedom, so workers are likely to stop what they're doing and interact with you. Although there is little pressure to "produce," these organizations tend to be highly productive. Leaders here hold their positions because they excel at overcoming obstacles and enjoy being mavericks. As bosses, they tend to be unworried (but a bit manic), freewheeling, and downright playful with their staff members. An advertising agency I worked with exemplified this kind of culture. I attended one of their staff meetings, which was conducted like a no-rules ping-pong game with multiple players, paddles, and balls all in excited motion at once. Despite the apparent chaos, they managed to come up with numerous possible ad campaign themes for their client.

Less well-developed Jester cultures, or good Jesters cultures that are temporarily under severe stress, can take shortcuts that

Table 5–4   The Experience of All Core Types in the Jester Culture

Core Type	Contributions	Difficulties
INNOCENT	Follows rules, keeps things going Desire for stability Optimism, enthusiasm	Lack of organizational rules, procedures. Does not like surprises and constant change
ORPHAN	Voices fears of too much change Reminds of vulnerability and dependence	Pessimism or woundedness at odds with this "don't worry, be happy" environment
SEEKER	Concern with issues of mission, meaning, integrity, ethics	Doesn't understand what's so funny; finds it difficult to lighten up
JESTER	Playfulness, brainstorming Willingness to problem-solve	Takes even serious issues too lightly. Doesn't know when to turn off gaiety
CAREGIVER	Sense of duty, responsibility, morality. Care and compassion	Burns out trying to pick up pieces others leave. Disturbed that others won't let themselves be taken care of. May feel irrelevant
WARRIOR	Sees direction, helps with strategic planning. Models discipline, hard work, completing projects	Confused by chaos. Feels that rug often pulled out from underneath
MAGICIAN	Will and vision Helps focus energy and creativity to get results	Frustrated that ideas often are not followed through
RULER	Takes care of business Develops policies, procedures Keeps things from spinning out of control	Is thrown off-balance by constant and rapid change in organization, lack of responsibility and clear authority
LOVER	Love and care for coworkers Commitment to organization and colleagues Intense, focused energy	Dislikes irreverence of culture, shifting commitments, goals, mission
SAGE	Has calming effect Remains detached from chaos, can give overview, good observation, and keep goal in mind	Dislikes the lack of vision, planning, and overviews. Finds it disruptive, difficult to get anything done

How Perceived	How See Organization	Survival Tips
Too traditional, rigid, and independent Needs to lighten up about changes	Chaotic, unstable, unpredictable, perhaps even amoral.	Enjoy the fun and play. Don't count on day-to-day sameness or security. Your "goodness" may be taken advantage of.
A worrier and complainer; paranoid; unpleasant	As "fiddling while Rome burns"	Complaining is likely to be laughed at. Take care of self, as no one else will here.
Too serious (like James Dean in a Marx brothers' movie)	Likes autonomy and lack of conformity but thinks it is too unprincipled	Help out with integrity issues. Know that your seriousness is unlikely to be appreciated.
A great playmate, fun-loving Smart, clever	The place to be. Not too demanding, innovative, highly creative, smart folks.	Use your smarts not only for innovation but also to be alert to stresses on the system that could put an end to all your fun.
Workaholic; uptight, too serious As trying to be "mom" or "dad"	Irresponsible Needs to be taken in hand, properly socialized, cared for	Don't try to clean up all the messes or details. Choose own work pace and style. Try to let go on occasion and enjoy yourself.
Someone who does not understand the game is played for fun, not to win	Needs discipline, focus, and a strong hand to keep on course	Forget disciplining the lot. Go about your business. When things fall apart or dissemble, you can help stabilize and regroup.
Too intense/serious Wants own way all the time	Creative but ineffective. Lacking in will to effect real change	Help carry some of best ideas to fruition. Don't let them fall aside. Take seeds, put energy into and nurture. Don't exhaust yourself or others.
Hopelessly uptight and rigid but can take care of the boring stuff	Out of control Needs to be better managed	Breathe a lot. Try to see underlying "order" in this chaos. Can help stabilize when called upon to pick up pieces.
Positive, energetic Works too hard	Unfocused but fun Enjoys lightness	Realize that what matters to you may not matter in culture. Know that nothing is sacred here, everything is made fun of.
As an odd character May be mistaken for Jester	Too many distractions, unnecessary activity Enjoys humor and detachment	Observe play and fun. Allow yourself to feel happiness and levity in culture. To teach: make learning fun, experiential.

result in inferior products and services. They also may find it difficult to complete their work by deadline, to deliver what they promised. Record keeping becomes shoddy, or even fabricated (because no one remembered to do it at the time). There are Trickster versions of Jester organization; that is, scams or flimflam operations in which individuals are charmed into buying inferior or worthless goods. Such organizations often try to snag buyers via their own greed: "Psssst! Hey, you! Want some waterfront real estate in sunny Florida that I just got at a great price from a poor widow who didn't know what it was worth?" (Of course, it turns out to be swamp land.) In such lower level Jester organizations, the sales philosophy is based on the old adages of: "Let the buyer beware" and "There's a sucker born every minute."

In highly stressed Jester organizations things *never* stay the same. People start to go crazy with all the change. These organizations are chaotic, unpredictable from one moment to the next. Just as you get used to something, the rug is pulled out from underneath you. Metaphorically, you find that it's safer to swing from the rafters than walk straight down the hall. It becomes impossible under these circumstances to meet deadlines. Accountability — to each other or clients — becomes a thing of the past. It also is almost impossible to follow up on the many good ideas people have generated. In-

---

ANALYZING YOUR ORGANIZATION

1. List the Jester scores you gave your organization:

_____

Specific areas:

_____

2. What strengths or weaknesses of the Jester Organization are similar to your organization?

+s: _____

– s: _____

stead, they are quickly forgotten. Unfortunately, this starts a vicious cycle. People stop producing good ideas because none of them come to fruition.

Leadership in disturbed Jester organizations is almost pathologically manic. Managers try one technique, then another, then another to correct problems. All their attempts come in rapid-fire succession. Unfortunately, none are tried long enough to take root and do some good. The out-of-whack Jester cultures are the first organizations to grab onto, then let go of, whatever is the current management fad. This happens over and over, until workers and leaders alike are jaded and cynical.

Because leaders run around, erratic and unpredictable in their commands, workers respond by becoming manic themselves. They rush around the office at great speed, but to little effect. Over time, this becomes quite discouraging. In not too long, the well of creativity dries up.

Summary of Jester Organizations

Strengths: High creativity; great flexibility; levity; ability to find ways around obstacles; lively, fun atmosphere. Mixing play and work; enjoying work.

Weaknesses: Unpredictable, jumping from one idea or strategy to another; manic; work doesn't get done, irresponsible, little or no planning.

THE CAREGIVER ORGANIZATION

I was called in to work with a public building services division for my region. The director there was a kind man, his staff a very pleasant group of people. Many of them had worked in this organization for a great many years. Their emphasis, to a person, was customer service. They were a high-functioning group, veterans who had survived many waves of governmental reorganization. Through all these disruptions they did two primary things: (1) the boss ran interference with the higher-ups so that (2) the workers could keep their noses to the grindstone and actually get something done.

Trust and employee morale were high here, an island of sanity in a sometimes crazy branch of government. This group had evolved over time a number of ways to keep-on-keepin' on, even when the system around them ground to a halt. I was particularly struck by what genuine affection they had for each other. I was also touched by how warmly they received me, an outsider, into their circle. I was quickly made to feel at home. These were dutiful people in a caring culture that actually rewarded those who did the day-to-day work.

This group had grown to enjoy constantly monitoring their clients' satisfaction — perhaps because their ratings had improved so steadily since they first instituted improvement efforts. When I asked why they took such evident personal pleasure in these reports, one person replied, to the agreement of all around, that it was a bit like receiving a thank-you note.

The purpose of Caregiver organizations is to care for, to somehow make life better for, others, particularly the less fortunate. A Caregiver culture is characterized by selflessness and service. Indeed, if you work in such a culture, you must guard against ever-increasing standards of giving that could result in burnout. Harmony, cooperation, and care are important institutional values. Your colleagues are likely to place more value on the good they do or on living up to their own ideals than on the size of their paychecks or their social status.

Caregiver systems are commonly found in "caretaking" fields, such as elementary and secondary education, child care, social work, nursing, and public service. Structurally, they are usually standard hierarchies, sometimes even bureaucracies with considerable duty-related paperwork. Problems in a Caregiver organization are often addressed by committees whose responsibility it is to thoroughly study the problem, weigh options, come to agreement, and recommend the best possible solution. Change does not come quickly because it is imperative to "do no harm," to take care of more rather than fewer people, and to carefully consider everyone's legitimate interests.

Strengths of the Caregiver workplace include cooperation, idealism, and stability. These organizations also tend to be socially responsible and conscientious about community issues. (For example,

Tom's of Maine actually *pays* its employees to spend time in community service.)

One of the major weaknesses of this kind of culture is its tendency to burn out employees. Other difficulties include conflict avoidance, low innovation, little institutional attention to appropriate image, status, or pay. These organizations expect their employees not only to work hard for little pay, but also to do so without complaining.

Caregiver cultures make decisions by putting a committee or individual in charge of an area. These people then have the responsibility of always keeping the best interests of clients foremost in mind. The primary values of Caregiver work environments include providing excellent service and doing so in a caring, considerate way. Indeed, *quality* is determined by how satisfied the customers are. Consequently, these kinds of organizations discourage their employees from being, or even from appearing, selfish.

Caregiver organizations expect employees to avoid conflict by sacrificing their own self-interest. What this often translates to in daily work is that people proceed cautiously and slowly, being careful not to step on anyone else's toes. Staff interactions tend to be serious, problem oriented, and focus on discussions of client needs. When conflict erupts, it is generally because there are honest differences of opinion about how to best serve those needs.

Caregiver cultures expect their employees to feel rewarded by the opportunity to help those who truly need their help. (The motto of this organization could easily be: "Do onto others as you would have them do onto you.") This is why you may feel that working in a Caregiver culture is a bit like volunteering in the serving line of a soup kitchen. The worldview here is that goodness is its own reward. This attitude sometimes is used to justify abysmal salaries. When change is forced on Caregiver cultures from the outside, the first issue always addressed is: "How will this affect our customers?" Change shifts into crisis in these cultures whenever workers are not able to provide adequate services to those for whom they are responsible.

The Caregiver organization tends to be slow moving, which is justified as necessary in order to avoid mistakes. However, when

Table 5–5 **The Experience of All Core Types in the Caregiver Organization**

Core Types	Contributions	Difficulties
INNOCENT	Follows rules, does what is told Attention to duty Enthusiasm	Burns out at Caregiver workload Faces disillusionment when addressing problems of Caregiver clients
ORPHAN	Shows compassion for human vulnerabilities (clients and staff) Complains when overloaded	Despair, because there is so much to be done, sees a bottomless pit. Feelings of powerlessness
SEEKER	Challenges rules and work standards; values individual versus community	Pressure to do "duties," to conform, to serve others rather than self
JESTER	Suggests "don't worry, be happy" Adds lightness and fun, creative ways around problems	Way too many rules and meetings Easily bored (then disruptive)
CAREGIVER	Dutiful, hard work No-nonsense attitude Dedication and follow-through	So dedicated to mission of organization that burns out
WARRIOR	Assertiveness Focus, prioritization of work efforts Action orientation	Too competitive in a cooperative work culture Impatient with slowness to action, committees
MAGICIAN	Ability to find easier, more efficient ways to get work done Models interdependence, equal respect for self/others	"Working smarter not harder" approach to work may be viewed with suspicion, as if cutting corners
RULER	Responsibility, decisiveness, ability to make tough decisions Prioritization of goals, resources, and tasks	Getting decisions made in a timely way with committees, overlapping areas of authority, tendency to avoid conflict
LOVER	Emphasizes love versus duty High energy, intensity	Intolerant of tasks or coworkers if don't like them Lack of support for Lover's intensity may lead to burnout
SAGE	Detached overview Attitude that, on same level, everything already OK	Too much unnecessary detail work/busy work Workloads too heavy

How Perceived	How See Organization	Survival Tips
Loyal, a good subordinate Dependency is another burden	As nurturing, a good parent Likes harmony and stability	Pay attention to how hard people around are working. Help shoulder the load, cheer them up and look to the future.
Whining, undependable, another victim to be taken care of Narcissistic, selfish	A place where one is taken care of or can avoid own problems via external activity	Don't criticize people's goodness and desire to do good work. Help them see the problems without being overly critical of them or clients.
Irresponsible, selfish, uncaring	Demands conformity Oppressive	Conformity and team work are expected. Help give a perspective on whether "good work" is really doing what it is supposed to be doing.
Uncaring, irresponsible, upsets order Lazy "Grasshopper"	Way too many rules and meetings, too serious, workload too heavy. As "ant"	Beware of appearing irresponsible Help lighten the burden everyone is carrying through good, but not biting, humor. Barbs do not work well here.
As one of the worker bees Can be counted on "Good" person	As a good place to do work that really matters, that makes a difference	Don't let organization use you up. Make certain caregiving extends to you and coworkers, not just clients — charity begins at home.
Loyal, hardworking Too pugnacious, combative, aggressive	Overly "careful," too hesitant to act Too "soft." Too easy to hurt feelings	Tread lightly. These people are dedicated, but tender-hearted. Help them shore up their boundaries so they are not taken advantage of.
Energetic, creative Could be seen either as a lifesaver or as insufficiently committed	Would take better care of clients if took care of employees Too slow to change	Be careful not to seem too "far out." Help this culture see where they can do more with less. Help maximize and leverage their good work.
Even handed, fair, responsible Appreciative of work done by coworkers	Responsible, orderly, harmonious, dedicated; or inefficient bureaucracy	Be careful not to appear pompous or overly-controlling. Make sure this culture uses all its resources well and doesn't "give away the store."
Compassionate, committed, charismatic Unpredictable; erotic Exhausting	Harmonious work environment, caring Noble mission; overly bureaucratic	Be aware that the Caregiver's form of love is "parent to child," not "equal to equal." Your intensity and eroticism may scare this culture.
Too philosophical/casual about meeting clients' needs	As trying to do too much for too many, results in burnout and ineffectiveness	Show your warm side. Do what you can to connect with coworkers. Then others will be better able to receive your detached, objective perspective

mistakes happen, considerable effort goes into correcting those errors before they reach the customer. If that is not possible, employees are expected to apologize profusely and make it up as soon as possible. It is not surprising that people burn out under this heavy burden. What creates the most stress, however, is when recipients of services — or coworkers — are not being treated well by the system.

The Caregiver culture approaches learning slowly, but surely, and with the strong motivation of making changes that will improve services for the clients. One of the ways it learns best is by soliciting and processing feedback from its clients about ways to improve services or products.

The More and Less Well-Developed Caregiver Organizations

In a well-developed Caregiver organization, the camaraderie and mutual respect are high, and the service performed is its own reward. Its employees are motivated from the heart; they receive enough energy from doing their work to keep on going. This quality provides plenty of emotional "glue" to hold the system together despite stresses on it. A primary distinguishing factor between higher and lower level Caregiver workplaces is that in the more well-developed Caregiver cultures the employees themselves are

---

ANALYZING YOUR ORGANIZATION

1. List the Caregiver scores you gave your organization:

   _____

   Specific areas:

   _____

2. What strengths or weaknesses of the Caregiver Organization are similar to your organization?

   +s: _____

   − s: _____

also well taken care of, that is, they have reasonable hours, pay, and working conditions.

Caregiver organizations tend to be caring workplaces, sometimes with a "community" feel — very pleasant and harmonious. People are courteous, kind, and loyal to each other, for example, greeting each other in the morning, asking about the health of each other's families, and checking on who needs help or a cup of coffee during the work day. Leaders in good Caregiver organizations tend to be parental (but not overbearingly so), socially responsible themselves, and work long hours. They are dedicated to the clients *and* their staff members, serving as champions to both in the larger institutional or social systems. Employees are expected to be conscientious, dedicated, thorough workers. By and large, everyone in the Caregiver culture tries very hard and is happy to do work that does so much good.

In less well-developed, or highly stressed Caregiver cultures, there are many problems. These include workaholism, burnout, low self-esteem, and low mutual respect. Employees tend to be paid poorly and work excessive hours. The system does not take particularly good care of its other resources either, sometimes "giving away the store" to needy clients. Even the strong of heart eventually leave such organizations, dispirited about the ideals that originally brought them to this caretaking work. High staff turnover is not unusual, because employees feel taken for granted and burned out from self-sacrifice. Another demoralizing factor is that, in order to maintain a pleasant environment, employees will go out of their way to avoid conflict. This often takes the form of passive-aggressive behavior; that is, people have complaints, but they don't voice them where they can do any good.

These systems also tend to be overly cautious and bureaucratic. For example, many people are needed to sign off on decisions. This can, of course, be carried to ludicrous extremes. I once worked with a government agency that required many signatures to authorize even small expenditures. It was not atypical for months to elapse before the first and final signatures were gathered. In one case, an important public event had actually come and gone before the paperwork permitting it had been signed! Indeed, workers in many

Caregiver organizations may have good cause to wonder if the paperwork is serving them, or vice versa. It sometimes takes on its own monstrous life and grinds activity to a halt.

In less developed Caregiver workplaces, leaders themselves tend to be slow to make decisions because the environment demands that they be cautious to a fault. The system insists that they protect themselves by preventing their staff from making mistakes. It is not surprising, then, that it takes so long for work to get done. The energy in such work environments tends to be low, as if workers are carrying a heavy weight. Morale also sinks when employees do not feel respected or cared for.

Summary of Caregiver Organizations

Strengths: Client service; harmonious, caring work environment; cooperation; "glue" that holds system together; socially responsible.

Weaknesses: Overburdensome policies; excessive paperwork; conflict avoidance; employee burnout; low pay.

THE WARRIOR ORGANIZATION

A colleague of mine was the director of a marketing department in a large group Health Plan. Unfortunately, as the city became crowded with new competing HMOs, her company began to lose ground in the marketplace. The next major season for corporate open enrollments loomed large. Then she hit upon an idea.

She divided the marketing territory in ways she felt were equitable, then split her staff into six teams. As a way to raise morale, to focus everyone on the task at hand, and to increase productivity, she set up a competitive "horse race." The prize, in addition to already established bonuses, would be a day at the racetrack. Although the whole staff would be treated to the outing, the team who enrolled the most new members would receive a large sum of betting money.

Teams were assigned racing colors, and a large racetrack mural was splashed across one wall. A frenzy of activity ensued. Every day at the same time the numbers were counted and the horses moved accordingly. One could practically hear the crowd roar as a different team's horse would take the lead. As a result of this good-natured competition, not only did this HMO have an excellent open enrollment, but the staff had a great time at the track when all their hard work was over.

Warrior organizations are highly competitive — both externally and internally. If you work in one of these highly energized systems, you will find they insist upon focused, results-oriented, goal-directed activity. Warrior cultures will reward you if you are loyal, disciplined, and hard working. They also expect people to simultaneously be tough competitors and team players. This culture insists that all staff members play by the rules. Workers need to be "winners" who constantly prove themselves. This can take the form of (1) improving your performance by externally measurable criteria, (2) rising in the hierarchy, and (3) increasing your salary, status, or power.

Problems are treated as obstacles to be overcome, challenges, and opportunities to compete and achieve. The bottom line is important, not only for its own sake, but also as evidence of a high-quality, winning team. Difficulties for these often successful organizations may come during periods of rapid economic or market changes when it is necessary to completely change the game plan — or the game itself — rather than just do more of the same faster, harder, or better.

Strengths of the Warrior culture include teamwork and strategizing for the future. People who seek to be rewarded well for their efforts, and who want an arena in which to prove themselves, are attracted to these kinds of workplaces. Warrior organizations are highly competitive and traditionally have done well in relatively stable marketplaces. Employees are expected to be self-starters and highly motivated; they need to have "fire in the belly." Most traditional management literature directs its attention and advice to the Warrior workplace culture.

Obviously, these systems also have their down sides. This includes a tendency to dualistic (either-or) thinking and a low tolerance for mistakes, which tend to be quickly punished. The Warrior culture also tends to be a bit oblivious to the social repercussions of

THE WARRIOR ORGANIZATION

its actions. For example, it may rationalize that if it did not cut down a forest, some competitor would. (Which may indeed be true, but this rationalization does not address the larger issue of resource management for the next generation.)

A problem with the Warrior culture's strategizing strength is that once a given strategy is in place, it tends to be inflexible and slow to change in order to meet the demands of a fluctuating environment. These work environments are not highly innovative nor do they require their leaders to be so. (It is said that generals tend to implement the outdated strategies of the last war, often resulting in tragic consequences for their troops.) Another difficulty is that the Warrior's natural competitiveness can sometimes spill over into rivalry between teams and departments that should be focusing on the good of the whole system.

The Warrior culture values winning above all, and understandably so. In warfare, winning and losing is the difference between life and death. Ironically, on a day-to-day work basis, this constant high-adrenaline work style can, itself, be a killer. People in these cultures are expected to be tough, loyal soldiers who need to "pass muster" and measure up to their supervisor's standards. Workers are, therefore, constantly prodded and tested by leaders to make sure they are strong enough to succeed when they go outside the culture to do its work.

Quality in this organization means delivering a better product faster than anyone else in the marketplace. Decisions are made in order to maintain a competitive edge, as quickly as possible, by the individual or team in charge. This is comparable to the field sergeant who is expected to make the immediate "right" call on the battlefield.

The structure of Warrior organizations tends to be lean and mean; they are efficient functioning machines. Waste and "fluff" of any kind are simply not tolerated here. For example, training is usually very practical, rather than focused on "touchy-feely" stuff, such as improving communications. The bottom-line question for everything in this workplace is: "How is this going to help me get my work done?"

Employees tend to have strong boundaries between "work" and the "rest" of their lives — that is if their work pace does permits a "life" outside of work. Interactions here tend to be very professional, to the point; any extraneous conversations tend to be about sports or politics or other "safe" nonpersonal subjects. Discussions are candid, often lively, and people debate issues on their merits.

In addition to a paycheck and bonuses, employees are rewarded with a chance to test and hone their abilities in challenging work situations. Change is not welcomed here, but this culture will work hard to adjust itself in ways that can improve its market performance. Crises occur whenever the Warrior organization is beaten by a competitor. At these moments, ripple effects are felt throughout the entire system. The new workplace priority then quickly shifts to making whatever adjustments are necessary to regain the market share. Unfortunately, this reactive stance often results in nonsystematic solutions. The organization becomes consumed with "ping-pong" adjustments and loses its balance and focus.

Mistakes are considered to be evidence of dangerous weaknesses and are usually handled as follows: whoever made the mistake is expected to step forward, admit it, and then shoulder the responsibility to make certain the error is corrected. However, what frequently happens instead is that a mistake is found and people play a "blame game" because it is much too risky to step forward and claim responsibility. Employees can become overly stressed by having to constantly be "right" and prove themselves again and again. They also can burn out when they don't have the resources to win ongoing internal competitions.

Working in the Warrior organization feels much like being on a sports team. Here leaders act as coaches who urge the team on, saying things like, "Just do it," "Go out and kill 'em," or "Where there's a will, there's a way." This system learns and makes adaptive changes by receiving feedback from market analysis, which, like sports rankings, shows whether the team is doing well or falling behind. Because the Warrior culture tends to have a lot of pride, it will exert every ounce of energy it has to rise to the challenge.

Table 5–6   The Experience of All Core Types in the Warrior Culture

Core Type	Contributions	Difficulties
INNOCENT	Follows commands exactly Optimism Sees possibilities	Does not like conflict or competitiveness Exhausted by pace
ORPHAN	"Squeaky wheel" who voices fears, sees problems	Trusting others or being trustworthy May not follow orders
SEEKER	Independent, avoids group-think of team Challenges rules	Expectation of team interaction, conformity, and obedience
JESTER	Creativity, especially alternate way around obstacles Sense of fun and play	Head-on collision of work ethic vs. play ethic Does not understand what is worth all this activity
CAREGIVER	Care and compassion for coworkers Sense of social responsibility	Burnout Being passed over for promotion due to lack of competitiveness
WARRIOR	Willing to work on the same team Loyal, tough, strong, self-starter Follows orders	Overly competitive Carries out strategies and commands, but doesn't necessarily think for self
MAGICIAN	Ability to find win/win solutions for conflict resolution Flexibility, creativity	Wants to "work smart" vs. "work hard" Frustrated by lack of receptivity to alternative ways of doing things
RULER	Harmonizes, reconciles any conflicting forces Appreciation of diversity	All the activity for the sake of activity Staying within lines of authority if don't respect supervisor
LOVER	Warmth towards coworkers, desire for harmonious work environment	Uncomfortable with internal competition/conflict Won't work as team if dislikes coworkers or project
SAGE	Calming effect Detached fairness Global perspective	Work environment overly active, difficult to think; feeling connected to/part of work team

How Perceived	How See Organization	Survival Tips
Good subordinate Too dependent, not leadership material As wimp or Pollyanna	Overly aggressive Too demanding, expects too much	Be careful to not appear naïve, overly optimistic, or more cheerful than serious. Expect to be prodded and poked to be toughened up.
As wimp or cut-throat Cannot be trusted	A place where you are either victim or victor. Competitiveness sets off fears	No whining allowed—you will be punished. Put complaints in the context of how to improve the product or the efficiency of the work processes.
Not a team player A loner, odd Not really committed to organization	Rigid, no room for individuality As group of "yes men"	Not being a team player will not go over well here. When speaking an unpopular truth, put it in context of how it will improve productivity.
Irresponsible Flake or lightweight Like "grasshopper"	Boring, no fun Not creative Like "ant"	Frivolity will not be appreciated. Help this organization with innovative suggestions to get out of any rut it's in.
Loyal, disciplined, hard worker A soft touch, not leadership material	Too much emphasis on competition vs. cooperation Hardworking team	While caregiving is appreciated by individuals, it is not rewarded by the system. Be careful not to be seen as a "bleeding heart."
Reliable, can be counted on A "good soldier"	As an excellent proving ground for self As a good team to play for	Your willing hard work is rewarded here. Be careful to define personal and professional boundaries so that you "have a life" of your own.
Good team builder and mediator Tough, hard worker Unconventional, odd	Rigid, dualistic. Likes power/energy. Hardworking, but often like gerbils on a wheel	May be seen as a "flake," too "far out." Be sure to show practicality of your suggestions. Grounded innovation can really help this organization.
Responsible, fair, decisive, self-directed Leadership material	Intolerant of diversity Tremendous discipline, focus, and energy	Be very respectful of others' boundaries. Do not overstep yours or turf wars will result. Fairness and stability are appreciated here.
Committed, energetic Erratic, unpredictable Too picky about assignments	Loyal to each other and organization Too much conflict	This culture has no time for "touchy-feely," "lovey-dovey" stuff. However, the Lover's intensity, dedication, and hard work are appreciated.
Loner, not a team person, overly philosophical, slow to action Fair, reliable	Too much busy work and spinning of wheels	Try to stay above the fray; your observations and detached perspective will be valuable. History lessons can avoid repeating mistakes.

The More and Less Well-Developed
Warrior Organizations

The well-developed Warrior organization expects its employees to be a winning team. Indeed, there are likely to be goals and standards to be met, management by objectives, constant training, pep talks, and measurement of individuals and work groups against both competitors and peers. Sometimes there are even organizational rallies. Employee rewards — salaries, bonuses, public and private praise, perks — are directly commensurate with the regularly tabulated results. People here tend to feel that they *really* belong, that they *do* have the best product available, and that their team is clearly the *greatest* one in their market's league: "We're number One!"

The high performing teams in good Warrior workplaces can themselves become "learning teams" which, in turn, help these cultures become learning organizations. These workplaces tend to be precision operations where leaders have clear priorities and brook no excuses. They look to hire disciplined self-starters, people who are eager and strongly motivated to produce. Alan Greenberg, Chairman of Bear Stearns, a Wall Street brokerage house, said it this way: "We are really looking for people with PSD degrees . . . poor, smart, and a deep desire to become rich."[1]

ANALYZING YOUR ORGANIZATION

1. List the Warrior scores you gave your organization:

   _____

   Specific areas:

   _____

2. What strengths or weaknesses of the Warrior Organization are similar to your organization?

   +s: _____

   − s: _____

In less well-developed, or highly stressed, Warrior cultures, the competitive drive is directed inward towards playing "king of the hill," rather than outward towards product delivery or sales. People become so competitive with one another that antagonisms develop, and they undercut rather than support each other's efforts. In these cases the trappings of the Warrior may replace its substance. This could manifest as activity for activity's sake or bravado toughness for show. Another characteristic of low-level Warrior workplaces is a rigid dualism and little tolerance for diversity among its staff members. Here "team" equals sameness or agreement. This homogeneity is a liability because it reduces the Warrior culture's resources.

Low-level Warrior organizations will not "coddle" their employees or tolerate frailty in any form. Indeed, they ruthlessly weed out anyone perceived as weak. This makes for a stressful "boot camp" environment. In these less mature cultures, competition exists at all levels for positions of power. On the real field of battle, it is imperative that foot soldiers know unequivocally who is in charge if an officer falls. In the day-to-day workplace, however, the hierarchical chain of command often leads to intense competitions for those few prized leadership positions — resulting in more bloodletting than is necessary.

Summary of Warrior Organizations

Strengths: Teamwork, focused energy, disciplined effort, results and action orientation, loyalty; pride in product and organization.

Weaknesses: Internal competition and excessive conflict, dualistic thinking, inflexibility, low tolerance for error, or human frailty.

THE MAGICIAN ORGANIZATION

The Central Minnesota Group Health Plan always seemed like a miracle to me. A large number of dedicated people had worked over a great many years, fueled only by their strong vision of what health care could be, to make this dream a reality. We faced one frustration after another. However, our tenacity finally paid off when we were able to secure capital, and two very brave MDs signed on with us. After so many years of being blocked from implementing our health care ideal, the group's energy spilled forward into tangible results. We attracted excellent staff of every kind. Membership grew with our reputation for competence and care. Once we got going, synergy resulted. It was almost as if we could do no wrong. As one board member commented, in amazement: "We've already accomplished everything we said we would do. What should we do next?"

I remember a board meeting early in our first year. The board knew things were working well, but they didn't quite understand who reported to whom. They asked me to bring in an organizational chart. This sounded like an easy task, but I found myself deliberating about it for a long time.

What I finally drew was the structural form that had evolved, a bit on its own, I might add. When I looked at it I was delighted. Then I stepped back; I had never seen anything like it before. The system had a center, from which the administrators served the rest of the staff, making certain that all activities were coordinated. Branching out from this center, like spokes from a wheel, were what we called the "pods" — functional work groups, such as nursing or the secretarial pool. Because staff members coordinated their own activities on a daily basis, I drew dotted lines between all these groups. In truth, only if there were difficulties did the center need to act to coordinate the periphery. What I had drawn looked much like a web.

When I revealed the organizational chart to the board, there was silence for several minutes. Then a flurry of questions ensued. One of the board members finally turned to the only other staff person present: our medical director. "Yes," he nodded, looking with some pleasure at our rather unique workplace design. "Yes, that's exactly how we work here!"

Magician organizations tend to be highly energized, focused, innovative, future oriented, and quick to respond to change. This makes them particularly well suited to survive the fast pace of our chaotic era, with its instant communication; increasing global economic interdependence; and rapid market, technological, and cultural changes. A Magician system tends to be flexible, easily adapting to a changing environment. Often these structures are modeled on natural, organic templates (like the "web structure" that spontaneously evolved at CMGHP). It is rarely a traditional hierarchy. Whatever its form, it tends to have a strong center and holds together well under stress. If you work in a Magician culture, you may find yourself assigned to specific work groups that change as the tasks change. Because of their learning perspective, Magician systems tend to be paradigm-vigilant — open to learning and altering their world-views.

It is not atypical for a Magician organization to begin with a charismatic leader who insists that responsibility and power be shared among its staff at all levels. This kind of workplace expects you to approach problems as if they were lessons to be learned and opportunities for personal and systemic growth. One of the great strengths of the Magician culture is that it sees itself as a whole and realizes that any change or problem anywhere affects the entire system.

Magician organizations wed strong will to high energy and creativity. They are clear about their goals, which are often something new and untried. Despite trying to do what other workplaces assume is impossible, the Magician system actually succeeds occasionally, especially if it paces itself and remains practical while reaching for its vision. If it does not, this culture will go down in flames. Whether it succeeds or fails depends on how mindful and respectful it is of the needs of the larger social and economic system within which it exists. Grounding in reality is critical to the acceptance of its new products or services, as the Magician organization may be so far ahead of its time that it has to "translate" what it is doing.

The Magician culture has many strengths for today's marketplace. Not least among them is its worldview that change is inevitable, its ability to thrive on chaos, its learning orientation, and its insistence on win/win thinking. Clear values, visions, missions, and goals are typical of these organizations, together with an intense will to achieve them. More than any other kind of workplace, the Magician bridges today with tomorrow by dedicating itself to turning innovative ideas into reality.

Magician organizations do, however, pay a significant price for this intensity. If you work in such a culture, you will soon learn that one of its weaknesses includes exhaustion of its employees, from whom it seems to expect miracles. These organizations are sometimes so far ahead of their time, or so significantly divergent from society, that the value of their products and services is simply not recognized. The motto of the Magician organization could be "The Future is now." Unfortunately, this philosophy often puts too much pressure on its workers to move into the future too fast, to change too much at a time.

Magician organizations often make a real mistake in assuming that all employees want to be empowered, and that you and your coworkers therefore will gladly assume responsibility for the good of the whole organization. However, when leaders and workers share the same values, vision, and mission, these act as a unifying field, a gravitational force that invisibly coordinates all organizational activity. Because this culture believes in synergy, it will encourage you to be clear about your own values, vision, mission, and goals so that you can optimize yourself while working within this system.

A product is considered to be high *quality* when it is an invention that the customer hasn't even thought of yet. This organization believes in W.E. Deming's saying that the customers do *not* always know what they want, but they are real "quick studies." This philosophy can translate to the not always successful "Field of Dreams" marketing strategy typical of many Magician organizations: "Build it and they will come."

Preferred interactions in these organizations include problem solving, brainstorming, and sharing insights in order to produce synergistic breakthroughs. *Dialogue* is sought rather than just discussion, because the system seeks and rewards nonsurface problem solving. This approach often results in paradigm-shattering intuitive solutions. Conflict is considered to be just being another form of energy. It is used, alchemically, to transform difficulties into breakthroughs. Conflict, therefore, is not a problem in and of itself. Rather, it is a *symptom* of underlying problems. This culture will encourage you to follow conflict through the labyrinth of related difficulties until you and your coworkers reach the "treasure," that is, together you expose the root cause of the problem and find an enduring solution.

Decision making is often a group activity, because it must include all those who could be affected by or who might have relevant input for that decision. These kinds of workplaces often have unusual and flexible reward and pay systems, for example, flexible hours, day care on premises, benefit menus. Moreover, the Magician system probably attracted you because you want to do meaningful work that is compatible with your personal talents, and is supportive of your own learning and development.

Your creativity will be highly encouraged here. Mistakes are considered not only to be inevitable, but also as potential opportunities for learning. The Magician organization harkens back to the original meaning of the word "error," that is, "to wander," in this case, in search of innovation. Systemic mistakes are used as early-warning signals. Therefore, no blame is assigned and you will be encouraged to come forth quickly with your problems. Indeed, this kind of culture has considerable potential to become a learning organization since it treats every event as a possible learning opportunity. In the first year of CMGHP's operations, a small group of nurses rather hesitantly entered my office one afternoon. As it turned out, they had a personal problem with one of the other nurses. After a bit of discussion, we hit upon a way that I could help them handle the situation. They were visibly relieved. "And by the way," I asked. "How long have you been agonizing about this?" When they confessed that they'd been going around in circles for several weeks, I told them only half-jokingly that I hoped they had suffered enough so that next time they wouldn't hesitate to ask for help.

The More and Less Well-Developed Magician Organization

A successful Magician organization uses its strength of will, considerable energy, focus, and clear vision not only to get work done but also to do it in the most efficient ways possible. It places a premium on creativity and sees the workplace as a laboratory where growth and transformation, both personal and professional, can happen for everyone in the system. Because one of its underlying assumptions

Table 5–7 **The Experience of All Core Types in the Magician Culture**

Core Type	Contributions	Difficulties
INNOCENT	Contentment with what is Stability Optimism, hope Sees possibilities	Uncomfortable with constant changes, work pace, and lack of hierarchical guidance Doesn't want to be "empowered"
ORPHAN	Helps grounding by naming limitations, problems, fears Gives perspective of much of society	Does not accept win/win possibilities or interdependence—sees it as a "con." Too much risk taking, too little security
SEEKER	Confrontational truth-telling Helps clarify who we are as organization changes/grows	Intensity is exhausting Withdraws when project, coworkers, management are too demanding
JESTER	Creativity, outrageous options Playfulness, lightening up Letting go of possibilities	Groundedness of organization—having to get results Expected to work hard, focus, and follow through
CAREGIVER	Care, compassion Responsibility; attention to details and follow-through Practical, "grounded"	Responds to intensity and seeming chaos by working hard to keep things together; can easily burn out
WARRIOR	Focus, discipline Action orientation helps bring product out into world	Competitive in a cooperative work culture. Orientation is win/lose versus win/win. Dualism versus seeing multiple options
MAGICIAN	Ability to vision. Personal and professional lives in balance Empowering of self and others Wants to learn and grow	Exhaustion of coworkers or staff Overextension Desire to live in future vs. present
RULER	Prioritization of tasks and resources Stability, order Can pull things together	Lack of control, pervasive autonomy, nonhierarchical structure. Rapid and constant change seems chaotic
LOVER	Appreciation of what already exists Commitment, care Passionate energy	Once attached to something or task, does not want change Dependent on good feelings to do good work
SAGE	Detachment from specific ways of doing things or specific results	Constant change is distracting Does not allow sufficient time to think/reflect

How Perceived	How See Organization	Survival Tips
Too dependent Resistant to change, growth, anything new	Tries to do too much too fast Exhausting, unstable Takes too many risks	Expect change daily. Optimism will be well received.
Saps power, self-defeating; must be handled with care	Incomprehensible Can't figure out what the catch is	Employ your capacity as a wounded healer to connect with this culture. For complaints to be heard, include possibilities for solutions.
Independent, autono-mous; insufficient will/focus/ commit-ment/energy	Allows great freedom and personal risk but pace too intense	Discussions of issues of meaning will be well received; autonomy will be respected; however, you will be ex-pected to be a part of community.
Creative, fun Irresponsible Too easily bored, dis-tracted	Likes unconventional-ity, constant change and creativity Too serious, intense	Brainstorming is prized here; how-ever, you will be expected to follow through. Humor that cuts others will not be tolerated.
Inefficient, too hard on self; caring, kind, loyal; slow response to change	Too far out, takes un-necessary risks Changes too much Respectful of workers	Working from the heart will be well received. Watch out for exhaustion or excessive demands. Don't let your good nature be taken advantage of.
Dedicated, disciplined Too rigid, aggressive Unimaginative; bangs head against wall	Flaky, far out Too soft on its opposi-tion	Intense work effort will be rewarded here, but cooperation rather than competition is insisted on. You will be expected to think of good of whole.
Dynamic, powerful (whether or not has title); sometimes too intense	As wave of the future As place that respects its people and helps them grow	Be careful not to overextend yourself and others. Constantly reality-test out-side organization to be sure there's still a string attached to this kite.
Inflexible, slow to change, authoritarian Fair, decisive, thinks of good of whole	Chaotic, exhausting Dangerous level of in-stability and disorder	Argue for change that is steady and reasonable, so that the whole system is not overwhelmed. Things will not be as orderly as you want.
Harmonizing force, linker, team builder Fantastic energy Sometimes erratic	Too much change Loves intensity and energy of mission	Your passion and commitment will have a good home here. Be careful to keep boundaries around erotic en-ergy, as it confuses relationships.
Cool head in difficult situations, good per-spective, fair, steady energy. Too uninvolved	Excessive attachment to results. Likes bal-ance of vision and groundedness	Think of the whole system, help peo-ple see how things are connected. You will be expected to personally connect to your entire work group.

is that everything and everyone are connected, this kind of workplace acts on the belief that to harm anyone is to harm oneself. The highly developed Magician culture views itself as a whole and as an integral part of the larger Whole. This makes the mature Magician organization both well integrated and of high integrity. It is respectful to its employees, clients, competitors, and the community in which it operates. It tends to be a constantly evolving system, typically on the cutting edge. It sometimes manages to use synergy and dialogue to accomplish miracles.

A less successful, or highly stressed, Magician organization changes too much and too often to produce significant results. It also can go off on a tangent, thereby squandering its resources. These cultures are sometimes overly attached to doing things a certain way: they swim upstream and put excessive stress on their workers. A lower level Magician workplace may also, like an eccentric inventor, not be connected enough to the reality of society's needs. This prevents it from making products that are useful, practical, or acceptable.

Because a Magician culture, as compared to the highly inventive Jester organization, tries to take almost every worthwhile idea to fruition, it can easily overextend itself. With too much on the

---

ANALYZING YOUR ORGANIZATION

1. List the Magician scores you gave your organization:

   _____

   Specific areas:

   _____

2. What strengths or weaknesses of the Magician Organization are similar to your organization?

   +s: _____

   − s: _____

burner at any given time, the system becomes overwhelmed. It then reverts to trying to work yet another miracle, pull yet another rabbit out of the hat, to extricate itself. Sometimes the magic works, but more often it does not.

In less mature Magician systems, I've seen leaders who either (1) are manipulatively charismatic, callously using up their people; or (2) who have taken up residence in their own future reality and have been written off by their staffs. Unfortunately, in the worst Magician environments, neither leaders nor employees acknowledge real-life limitations. It is not long before they collapse, sometimes taking the dreams, and financing, of others with them.

Summary of Magician Organizations

Strengths: High energy, creativity, flexible, innovative, very adaptive structures, strong vision plus practicality, acceptance of change as a constant.

Weaknesses: Too future-oriented, expects miracles from workers, often has ineffective marketing, overextends itself.

THE RULER ORGANIZATION

This elegant hotel has been in business for more than a century. It caters to corporate travelers and wealthy tourists. A friend of mine, one of the former, is in town for a few days. We set aside a time for dinner, after which I'm going to take him on a walking tour of the area.

My car is parked by a courteous valet. I admire the hallway as I enter. Large baskets of fresh flowers on white marbled stands sit in front of gilded mirrors, which multiply their effect. From the ceiling hang beautiful old European tapestries.

When I buzz his room, my friend informs me that he is running behind schedule. He asks me to please wait, if I would be so kind, in the hotel's lounge. I walk in and take a comfortable seat, since it is a cool day, by a roaring fireplace. This is a spacious room, with rich mahogany paneling. Although other people are in the room, conversing in small groups or couples, it is relatively quiet. I settle in to my well-cushioned chair.

A waiter comes over to me. Before I can open my mouth to order, he asks me to leave the room. I am informed — somewhat disdainfully — that this hotel has a dress code, which my casual weekend gear does not come close to meeting. I feel a bit like a scully maid who has been reprimanded for leaving her station. I gather my things and leave the room in as graceful a fashion as I can manage.

For another ten minutes I wait outside the lounge. I casually peruse the windows of expensive gift shops, which display designer dresses and sequined ball gowns. The staff inside look my way but once. I watch women in silk dresses and men in rich dark suits appear from the old-fashioned, manned elevators, then enter the hotel's restaurant or lounge.

Eventually my friend bursts off the elevator, spilling apologies for the delay. I am delighted to see that he too is in jeans! The concierge looks at the two of us, appearing poised to keep us from entering the several sections of the hotel that have a strict dress code. We laugh and exit for our walk in the nearby park.

A week later, I am invited to an informal meeting at the very same lounge. This time I have just completed a lecture and arrive in full business gear. The same waiter, who of course does not recognize me, escorts me to where my friends are seated, and most graciously asks to take my order.

Ruler organizations are stable, productive, orderly, and function smoothly with well-considered, timely procedures and policies. They are usually hierarchical and often bureaucratic. If you work in a Ruler system, you will notice that the "currency" here is power — both internal and external, which is why it is not unusual to find Ruler cultures among our most powerful governing, political, and financial institutions. Such organizations convey their felt sense of authority and importance in many ways, including their offices, marketing literature, and interactions with other organizations. Sometimes they can border on the pompous. For example, I remember one bank that unabashedly advertised itself as: "The most important bank in the most important city in the most important nation in the world." These organizations often have a well-established history of a sterling reputation of which they are, understandably, quite proud. Fortunately, many Ruler workplaces are also mindful of their social responsibility; they see themselves as contributing significantly to the public and their own community's good. For example, some give a percentage of their profits to, or host black-tie fundraisers for, charity.

If you work in a Ruler culture, you will find that its lines of authority are clear and that it tends to approach problems in an orderly way. The system has well-established procedures that you are expected to adhere to like a dutiful subject. However, due to this workplace's preference to maintain stability via its measured pace, it may have difficulty adapting to rapid market or other change. Its degree of internal diversity will be its saving grace during such times.

Ruler organizations have many strengths. They are widely accepted as being at "the top of their class," with a long history of accomplishment, the wealthiest clients, and one of the most impeccable reputations in the industry. This gives them a lot of room for error.

The potential weaknesses of the Ruler culture include a bureaucracy that can become overly rule-bound. To some extent, it inadvertently rewards self-involvement, self-protection, and unkindness to anyone inside or outside the system who does not have money, power, or prestige. So much attention is paid to one's place in the hierarchy that, too often, even excellent suggestions from lower level employees are simply dismissed. In these ways, the Ruler culture can become so removed from the reality of most people's lives that it eventually distances itself from its market.

A primary value in the Ruler culture is prestige — your individual prestige within the system and the organization's prestige within the marketplace. Employee insubordination or the ignoring of written (or unwritten) rules will not be tolerated here. If you do not have an academic degree from the best schools, or the "proper" cultural background, you can easily find yourself committing some kind of fatal *faux paux.*

This kind of workplace defines *quality* as producing top-of-the-line products or services. As a result, its market niche is often for the elite. Decisions are made in these systems by the senior person involved, although the issue may first have to meander through a thorough, long-established organizational process. The structure of Ruler organizations is designed to maintain existing order. It is typically a pyramid with well-delineated authority and extremely clear political lines. Conflict will erupt if you cross these lines, although that conflict may last only as long as it takes for your superior to execute the workplace equivalent of: "Off with their heads!"

When there are problems, the subordinate person usually defers immediately. An alternative mode of conflict resolution is for the subordinate to try a well mannered deferential persuasion. Only in the most extreme circumstances should you challenge a superior, as this carries great risk, similar to a political coup. You may find that you spend much of your time clarifying procedures so that you do the right thing, don't ruffle feathers, and are able to complete your work in a timely, "politic" manner.

The motto of Ruler organizations could be: "Born to Rule." Indeed, the Ruler culture is reflected in its aristocratic aura of expensive suits, elegant furnishings, and spacious offices. People are typically attracted to Ruler organizations because they want to be part of a well-established, highly respected, historically stable organization, with all the security, money, power, and prestige that accompany it.

However, the times are certainly changing. Many Ruler workplaces are at risk nowadays precisely because they respond to change so carefully and so reluctantly. Typically, Ruler organizations think things are fine just the way they are, and they will try to maintain the status quo as long as possible. This is understandable. If we look at history, there have been precious few rulers who have willingly participated in their country's revolutions. Because they sit at the top of the economic, political, and social pyramid, Ruler cultures have the most to lose if the entire system is overturned.

Therefore, crises in Ruler workplaces are most likely to be caused when the current order is threatened. Because these systems spend so much energy safeguarding themselves from instability, they are not particularly forgiving of mistakes. In fact, mistakes are considered to be so dangerous that if they are made by superiors, subordinates are often expected to assume blame on their behalf. This is a bit like a chess game in which the lower ranking piece is "sacrificed" as part of a deliberate strategy to save royalty. It is not uncommon to see this strategy in play when Ruler systems enter negotiations with other firms.

If a mistake is serious enough, anyone's power within the organization will be reassessed. However, Ruler organizations are loathe to let anyone outside their system know they are having difficulty. This secrecy can exacerbate the problem, as difficulties compound while problem solving and change are avoided. When these systems finally do ask for help, it tends to be of well-established, high-prestige consulting firms or "gurus" in a field, with an expectation of complete confidentiality. In fact, advisors to Ruler organizations often keep their client lists confidential. This caution is based on the historical precedent that for a king to admit frailty is to invite a revolution. However, Ruler cultures can become learning organizations when they listen to wise leaders or advisors who help them challenge the long-held paradigms and practices that have served them so well in the past. Then the Ruler organization can join in the evolution occurring around them, rather than become a casualty of the revolution.

The More and Less Well-Developed Ruler Organizations

The best Ruler organizations treat staff in a fair, even-handed way. Employees are seen as a valued resource who need to be carefully stewarded and "developed" so that their talents are put to good use. Diversity is not only tolerated, but is respected and actively sought. Staff are neither overloaded nor underutilized. They have sufficient guidance from an attentive management, who reinforces the feeling that their work is both worthwhile and appreciated. A premium is placed on getting the job done right and on time. Projects are planned and managed with one eye to the overview, and the other eye to securing the necessary resources. Work tends to proceed in a straight line fashion from inception to successful completion.

Table 5–8 The Experience of All Core Types in the Ruler Culture

Core Type	Contributions	Difficulties
INNOCENT	Follows rules, does what is told Enthusiasm, hope, sees "silver lining"	Does not understand (or denies) politics, power shifts Because overly trusting, may be taken advantage of
ORPHAN	Can be motivated by power, status "Squeaky wheel"—gives early warning signals for problems	Feelings of powerlessness May not follow rules Trust (both ways)
SEEKER	Confrontational truth-telling Independent thinking	Does not value "currency" of organization (power/prestige) Chafes at authority
JESTER	Playfulness, creativity Irreverent truth-telling Sense of humor	Does not get work done Not motivated by power or prestige Easily bored, disruptive
CAREGIVER	Care, compassion, warmth Social responsibility Loyalty, attention to detail work, follow through	Does not like power conflicts Passivity Won't delegate easily, so burns out
WARRIOR	Preference for action Decisiveness, focus Discipline, loyalty	Diversity in organization Dualism conflicts with the variety of opinions/people
MAGICIAN	Ability to create synergy from diversity in organization Flexibility Change-agent skills	Lack of willingness to change Lack of intensity, synergy Pace is too slow
RULER	Stewards resources well Keeps things in order Sense of place within the organization	Authoritarian Overly status conscious Inflexible
LOVER	Passionate commitment Energizes coworkers Charisma, intensity Warmth, caring, a "linker"	More likely to do what wants than what told; not motivated by power and prestige; lack of warmth, love in organization
SAGE	Ego detachment, objectivity Global perspective, long-range planning	Getting tasks done/details attended to; not motivated by power/prestige

How Perceived	How See Organization	Survival Tips
Not management material; overly dependent, needs guidance Naive	Orderly, stable A good (or bad) parent	You will be expected to be deferential and obey the rules. However, your optimism and naivety may cause superiors to dismiss your opinions.
Self-destructive; needs monitoring, guidance; cut-throat in power struggles	May provide security or feel like jail	Don't expect extra attention; whining will not pay off. Avoid putting on airs. Your compassion can provide connection to those with less power.
Loner, independent, not a "yes" man Not really committed to organization	Values diversity, listens to staff Overly authoritarian, hierarchical	Don't look for a lot of freedom. Choose carefully the time and place for truth-telling to make sure you are heard by those in charge.
Irresponsible, unmanageable, leaves tasks unfinished Creative, good ideas	Boring, self-serious, overbearing, inflexible	Traditionally, jesters told rulers hard truths with humor; however, proceed with caution, as these systems are not known for their sense of humor.
Willing to work hard, tends to overdo Cares about job and coworkers	Orderly, stable Appreciates workers but could be warmer; too rigid, unfeeling	You may be treated as a servant. Stay conscious of your boundaries so you are not misused. The quality of care you bring is a real gift.
Overly aggressive Impulsive action Motivated by measurable rewards	Stable, productive, but slow to action A hodge-podge, not a real team	You are expected to be a "good soldier" and follow orders. Be careful not to be too quick to action. Wait for commands from your superiors.
Flaky, tangential Lots of good ideas "Quick on feet," manages transitions well	Inflexible, authoritarian, cumbersome Diversity is greatest asset	You can function best as advisor about the future. Expect resistance to change. Breathe whenever you're frustrated by the slow pace.
Aristocratic, sometimes snobbish; someone who belongs here A "born" leader	Excellent reputation Good to have on resume; the "right neighborhood"	Stay clear about lines of authority and don't overstep yours. Others may consider you snobbish. Don't put on airs or be condescending.
Erratic; focused, intense, energized if likes work Prone to burnout	Diverse and appreciative of talent; indifferent and lacking in warmth/care	You will probably be viewed as a "loose cannon" who needs to be controlled. However, your energy can infuse life in a brittle, dry system.
Odd, a loner Objective, wise, fair Gets tangential if left alone for too long	Stable, orderly, thoughtful; too much management and conflict over authority	You can play a mentoring and advisory role. Remind people of the system's needs so that politics do not dominate decision making.

Ruler organizations often have considerable wealth, a reputation that helps to ensure their continued success, and a very civilized work environment. Leaders tend to have an aristocratic manner and the best credentials in their field. Employees are generally respectful, well-mannered, and behave according to their designated position.

The less well-developed, or highly stressed, Ruler organizations are authoritarian, inflexible, and clogged by their own bureaucracy. They tend to lack the staff diversity that characterizes more successful Ruler cultures. Instead they hire only the "right" kinds of people and discourage diversity of opinion. The chosen ones, because they so much want to belong to this high-prestige group, often simply follow the rules and do as they are told. Such workplaces tend to foster elitist leaders who treat employees as serfs. The worst of these cultures are tyrannical, flaunting and often abusing the power they do have.

Highly stressed Ruler systems will dig in their heels when change comes their way. They are slow to recognize problems because no one dares tell the "emperor" the truth. Their protocol is so burdensome that it grinds them to a halt. Over time, favoritism replaces competence and credentials as the criteria for management

---

ANALYZING YOUR ORGANIZATION

1. List the Ruler scores you gave your organization:

   _____

   Specific areas:

   _____

2. What strengths or weaknesses of the Ruler Organization are similar to your organization?

   +s: _____

   − s: _____

selection. Another symptom of the less well-developed Ruler organization is status conscious leaders who overly stress the system by demanding costly perks and prestige symbols. This further widens the gulf between the haves and the have-nots. Interestingly, employees in these workplaces can be even more snobbish than their leaders, sometimes behaving in disdainful ways to customers and putting on airs as they jockey amongst each other for position and favors.

Summary of Ruler Organizations

Strengths: Excellent reputation, stability, prestige and power, orderly internal procedures; careful stewarding of all resources.

Weaknesses: Slowness to change, overly rule-bound and status conscious, inflexible structure, rigidity impedes communication.

THE LOVER ORGANIZATION

As I walk into the campaign office, it is a-buzz with activity. The candidate, a friend of mine, is a popular woman who is challenging our area's congressional incumbent. She and her staff have built a high-energy, grassroots campaign. People work around the clock, even eating at their desks. And nobody works harder than the candidate herself, who started this morning at 6:00, shaking hands at a factory gate. She feels passionately about the key issues in this campaign and speaks eloquently from her heart.

Her reputation is one of high principles. This presents some contrast to the long-time incumbent who has received contributions from special interest groups of every imaginable type. He also is a bit of a chauvinist. Every slightly misogynist comment he makes has the unintended effect of infusing his challenger's campaign with another bolt of full-tilt energy. To quote from The Blues Brothers, these people feel that they're on a mission from God.

Tonight I am one of dozens of people there to stuff envelopes for a mailing. Other volunteers include students from several local universities, some high school students, a few business people, several members of a union that has endorsed this candidate, many of her social friends, and some old-time political junkies. Quickly we strangers, people from such different walks of life, are in animated conversation about local and national politics.

After a few hours, we complete our task. I say good-bye to my new acquaintances, then walk to the front of the office to get my coat. As I do, I pass a large calendar board that counts down the days to the election. The campaign manager, who is adjusting the count at the end of the day, thanks me profusely while in the same breath asking when I can return. The candidate also sees that I am about to walk out the door, drops what she's doing, and comes over to thank me with a big bear hug. On the way home I hear myself think, "Yes." I decide to rearrange my schedule so I can help out again sometime later in the week.

The Lover organization seems tireless in its efforts to fulfill its mission. If you work in a Lover culture, it is probably because you were attracted to that very mission. By and large, workers here truly enjoy their job and their colleagues, often with feelings that border on passion. This kind of workplace expects everyone to be cooperative and emotionally honest. A harmonious environment is characteristic of Lover organizations where people appreciate and support each other's work. You can easily form friendships here that last a life time.

Because Lover cultures are so intense and focused, they can create staff burnout. This is not so much a problem if the organization has ongoing employee support systems that serve to defray stress as it builds. You will find that the Lover culture pays a lot of attention to its employees and embraces cutting-edge training that focuses on people issues. Another advantage this kind of culture has is that people do not hesitate to help each other out, sometimes covering for someone who collapses temporarily, much as if they were running a relay race together.

These organizations are often formed around charismatic leaders, as in the above-mentioned case, but the work is carried out in a democratic fashion. Lover structures tend to be atypical: e.g., a web structure or flat and egalitarian, changing form not only according to the needs of the mission, but also bending to meet the personal desires and affiliations of staff members. Sometimes the forms of these systems shift depending on who wants to work with whom on what projects. Even if it is built as a hierarchy in name, the Lover culture tends to operate in a power-sharing manner. Consensus is clearly the preferred decision-making model here, and sometimes it is used to a fault. Fortunately, you will find that the time you spend coming slowly to decisions as a group is usually recouped in the implementation phase, because you and your colleagues uniformly support the agreed-upon approach.

The Lover organization does not like conflict and has difficulty dealing with it when it arises. After all, it attracts people who would much rather love than fight each other. Consequently, there is a tendency to avoid problems until they get out of hand.

Unfortunately, this kind of system is vulnerable to even one difficult employee. I once met such a staff person, whom her colleagues referred to as Nurse Jekell/Ms. Hyde. Indeed, the "rotten apple in the barrel" can wreak havoc in Lover cultures. This is why careful hiring, probationary periods, candid evaluations, employee assistance programs, appropriate firings, and regular staff meetings to air issues are absolute musts for this type of workplace.

When problems arise, the welfare of individual employees and the *process* of problem solving are considered critical to the organization's success. How work gets done is thought to be as important as, and largely determinant of, the organization's bottom line. Michael Hammer describes this as "process-centered work." In *Beyond Reengineering: How the Process Centered Work Is Changing Our Work and Our Lives*, Hammer says, "Process-centered work can help satisfy everyone's hunger for connection with something beyond themselves and their own needs."[2] The Lover organization focuses on building connections among its staff members; this makes it extremely resilient, able to hold together despite severe stress.

Although not a common culture, Lover workplaces have many strengths to recommend them. These organizations inspire fierce commitment, almost as if employees are fighting a "holy war" in the marketplace. Lover cultures allow their workers an emotional life, and they devote resources to employees' personal and professional development. The energy of this system is usually so high because everyone is completely "on board" for the ride.

The downside to the Lover culture is that it may de-emphasize production and results. Its need for consensus also may result in tortured decision making, partly because people hesitate to hurt other's feelings. When conflict does erupt, it can stop everything. Although reluctant to fight, people who are attracted to this kind of workplace tend to be fierce when they do. Staff divisions can result that are irreparable. In general, you may find the emotional intensity of this culture exhausting. Workers and leaders are expected to feel so strongly about the organization's cause that they give their *all* for it.

When I walked into the San Francisco Greenpeace office many years ago, I was struck by a huge mural that spanned an entire wall. It showed a large Russian whaling ship on one side and the tail of a diving whale on the other. Between these two giants was a tiny rowboat with Greenpeace volunteers. Lover organizations can inspire people to be so devoted to their cause that they will gladly put themselves into this kind of danger. This zeal can be carried to excess if individuals merge their identity with the cause of the organization until they become symbiotic. Losing appropriate boundaries turns workers into fuel for a system whose passion will consume them.

Clearly, Lover workplaces do not tolerate indifference or apathy. People believe completely in the "rightness" of their cause. Exhaustion is a real danger in this culture, as people treat their work as if it were a noble crusade. What is amazing is how such dedication to a cause allows people to burn the candle at both ends for as long as they do.

Because you are surrounded by "soul mates," you are likely to develop strong personal connections with other staff members; sometimes even intimacy. It is not surprising then that dialogue can readily occur in these cultures. By and large, both leaders and workers feel rewarded by the opportunity to work for something they intensely believe in, and with colleagues they truly treasure.

People here tend to have strong emotions that run hot or cold. For example, change is either whole-heartedly embraced or fought, depending upon the following factors: how it affects the mission and whether or not it will break up current friend-based alliances. For example, no one is going to want to move to an office that separates them from the people with whom they enjoy working. In this kind of workplace, people are expected to "cut each other a lot of slack." Mistakes are easily forgiven. People quickly apologize and then work together to set things right. This attitude, along with the Lover organization's deep desire to do everything it can to achieve its mission, contributes to its becoming a learning organization.

The More and Less Well-Developed Lover Organizations

John Ruskin once said that "When love and skill work together, expect a masterpiece." The shared passion for the Lover's organizational purpose and the synergy of staff relationships release great amounts of energy for the work at hand. Indeed, the atmosphere fairly tingles with positive attitude, enthusiasm, and enjoyment. The workplace itself is usually quite "humanized," often colorful, sometimes beautifully decorated. It is common to see individual work spaces personalized with family photos and plants or children's drawings. Excitement abounds. People make a point of celebrating their successes. Assertiveness and honest communication is insisted upon. Frequent, regularly scheduled problem-solving sessions are part of the preventive maintenance that heads off trouble and keeps problems from crossing the danger threshold. Consensus is preferred; however, leaders have the authority to take immediate action, if necessary, for the good of the whole system.

Displays of affection are not uncommon in these workplaces. Staff members actually hug each other — an activity that would send people in other workplaces scurrying to the human resources department for advice on how to handle sexual harassment. It's not uncommon for employees to have personal relationships outside of the workplace with other staff members or clients. The Lover organization assumes that everyone has relatively equal standing, and that employees are all grown-ups capable of making their own decisions about such things. In other workplace cultures, for example, the Caregiver organization (which assumes a "parent–child" relationship with subordinates and clients), such behavior would be horrifying.

Table 5–9 *The Experience of All Core Types in the Lover Culture*

Core Type	Contributions	Difficulties
INNOCENT	Optimism, hope, trust Contentment with what already exists Positive energy	Dislikes lack of conventionality Can easily be taken advantage of
ORPHAN	Ability to define problems clearly and force attention on them	Hopelessness dissipates energy of self and others Creates internal conflict
SEEKER	Independence, which prevents group-think	Commitment required Intimacy expected Consensus decision making
JESTER	Playful irreverence Lightens up seriousness Creativity	Does not understand what is worth getting so "worked up" about. Problems with commitment and workload
CAREGIVER	Sense of duty, willing to do what needs to be done, even if distasteful	Will burn out quickly if assumes this culture's approach to work but keeps passivity and conflict avoidance
WARRIOR	Willingness to confront Assertiveness Action oriented Toughness	Competitor in a cooperative environment, like bull in china shop
MAGICIAN	Flexibility Conflict resolution, mediation, and communication skills Vision	Conflict avoidance saps energy of efforts; wants more and faster change
RULER	Stability, order Prioritization	Being "peers," consensus system, power sharing Intensity and type of energy is confusing
LOVER	High energy and commitment Capacity for caring, honest interactions, and intimacy Ability to dialogue	Exhausts self and others Erotic energy can cause confusion in staff relationships
SAGE	Detachment Equality consciousness	Finds crusading attitude to be distasteful and inappropriate Passionate energy is disconcerting

How Perceived	How See Organization	Survival Tips
Naif who needs love, protection, and guidance	Warm, caring. Too intense, exhausting. Dislikes consensus, prefers authority	Maintain personal boundaries so you are not swept off your feet by the charisma of coworkers. Cheerful optimism will be appreciated.
Wounded individual who needs a lot of TLC, or rotten apple in the barrel	Does not understand where energy comes from or why. Sees consensus as a "con"	Although it may not be appreciated at first, your gift for reality testing will keep this organization from going overboard.
A loner, indifferent Not warm or caring Not really part of group	Excessively enthusiastic conformers. Exhausting, unreasonable expectations	Help this culture avoid "group-think." Be aware that workers here may not respect your desire for separateness.
Irreverence is disruptive; unreliable, does not complete tasks, lets down coworkers	Uncomfortable with passion, intensity, and work expectations	Your ability to brainstorm will provide more than just the "one right way" to do things. Be careful not to appear irreverent toward the "holy cause."
Dedicated, responsible, but works out of duty rather than love Lacking in energy	Likes its warmth, care, cooperation, harmony; somewhat erratic in getting results	Your desire to take care of the less fortunate may conflict with democratic ideal of this culture. Maintain solid personal boundaries.
Combative, overbearing, unkind Disciplined, hardworking, committed	Slow to action Intense, energized Too sensitive to hurt feelings	This "touchy-feely" culture may make you very uncomfortable. Your action orientation and willingness to fight for the cause will be appreciated.
Willful, stubborn Creative Assertion forces problems to surface	Slow to action Inflexible Loves energy and power sharing	This culture will value your vision and "win-win" approach and your ability to mediate conflict. But it may not be open to alternate approaches.
Authoritarian, bossy, domineering	As a "love-in" rather than a workplace Erratic, unpredictable	Your desire for clear lines of authority will be frustrated. However, your sound judgment in resource use can keep it from "giving away the store."
Inexhaustible worker Dedicated to the cause Will give "all" Democratic	As a meaningful, important place to work A worthy mission; a "holy" cause	Avoid burning the candle at both ends. Take care of yourself — there is always more to be done. Maintain personal-professional boundaries.
Too uninvolved, uncaring, detached Fair and judicial in conflict resolution	Too attached to ways of doing things or to specific results	People may find your emotional detachment puzzling, even offensive. You can help them step back and obtain a more global perspective.

In highly stressed or less well-developed Lover organizations, there are underlying, unstated power struggles that result in a fragmentation of affiliations and the setting up of different camps. Internal conflict prevents the organization from getting any work done. In the worst cases, civil war ensues, and the organization is ripped apart. Alternately, people can avoid confrontation until the problems are crippling. This avoidance can manifest as "groupthink" which blunts the natural intensity and focus of this kind of organization. Repressed feelings eventually explode in ugly ways. In highly stressed Lover organizations, the decision-making process becomes irrational, emotional, rather than fact-based. Leaders and workers are uncompromising, even fanatical, about their beliefs and opinions, and are excessively demanding of each other.

Summary of Lover Organizations

Strengths: Highly energized, cooperative, committed to a shared purpose, consensual decision making, work process orientation.

Weaknesses: Exhausting, avoidance of conflict *or* excessive, hateful internal wars, de-emphasis on product, slow and/or irrational decision making.

ANALYZING YOUR ORGANIZATION

1. List the Lover scores you gave your organization:

   _____

   Specific areas:

   _____

2. What strengths or weaknesses of the Lover Organization are similar to your organization?

   +s: _____

   – s: _____

THE SAGE ORGANIZATION

The director of a research division of a large pharmaceutical company has asked me to help his organization establish cross-functional teams. This is a department that spends its time testing drugs that may or may not ever reach the market. They are a well-funded group, with a reputation — even among federal regulators — for integrity and impeccable research. As I am given a tour of the facilities, I notice that the laboratories are spacious and sparkling clean. The halls and offices we pass are quiet. When the director introduces me to key staff members, I feel that, although they respond pleasantly, I am disturbing their revery.

This a very cerebral group. It has more PhDs, MDs, and post-docs than I have found anywhere outside a university department. The leader here is interested in creating a "learning organization." He realizes that his group needs more basics before they can approach that level of functioning. Although his people have been trained in TQM fundamentals and enjoy using Statistical Process Control techniques to measure their work processes, they still tend to work too much in isolation or in small, functional workgroups. These individuals seem to respect each other greatly and get on very well. The leader is right, though. They do not appear to have sufficient interaction or cohesion among the different workgroups to move on to the next level of organizational development.

Indeed, I find the staff reluctant to "waste time" at a seminar on team-building. My first job appears to be giving them an experience of the "efficiency" of cross-functional teams. I talk to them about the research on team dynamics and systems learning. I ask them to "experiment" with me. By the end of the first day of this three-day seminar, they are completely on board.

The Sage culture emphasizes planning, analysis, and clear, logical thinking. If you work in a Sage organization, you will find that it tends to treat its employees fairly and respectfully. It is quite intolerant of pettiness, egoism, and conflict. It has no time for internal politics. The work of these workplaces is often *thinking*, for example, governmental policy formation. Employees at all levels of the organization tend to be given sufficient time, independence, and quiet to do their jobs. It is not uncommon for Sage work spaces to include designated "quiet areas": on-site meditation rooms or corporate gardens where individuals can walk and contemplate their assignments. Working in a Sage organization, then, is a bit like studying in a library; it causes considerable stress when circumstances prevent people from having the quiet time they need to do their real work of thinking.

If you are hired by a Sage culture, it is because you are considered a "grownup" — self-sufficient and able to handle all your work, including the necessary details. Leaders are expected to provide the vision, context, planning, and overview for everything that is done here. Performance evaluations are regularly scheduled and tend to be quite candid. This culture considers criticism to be a gift, one that is necessary to learning and improvement. In Sage workplaces, you will find that problems are approached in a emotionally detached way. People are really seeking the right answers and do not usually have a strong investment in particular outcomes. The goal, here, is Truth with a capital "T." These organizations gravitate to systemic, holistic, long-range, comprehensive solutions. Decisions are made on the basis of data and philosophical considerations. This calm, steady, thoughtful approach is usually an asset when responding to change. However, it can become a liability if problems are analyzed so much that necessary action is delayed or no action results at all.

The strengths of the Sage culture include its ability to approach issues objectively and its detachment from specific outcomes. This even-handedness tends to result in long-lasting decisions that take all factors into consideration. On the other hand, as a work environment you may find it somewhat cool, with a lack of emotional cohesion and linkages between staff. Moreover, sometimes its "ivory-tower" perspective keeps it from being attentive to bottom-line issues. After all, financial matters pale in comparison to the great thoughts you're having until your neglect threatens to result in loss of funding!

Sage organizations try to arrive at perfect solutions. As this is not an easy task, sometimes these workplaces become paralyzed during their attempts. *Quality* is attained in Sage workplaces by consistently meeting high standards, by continually gathering feedback from customers, by monitoring the efficiency of work processes, and by being within the quality control limits for a given product or service. Logic, intelligence, and careful thinking and speaking are prized in these cultures. Here you would be expected to thoroughly research, even footnote, arguments and discouraged from offering any solutions that appeared "simple-minded." Indeed, this kind of culture distrusts anything that (or anyone who) appears too easy, too quick, or too glib.

Sage cultures tend to have rationally determined structures that are adjusted in order to optimize the organization's work. Therefore, they can be either hierarchical or nonhierarchical. Sage organizations tend to select leaders who are content experts, such as the physician who has published the best research in that field. Other managerial criteria, such as knowing how to get along with people, are not priorities.

Conflict is uncommon. You will find that your colleagues tend to be unemotional about disagreements up to a point. They will, however, retrench if you challenge their expertise, research, ethics, or objectivity. Conflict is avoided because it is considered to be unnecessary and time consuming. It is handled first by fact-finding, then analysis, and detached decision making. If necessary, impartial third parties are brought in to settle the dispute.

It is not uncommon to find people in these cultures thinking out loud with each other, sifting through the facts together or discussing interesting concepts with colleagues. Sage systems attract individuals who want intellectual challenge and stimulation.

Change is approached in a matter-of-fact manner. It is first examined for its cause, then potential long-range impact on the organization. After that, it is responded to in a way that is not piecemeal, and that, therefore, is likely to endure.

The best forms of the Sage culture welcome challenges to their paradigms. I was very impressed by astronomers' exhilarated reactions to photos from the Hubble telescope that, in many cases, threw out years of their life's work. I thought the excitement of these individuals reflected the true scientific approach. Similarly, if a Sage

Table 5-10   *The Experience of All Core Types in the Sage Culture*

Core Type	Contributions	Difficulties
INNOCENT	Cheerfulness Optimism Trust, hope Beginner's mind	Expected to work independently, to be "grown-up" Organization demands development, growth
ORPHAN	Presentation of problems in early stages; helps keep organization attached to "real world" Compassion	Expected to be an adult, must sink or swim; pettiness, ego conflicts not tolerated
SEEKER	Autonomy Integrity Concerned with issues of meaning	Degree to which held accountable Seeing larger truth vs. personal truth Angst not tolerated
JESTER	Playful truth-telling Creativity	Emphasis on planning Calm, quiet
CAREGIVER	Warmth, caring, linkage with co-workers Self-sufficiency	Could burn out trying to fulfill emotional needs that perceives in coworkers
WARRIOR	Discipline, focus, loyalty, decisiveness; action orientation	Organization dislikes conflicts of any kind, always plans and thinks before it acts
MAGICIAN	Change agency Mediation, communication, conflict-resolution skills	Your action orientation exhausts and alienates the more reflective coworkers
RULER	Prioritization Decisiveness Attention to details/follow through	Need for control, authority over others; organization often does not see nose in front of face
LOVER	Emotion, attachment, passion, caring Cohesion, linkage with coworkers	Workplace has "wet blanket" effect; robs of energy
SAGE	Mentoring new people Calmness Detachment, fair perspective	Lack of emotional connection to other staff members Work too much in isolation

How Perceived	How See Organization	Survival Tips
Pleasant, but naive Needs too much supervision	Pleasant, but cool Somewhat confused by what is expected	Think before speaking. Temper enthusiasm. You can learn a lot in this culture if you allow yourself to be a student.
Unusually needy person; if doesn't respond to opportunity, will be replaced	Cold, uncaring Does not give you enough of a chance	Complaining and disputes are not welcome. This culture may not seem compassionate, but it will address problems you bring before it.
Insufficiently productive; not quite a grown-up	Allows independence and freedom to do own work	Remember that your "truth" is not necessarily the whole "Truth." Your opinion will be heard and taken into consideration.
Childlike, fun Unpredictable Not reliable	Boring, dull Too quiet, serious	This culture is receptive to new ideas as long as they have a potential purpose. Humor tends to be a bit dry; hilarity and uproar are discouraged.
Responsible, self-sufficient; tries to take care of self by taking care of others	Treats people well but too cool Too much "head," not enough heart	This culture needs the "glue" you provide, as it may neglect staff needs. Argue for your concerns within the context of the whole.
Combative Needing to be "right" or to win Hardworking	Productive Too much planning, too little action Weak, too easygoing	Competition is seen as being divisive. You are likely to be frustrated by lack of action. Take care to plan and justify your actions before you act.
Too attached to particular outcomes. Unpredictable, disruptive	Overanalytical Organization's pace is too slow	You share with this culture a desire for learning the truth. Your charisma is likely not to be understood or trusted.
Good on details and follow-up Too rigid	Orderly, stable Too cerebral	This system can benefit from your attention to resources as it can be too much an "ivory tower." You share desire to work for the good of the whole.
Illogical Overemotional Unpredictable	Overanalytical; values mind over heart Too easygoing about life and death situations	You are likely to be considered irrational, overly emotional and a loose cannon; tone it down. This system can use your liveliness.
Efficient Intelligent	A place where you can think and get real work done without disruptions	Remember that "all work is relationships." Take care to really connect with others so that the whole organization is successful.

organization is open to new information, change can result in a quantum leap in understanding. Crises are caused in these organizations when they can no longer see the big picture, or when they refuse to examine or renew their paradigms.

When mistakes occur in Sage systems, first the error is analyzed and the root cause found. Then a systemic correction is proposed, studied, and finally implemented. Walter Shewhart's Plan-Do-Check-Act cycle describes a typical work process in many Sage cultures. These systems can become "learning organizations" by employing their natural strengths of observation, introspection and reflection. When a certain level of attention and responsiveness to the environment and its own staff members is added to the mix, the Sage culture can soar to new heights.

The More and Less Well-Developed Sage Organizations

A successful Sage organization is a pleasant, calm, easygoing, yet productive place to work. Leadership is fair, approachable, and relatively unflappable, even during times of crisis. Ongoing evaluation is conducted in such a constructive manner that it helps employees feel they are really "seen." There is a gentle acceptance of

---

ANALYZING YOUR ORGANIZATION

1. List the Sage scores you gave your organization:

   _____

   Specific areas:

   _____

2. What strengths or weaknesses of the Sage Organization are similar to your organization?

   +s: _____

   − s: _____

human frailties and a recognition of the need to establish some emotional bonds between people as a way to support theoretical or philosophical consensus.

Mature Sage cultures create pleasant, quiet workplaces. They tend to have work processes that are logical, clear, direct, and understood by all participants. Consequently, people work together efficiently. These workplaces develop good internal processes for gathering feedback. Much attention is paid to optimizing the whole system. Leaders are sought who always keep the big picture in mind. Sage cultures and the people in them tend to be captivated by ideas, models. Employees are prized who are intellectually alert, and who themselves can remain detached from specific outcomes.

The least successful Sage organizations are so emotionally detached and analytical that they feel inhuman and are cold, uncaring places to work. They also may not be sufficiently in touch with the rest of the world to keep from going off on unproductive tangents. Other lower level Sage organizations may be perfectionist and analyze things to death. Examples of less well-developed Sage organizations include workplaces where intellectualization is used to trivialize interpersonal issues, to justify reprehensible behavior (sexism, racism, etc.), or to avoid facing emotionally difficult situations.

In such organizations, hypercritical interactions would prevent you from expressing your real thoughts and feelings. Intellectual debate is sometimes used to mask personal pain. In such Sage organizations there is little "glue" between people. Employee policies are inadequate or nonexistent. Conflict seethes below the surface but is repressed as "petty." Leaders seem to have their heads in the clouds and are as distracted as the absent-minded professor. As a result, employees respond by distancing themselves; they go about their work in an emotionally shielded, sometimes even robotic manner.

Summary of Sage Organizations

Strengths: Planning, logical work processes, fairness, objective; systemic, holistic approach to problems, seek feedback and truth.

Weaknesses: Too detached, overly analytical, inaction, lack of emotional cohesion and staff linkages; hypercritical; perfectionist.

NOTES

1. Alan C. Greenberg, *Memos from the Chairman*, Workman Publishing, New York, 1996, p. 19.
2. Michael Hammer, *How the Process Centered Work Is Changing Our Work and Our Lives*, HarperCollins, New York, 1996, p. 69.

PART IV

Riding the Waves of Change

6

The Dynamic Forces of Change

God grant me
the *serenity* to accept the things I cannot change,
the *courage* to change the things I can,
and the *wisdom* to know the difference.

This chapter outlines how change typically affects each Core Type and Core Culture. It examines how we as individuals and how our organizations can more gracefully "ride the waves" of change.

The truth is: change is often painful, whether we experience it in our personal lives, our professional lives, or the lives of our organizations. It is especially difficult when it is forced upon us, taking us in directions we do not choose, calling upon us to "grow" when what we really want is to stay the same. (Even when our current circumstances are not all that great, we tend to assume that the devil we know is better than the devil we've not yet met.)

In *Magic at Work*, Carol Pearson and I talked about the difficulty of living in the *In-between*. Even though change guarantees that when one door closes, another will open for us, we all know that "the hall between can be hell."[1] Whether or not we cooperate with change, it will take us in and out of various phases of our lives as we, our work environments, and the people around us shift, learn, and grow.

Working from Your Core is designed to help you gain the *serenity, courage,* and *wisdom* you will need to work with — rather than "manage," "control," or "drive" — the three dynamic forces of change. Great wisdom lies in understanding that trying to manage change is roughly equivalent to trying to manage the weather. Our desire to control change reflects our (quite understandable) fear and frustration about how freely these powerful forces move around and through us, in whatever ways they will.

Change is usually more painful when we resist it, when our pride or strong will take over and we swim against the waves coming towards us. I am not suggesting that we stand by passively while the forces of change do whatever they will with our lives or workplaces. It is up to all of us to find ways that we can work *with* the forces of change, so that we minimize their negative impact and maximize their potential for good in our lives and work.

THE THREE DYNAMIC PROCESSES OF CHANGE

There are three classical forces of change: *Creation, Destruction,* and *Sustenance.* Since ancient times and across a great many cultures, we hear stories of these three processes. Sometimes they are represented as triple gods or goddesses, for example, Christianity's Holy Trinity, the triple goddess Morrigan of Ireland, and the triple Devi of India (Kali, Lakshmi, and Saraswati).

The processes of change move through and animate the Core Types and the Core Cultures. They call upon us to constantly balance the kind of heroic action *and* heroic inaction that is described in the serenity prayer above. These three forces are *constants* that affect everything in our work lives. *They exist both inside and outside us,* therefore they affect us individually, organizationally, nationally, and globally.

I find it helpful to think of the Core Types, which wear human faces, as nouns and the forces of change as verbs. Or, to borrow a metaphor from quantum physics: if each type is a *particle,* then the processes of change are *waves*. For example, "The *Jester* in me is *creating* an exciting new product." You will find that when you become aware not only of what Core Type is most active in you, but also which of the three processes of change is moving through you, you will be able to behave more wisely in any given situation.

This is because each Core Type employs each of the processes of change differently. For example, if you want to create a new product, you may decide that what you most need right now is the Warrior's focus, discipline, and willingness to put in extra hours, and perhaps also the Innocent's optimism that all this effort will eventually pay off. Similarly, Core Cultures benefit greatly by deliberately using each of the three processes to augment their strengths. For example, a Caregiver's workplace could choose to better *sustain* its staff by monitoring and limiting their overtime hours; simultaneously it could *destroy* or significantly reduce a program that was putting a disproportionate demand on its total resources. In both these ways, the organization would augment its overall viability. What is important is that we and our workplaces *consciously* tap these processes of change. Otherwise we will suddenly notice that we have gotten ourselves into trouble because we have unconsciously overused or underused our resources.

The three forces of change work alone and together, sometimes so folding in on each other as to make it difficult to discern where one begins and the other ends. Paradoxically, they are at the same time three distinctly different forces *and a unified force* (very much like the three-in-one gods and goddesses). All life has a birth, a plateau, and then it decays. Biologists describe this natural tendency as an "S-curve." The only way that entropy will not set in prematurely in a life form is if it remains an *open system*. In much the same way, when we consciously allow ourselves to remain open and move *with* the forces of change, we continually regenerate our lives and work.

Paying attention to all three processes, keeping them in fluid balance, makes ourselves and our systems more vital. This translates into daily action in which we quickly let go of what is no longer appropriate, do what we can to sustain what is working well, and create new life by interacting with our surrounding environment.

When we cooperate with all three dynamic forces, we participate in our own evolution. We learn and adapt. This helps us avoid the need for more radical, dramatic upheavals. For example, you may notice that you are no longer performing well in one aspect of your job. Simply put, you are bored with it. You can be proactive: find another way to do the task, or talk to your boss about your difficulty. Or, you can avoid the issue entirely until your sloppiness causes a reprimand — or worse.

CHANGE AND SELF-MASTERY

Biology teaches us that all adaptation to change has to be in service of the self. That is, we need to stay who we are, integrated (as determined by our core identity). Otherwise we change so much that we become unrecognizable to ourselves: we "fragment," we fall apart under the stress of change, we lose our Self. The best way to work with change is to move into it from our Core, approaching it consciously so that it can lead us to whatever needs to be done right now.

One of the difficulties I see in organizations, and also in our personal lives, is that change seems to be happening too rapidly for most of us to cope well with it. Charles Handy, Peter Drucker, Tom Peters, and many other great thinkers have described our era as being one of *discontinuous* change. To give a sense of how up-tempo life has become, we need to realize that for most of recorded history, and even up until the invention of the steam engine in the 1800s, people could travel at only *three miles per day*. Since that time we have taken quantum leaps forward in the speed of travel and communications. One difficulty we face now is that, as a species, our technology has outpaced our own evolution. Charles Handy describes our current dilemma well:

> Change is not what it used to be. The status quo will no longer be the best way forward. The best way will be less comfortable and less easy but, no doubt, more interesting — a word we often use to signal an uncertain mix of danger and opportunity. If we wish to enjoy more of the opportunity and less of the risk, we

need to understand the changes better. Those who know why changes come waste less effort in protecting themselves or in fighting the inevitable. Those who realize where changes are heading are better able to use those changes to their own advantage.[2]

At any given time all three dynamic forces of change are weaving themselves through our lives and work. We can easily tell how well we're doing with the forces of change by noting how stable we feel internally, despite the chaos around us. We all will have countless opportunities to sharpen our skills in this area. For example, if your company is downsizing, sometimes it will be appropriate to move with the forces of Destruction, letting people go and helping them along in that process of change. Or, if Destruction has become excessive, depleting the overall life force of the organization, you may instead need to find ways to support those employees who are leaving and buoy up those who are being left behind to pick up the increased work load. Or, you may decide that it is high time to turn the tide in this change cycle by refocusing on a new, creative market effort.

By working from your Core you can more easily sort out which dynamic force is acting at a given time, and when the balance of change needs to shift in another direction. This takes vigilance — deliberately shining some focused attention on these processes, which otherwise remain hidden from view. Unfortunately, there are no cookbooks for dealing with the volatile, fluid state of change. There is no knowledge — only wisdom — that is adequate to guide us here. The good news is that over time, our attention to the forces of change will lead to work decisions that are enlivened with the kind of wisdom that is described in the serenity prayer.

THE IMPLICATE AND EXPLICATE ORDER
IN CHANGE

Physicist David Bohm described life as a fluid state of implicate (*enfolded*) and explicate (*unfolded*) order. We can see what has unfolded because it is visible to us now. What is enfolded are the possibilities that exist, but in latent form, below the surface. (Before a tightly closed flower blooms, we can't see all its petals, even though they are there.) The concept of a *holomovement* between an implicate and explicate order is a helpful way to think about the ever-fluid state of change.

If we look at our lives and our work, we can quickly see that they are in constant movement between Creation, Sustenance, and Destruction. Because all of these processes are necessary for Life, none is inherently better than the other. This is not to say that you and I won't have strong personal preferences about which process we want to happen at any given time! (In the great scheme of things, this is probably why we, with our limited perspectives and biased self-interest, are not allowed to play God.) Creation is not only the bringing into being of something beautiful but also the irresponsible birthing of more than we can feed. Destruction is not only the feared face of Death but also the courageous letting go of a part of our lives that no longer works for us. Sustenance is not only Mom's delicious chicken soup, but also a guest who doesn't seem to realize that it's way past time to leave.

The difficulty is that if any one of these powerful forces of life is used either insufficiently *or* to excess, it will cause an imbalance in the whole system, which then will initiate a shift into another of the change processes. These three forces are actually an interwoven holomovement, each one leading to — and setting up the need for — the next. In a very real way, each process does contain the seeds of the others.

> In Sustenance are the seeds of Destruction
> In Destruction are the seeds of Creation
> In Creation are the seeds of Sustenance

The following story illustrates how you can use the three processes of change to better understand what's happening in your work.

I had been working with an area health-care client for the past two years. We had established an exciting TQM effort, including getting all the staff enthusiastically on board, establishing hard-working cross-functional teams, and training facilitators. In year three of our project, we were scheduled to conclude my tasks by turning over more and more responsibility in-house. But the client became erratic about returning my calls; he stated that other events were taking precedent, that our concluding efforts would have to be postponed.

I watched all this from an enforced distance. The teams were not using their facilitators, and some were starting to have significant difficulties. One fell apart completely. The Caregiver part of myself wanted to rescue them and the fruits of their good labors. I wanted this organizational effort to be sustained, so for some time I continued to call the client. Finally, I recognized that I was oversustaining.

So, one morning I decided to take a few moments to contemplate the situation. I took a deep breath and went into my Core. I called upon my inner Sage for advice. This gave me a more emotionally detached perspective with which to view what was happening. What I eventually realized was that the process of Destruction, of letting go, was what was called for here — not Sustenance — but gently and respectfully, through my calm Sage rather than the insulted Warrior or concerned Caregiver. As I thought more about the situation, I had to admit to myself that (1) we had done excellent work together, and (2) although our contract called for another year of consulting, it really wasn't necessary. We both would be continuing with the relationship only out of contractual duty.

I was already heading in a significantly different professional direction. To continue this effort — to oversustain it — would hold me back. The more I worked against the dynamic life forces, the more difficult it would be to end this professional relationship. I could hold on, or I could be gracious and let go. It answer became obvious: I needed to leave this old work behind so that I could focus my energy on creating new work.

The rest of this chapter describes how each of the ten Core Types and each of the ten kinds of Core Cultures use these great powers of Sustenance, Destruction, and Creation for good or ill. Hopefully this information will help you and your organization more easily ride the waves of change.

SUSTENANCE

I believe that, in our rapidly changing workplaces today, we pay the least attention to the positive aspects of the life-*sustaining* force. Sustenance is the link between Creation and Destruction. Sustenance is whatever keeps us alive: things we tend to take for granted, such as gravity, the safety of the roads we drive on, the eyes and ears that help us navigate our world, clean water, the opportunity to work, laws that govern our society, or the kind touch of a family member. Sustenance is the food we eat, and also the nutrients it contains. It is our supportive friendships and working relationships. Sustenance is the life-force that makes us put money in our savings account, the instinct that urges us to hire a security guard for that dark employee parking lot.

When we don't have enough Sustenance, we die. Slowly. From hunger or thirst or lack of meaning. Unfortunately, in an era of "lean and mean" business practices, it is Sustenance that is now often lacking in our work lives. This is why so many of us describe ourselves as feeling "starved" in our jobs; it is much more than a metaphor. The support systems, the hidden infrastructure, and the good manners of business are often the first to go when our organizations are put under stress. Because Sustenance so often cannot be seen or quantified, this process is often ignored as we pour energy into taking care of crises. We try to stave off Destruction and/or increase Creation. Meanwhile the life-blood of the organization is drained. Trust and cooperation are eroded. Employees respond to management with resentment and less productivity. Not only a *lack* of Sustenance, but *over*sustenance can lead to an individual's or a system's demise. Trying to hold on when it is time to let go will always backfire, as the interwoven forces of change will move on with or without our consent.

In general, Sustenance is augmented on a personal level by noticing and feeling gratitude for what we *do* have, rather than focusing on what we lack. Sustenance is often so subtle that its continuance is taken for granted. (The old song is right — you usually don't know what you've got 'til it's gone.) As things change around you in your workplace, you can pay attention to, then move proactively to sustain the things that are important to you. You can also increase the force of Sustenance in your work life by employing the sustaining aspects of each of the Core Types and the Core Cultures.

Sustenance and the Core Types

The *Innocent's* hope and optimism not only help us, but also others around us, to keep going, to be sustained through tough times. Cheerfulness gives comfort to our colleagues. The pristine faith of the Innocent nurtures and sometimes even draws miracles to it (for example, the help of others who don't want to see the Innocent fail).The Innocent in each of us keeps the child within feeling safe. It holds onto security, and also attracts safe places and people to it. Not seeing or being hampered by real limits can keep the Innocent involved in a project long after others would have given up. Sometimes this is great; at other times it has an oversustaining effect. On the clearly negative side, the Innocent may want so much to prolong our current situation that we won't adapt to changing circumstances. The Innocent can also sustain problems by (1) denying they exist or (2) denying their effect. This is how the Innocent enables bad situations to continue unchallenged.

The *Orphan's* compassion has a healing effect on everyone — the person to whom it is directed, everyone who witnesses it and, also, the Orphan itself. The quality of compassion is so nurturing because it gives us an understanding of our humanity and fallibility. The Orphan's wound serves to bind groups together around shared difficulties. Obviously, this can be good or bad. At a certain point, however we start oversustaining our focus on our wound, confusing it with our identity. (I've seen this happen in substance-abuse or victim support groups.) Our self-pity or pity for others can be a negative sustaining force, causing people to continue in partial identities or self-perpetuating cycles, where they see no way out.

The *Seeker*, with its relentless search for meaning, sustains meaningful work, a life purpose, and worthwhile relationships. The Seeker is determined to maintain integrity and principles. Because the Seeker in us feels that we are unique, it supports our personal boundaries within the context of the group: "I am not my tribe. I am an individual. I have my own ideas." This sustains a sense of separation, of who we are versus others within the community. When the Seeker in us speaks our own truth, we can encourage others in their own search for clarity and meaning: "I'm not crazy . . . others think there's a problem here too." The danger is that the Seeker can oversustain us in our search for the ideal, thereby having us windup with nothing to show for all our wanderings.

It has now been amply demonstrated that laughter heals. Yet I rarely find the *Jester* bouncing around hospital corridors. Good humor keeps our hope alive, helping us endure despite difficult circumstances. Levity enlivens situations that otherwise would bog down. The Jester can help us shed light on what is true so that we can see it more clearly. It can also lighten things up while we look at what does and does not work. On the negative side, the Jester can use trickery or clever manipulation to get others to support us in ways that are not in their best interests. The Jester can also use its considerable charm and wit to excuse and protect bad habits, as does the witty alcoholic.

The *Caregiver* is often assigned the task of community sustenance, doing selfless service, the usually thankless nurturing tasks that keep societies, organizations, families together. This Core Type tends to give whatever is necessary to help our infant projects first survive, then thrive. The support given is frequently physical and emotional. The Caregiver in us can be buoyed up, energized by this giving of the self. Up to a point. When Caregivers oversustain, the damage is dual. No only do we burn out, but we have enabled others to stay dependent rather than learn how to become self-sufficient. When the Caregiver finally collapses, both are left stranded. This same phenomenon can also be observed with Caregivers who make ourselves "indispensable" in our organizations.

The *Warrior* sustains life itself by keeping appropriate boundaries in place, much like cell walls, which protect the internal workings of the cell. If its boundaries are penetrated, the cell will die. The internal Warrior maintains our mental, emotional and physical walls against those who would harm us. The Warrior "watches over" our psyche while we are busy doing other things. It provides early warning signals, such as anger and fear, to let us know that something dear to us is in danger. The Warrior's protective stance helps us define what territory is ours versus someone else's. It encourages us to put up a fence around our property so as to keep out predators. On the negative side, the Warrior may tend to oversustain by being overly protective of everything within our domain. It may have violent, knee-jerk reactions to protect whatever currently exists, including that which is rotting. This could take the form of defending inequities in the current system that actually threaten the viability of our future.

The *Magician* nurtures us by helping us find balance in our lives. It supports us in claiming the power we have to heal ourselves from the inside out. This personal power, in turn, sustains us in our efforts to manifest whatever is important to us in the world. The Magician also supports us with its worldview of prosperity. It shifts our perspective so that we focus our energy on increasing the resources available to us (much like one candle lighting another) rather than settle for dividing up a limited pie. This Core Type helps us recognize and augment the many gifts we already have. The Magician can oversustain by using its powers to support an old system beyond its usefulness. It can also have us use our magical gifts inappropriately, for example, for personal gain.

The *Ruler* is charged with maintaining order and peace in our kingdoms, whether home, work, or community. Its responsibility is to keep our world as stable as it can be. To this end, the Ruler in us enforces a personal code of behavior, establishes rules and routines, and stewards our resources. The Ruler manages the wealth of our kingdoms so that prosperity is enjoyed by all who live and work there. This careful stewarding of our natural resources and talents allows us to flourish, our wealth to grow. However, our Ruler can oversustain by repressing natural growth, diversity, or change in order to maintain our current status and the existing order. And, as has been seen throughout history, the unwise sustenance of the old order for too long can lead to repression of, then revolt by, the disenfranchised.

The *Lover* sustains us with its fierce dedication and commitment, and its willingness and ability to burn the candle at both ends. Its strong emotional support often provides the glue that keeps our relationships and organizations together under stress. The Lover also nurtures us personally by stimulating our awareness of the senses, our fondness for and enjoyment of all things beautiful. However, this Core Type, with its tendency to make such strong attachments, can easily oversustain, prolonging relationships or projects beyond their natural life span. This part of ourselves will go to great lengths to protect and maintain whatever or whomever we are committed to. The Lover tends to ignore all the warning signs, trying instead to keep things as they have always been, even when the job or relationship needs to be let go of or completely recreated.

The *Sage* sustains us with its ability to plan for the long haul and overview the entire system. The Sage supports us and our efforts with its objectivity, its data, its willingness to study and research. The Sage's ability to reflect and keep calm despite surrounding chaos sustains our center of gravity so we don't completely fall apart. The Sage can oversustain as well: we call this "analysis-paralysis," the inability to act because we have become mesmerized by our own planning or research. The Sage can easily immerse us in the complexity of a problem or gaze too long at the whole system, trying to figure it all out. The Sage can also get us into trouble when, after finally designing the "perfect" theoretical system, it puts something in place and keeps it there despite evidence that the plan is not working particularly well in reality.

Sustenance and the Core Cultures

The *Innocent* Core Culture tries to sustain the best parts of the past — its traditions and job security — as it moves into an uncertain future in an uncertain world. It wants to protect civility and good manners and a family feeling in the workplace. Unfortunately the Innocent work environment is too often guilty of undersupporting innovation and maintaining too tight a grip on the past. It rarely moves easily out of continuing to do what it has always done, thinking this to be the best of all possible worlds.

The *Orphan* organization will sustain, at all other costs, its ability to survive. This often translates to a strong bottom line and a tough image. In the lower forms of this kind of culture, what tends to endure are turf battles and grudges. Workers remember who did what to whom and when, and feel betrayed by management (or vice versa). What tends to be undersupported here are the people who are suffering — those who have been weakened by this system's difficulties. It could be argued that, in Darwinian terms, this is just survival of the fittest. A counter argument is that a lack of sustenance does *not* lead to individual, organizational, or species evolution. In higher level Orphan workplaces, compassion is the nurturing force that holds people together despite all difficulties. The realization that we're all in the same boat — and that we've managed to survive in the past — are also sustaining forces in Orphan cultures.

The *Seeker* organization most wants to sustain its uniqueness and the employee independence typical of its work environment. It is not particularly good at buoying up workers who need a lot of attention, as it expects them to function on their own. A Seeker culture can better maintain itself by developing a strong core identity that holds together its disparate parts and independent people. This can help it adapt more readily to changes in the environment, which, if too severe, will cause this culture to fragment along the lines of its internal special interest groups. In its best forms, a Seeker system fosters free-thinking, experimentation, collegiality, and interdependence. In its worst forms, it prolongs too much separation, which results in fragmentation of effort, alienation of departments and individuals, and an overall lack of organizational cohesion.

The *Jester* organization will sustain its freedom, a fun work environment, and innovation at any price. It tends to promote excitement and hilarity, often at the cost of deadlines or quality. It tends to undersupport the structure or procedures necessary for its own productivity, too often changing things midstream, or abandoning a project in process for another that is more appealing. It also often does not prolong an effort much beyond its first obstacle; that is, when it has stopped being fun. The force of Sustenance can help this kind of culture adapt: by having it consider how it is to carry its brilliant ideas through to completion and by making certain it produces what it said, when it said. Sustenance can also help this culture by having it pause and contemplate what it actually can sustain over time, that is, to make certain it is not taking on more than it can see through. The worst forms of Jester organizations will ignore how much hard work is needed, right now, to pull the fat out of the fire (much like Nero fiddling while Rome burns).

Caregiver cultures want most to sustain the good service they give their clients. Indeed, this kind of organization is willing to sustain client service, often at cost to its own employees, who ironically, it often undersustains (as reflected in wages and working conditions). Caregiver systems value selflessness in employees, but often do not reward this trait, apparently assuming that goodness is its own reward. The best ways Caregiver workplaces can nurture themselves are by not "giving away the store" financially and by developing an infrastructure that prevents its employees from burning out. In its worst forms, this culture sustains the belief that "good" employees are those who give of themselves until there is nothing left. As illogical and cruel as this sounds when spoken out loud, the unwritten assumption in some Caregiver work environments is that anything less than martyrdom is inadequate. This culture also runs into difficulties when it continues burdensome structures and policies as protections for clients.

Warrior organizations sustain competition as a way of sharpening skills and sorting the wheat from the chaff. Loyalty, teamwork, and discipline are sustaining traits within this culture. The Warrior workplace has great staying power, and a willingness and ability to endure. Healthy personal and professional boundaries are respected within this kind of culture. Staff members are motivated by pep talks, challenges, and internal competitions. Rewards are given in accordance with production, which tends to encourage individual versus team efforts. Problems occur when the Warrior culture maintains an outdated strategy, that is, when it does more of the same thing faster, rather than reassess and shift gears entirely. This system may also maintain boundaries that are no longer helpful or appropriate. It also tends to undersustain, sometimes even ignore, the emotional needs of its employees.

Magician cultures are sustained by a vision that is "grounded" it in reality. This kind of workplace is also supported by flexible, innovative structures and results-oriented management. Often, the charisma of a visionary leader is a strong force that holds the organization together despite the uncertainty and chaos around it. Because the Magician organization often has ideas that are premature for its society, it needs a strong sustaining infrastructure that will provide staying power for the long haul. The Magician culture also needs alternate ideas, "plans B and C," or it could collapse while the world finally evolves to recognize its wonderful product. Another danger is that this culture will not sufficiently maintain its connection to its industry or societal environment. This often takes the form of insufficient or ineffective marketing. In the worst cases, the Magician organization undersustains its people, burning them out while simultaneously expecting them to work miracles.

Because the *Ruler* organization is at the top of its industry, it understandably wants to maintain the status quo. It guards both its reputation and the existing order of things. Its heavy bureaucracy and complex internal systems perpetuate its current form. A careful, measured work pace also helps protect this kind of system in the face of too rapid change. Ruler cultures tend to be solid organizations, not easily blown hither and thither, who steward their resources well. However, when these structures are not regularly reviewed and renewed, they will rigidify and be unable to move with the times. Another difficulty in Ruler work environments is that classism and stratification of employees often prevent the free flow of information. The culture, then, loses potentially sustaining gifts from those many individuals who are not in the "right" leadership positions.

In the *Lover* culture, intimacy and emotionally easy interactions provide the glue that keeps this kind of organization together. The intense dedication to the Lover organization's cause can sustain this system's effort for a very long time. The consensual decision-making process means that decisions have full support, and therefore, real staying power. An unwillingness to confront coworkers in this culture sometimes means that people remain overly long in their positions when they should be moved or retrained instead. Also, it is not uncommon in Lover workplaces for the decision-making process itself to be excessively prolonged. Because consensus often requires so much time and the involvement of so many people, problems can continue unaddressed for too long.

Sage workplaces do everything they can to sustain a calm, quiet work environment where people can think. Another goal of this culture is to maintain interactions that are objective and fair. A major strength of the Sage organization is its systems perspective, which is supported by its vision, contemplation, and long view. The factors that preserve this kind of culture are its willingness to mentor and teach new employees, thereby passing on history, information, and modeling of the expected work style. Sage cultures can get into trouble when they do too much planning and analysis, which leads to slow action or no action at all. They also have a tendency to undersupport the emotional life of staff members. This can result in the Sage workplace becoming a hollow, uncaring work environment that is too brittle to withstand stress.

DESTRUCTION

We rarely welcome the force of Destruction with open arms. Destruction ranges from a gentle letting go of a friendship that both people have outgrown, to losing the great love of your life, to the untimely death of a good neighbor, to the complete ravages of warfare. In the workplace we see the process of Destruction when we complete a project, edit a manuscript, or lose a job. The Statistical Process Control (SPC) techniques used in Quality efforts are a proactive form of Destruction. We employ these tools to help us avoid a slow erosion of productivity and avert crises. SPC and other evaluative or research tools help us work with this force of change by making us take a step back, objectively observe, then eliminate activities that are inefficient.

Destruction gets rid of whatever no longer works well in our lives and work. It works gently if we cooperate with it, and sometimes violently when we do not. Destruction is Nature's way of saying "No more," of weeding its own garden in order to prepare for new growth. Destruction is frequently hard on individuals, such as the person in charge of that non–value-added task who is slated for layoff, or the poor antelope who gets eaten by the lions. However, it is a vital process necessary for the good of the whole system.

Inadequate Destruction leads to overgrowth or the wrong kind of growth, which then requires a more radical form of Destruction to correct the situation. On the other hand, excessive Destruction may go so far that there is insufficient life force left to continue the natural change cycle. This is reflected in the nonjoke making the rounds about severely down-sized organizations: "Will the last person left please turn out the lights?" Or, as Peter Senge warns leaders, the danger in trying to make your organizations "lean and mean" is that they may wind up "gaunt and dead." The regenerating, open-system cycle of dynamic change can be terminated if there is an insufficient thread of life upon which to return. Entropy is then complete.

In many cases, however, Destruction has the positive effect of wiping the slate clean so that something new can be written in its place. Destruction is a prerequisite for successful Creation.

Destruction and the Core Types

The *Innocent's* optimistic attitude helps us break through limiting mental barriers that hold others hostage. It can destroy illusions by presenting new possibilities, new energy, and a beginner's mind. The Innocent in us may act as a whistle-blower, naively thinking that this behavior will be rewarded by superiors, when in truth we are more likely to be punished for inadvertently rocking the boat. On the negative side, the Innocent's denial or escapism can prevent us from seeing reality, or allow us to wander into dangerous situations where we will be taken advantage of or otherwise harmed. The Innocent's trait of denial can also have a degenerative effect by ignoring, and thereby, enabling the bad behavior of others.

The *Orphan* helps us destroy what needs to be eliminated with its complaining, its pointing out of real problems. This Core Type's compassion can dissolve the artificial barriers that separate people who, if connected, could help each other. The Orphan can over-destroy by playing too long the roles of either victim or victimizer. And as was described in the story about the child who cried "Wolf!," it can get us and others into trouble by complaining indiscriminately, blaming others, or trying to tear down the system within which we work.

The *Seeker* helps us let go of old ways, inappropriate parts of our work, lives, and community, so that we can discover who we really are, live more truthfully, and say "No!" to what does not fit for us. However, when it lets go of its own old life, the Seeker can also demolish the lives of others. Sometimes this is positive for those left behind and sometimes it is negative. The Seeker's destruction can take the form of a boss who leaves for another job with little notice, throwing his or her department into so much uproar that things fall apart. Or, alternately it could happen that what is destroyed is the workers' overdependency, and that they wind up completing the work on their own. The Seeker can destroy excessively by determining that, since nothing and no one matches our ideal, we have to leave one job (spouse, town, country) after another.

The *Jester* in us typically does not find it hard to let go of one thing for another. Its irreverence and belief that rules were meant to be broken makes this part of us act as a disruptive, challenging force much of the time. While this is a good approach when a particular part of the workplace really does need to be revamped, as a matter of course, it results in chaos. The Jester's distaste for pomposity leads us to puncture our illusions with humor. It also tends to eradicate group thinking and lies, and does not allow us to conform to political or social niceties. However, the Jester can destroy negatively when we use our humor as a weapon, cutting others to the quick, leaving invisible wounds. Clearly, the Jester is capable of wreaking havoc in the work environment, for instance, by causing "uproar" for entertainment, simply because it is bored.

The *Caregiver* destroys positively with the gift it most hates to give, *tough love*, the termination of caretaking that has become enabling. In such ways the Caregiver helps us to gently but firmly weed our gardens, destroying other plants so the preferred ones have the space they require to grow and survive. Caregivers sometimes need to eliminate the bad habits of those in charge, for example by saying "no," by teaching manners, respect, and discipline, and by keeping people from hurting themselves. This Core Type is often willing to sacrifice and surrender its own interests, its own welfare, for others.

However, its gift of care can have an unintended, degenerative influence when it is misplaced or excessive, disabling the recipient and draining the Caregiver. In the worst cases, Caregivers can *take* by giving, that is, we can manipulate others by serving them until the recipient of care is deeply indebted to us and thereafter subject to our will.

The *Warrior* in us confronts and fights bullies, annihilating those who attack us, our communities, or others whom we are supposed to protect. It dismantles boundaries that no longer are appropriate. It helps us let go of bad habits by first forming, then sticking to, new habits. This is the part of us that willingly surrenders our own life in order to save a comrade, our community, or nation. On the negative side, the Warrior can harm or kill others, taking no prisoners and spilling innocent blood in its march to victory. The destructive force of the Warrior is often personified in organizations by "hatchet men" — those people who are designated to fire others or be the bearers of bad news.

The *Magician* destroys limiting paradigms, lifting the veil of illusion that keeps us from clearly envisioning the future. This Core Type can act as a lightning bolt to jolt us awake, then empower us to remove old habits, outdated ways of being. The Magician can use its charisma to draw us into letting go of the safety of our old world, then leaping into the unknown of the next. However, the Magician can harm us in this process if we, like the sorcerer's apprentice, are not yet skilled enough to manage and control our own power. This part of us can manipulate others by overpowering their free will. The Magician can also be so impatient to push into the new world that we demolish the good of the present in the transition process.

Rulers in mythology sometimes allowed themselves to be sacrificed so that the kingdom would have new life. This ritual "killing of the king" is regularly acted out even today in corporations whenever the board or staff believe that the organization needs a new lease on life. The Ruler in each of us keeps order by acting as a judge: eliminating what is expendable and throwing it out, by prioritizing what is important, and by getting rid of the "fat" in a system, any out-of-date rules, or excessive layers of bureaucracy. The Ruler, particularly a new Ruler, can raze the old order so as to make way for the new. In almost all cases, Rulers deal harshly with real threats to stability, often responding with the equivalent of "Off with their heads." This includes punishing ourselves or others who are out of line or who disobey orders. The Ruler represses, kills, or expels from the territory anyone or anything that threatens the welfare of the kingdom.

The *Lover* destroys our sense of a separate self by having us surrender so that we give ourselves completely to another person, our work, community, or a great cause. This removal of barriers allows us to feel completely at one with our chosen worthy other. Clearly, this can become destructive if our sense of an individual self — our ego boundaries — are destroyed. Indeed, this results in symbiosis, where we lose ourselves completely, forgetting who we are, our self-worth, even our own needs, in our desire to fulfill someone else's. Such overattachment to a person, idea, or project can have the deadly effect of consuming our Self.

The *Sage's* clear, detached evaluation, planning, and analysis pinpoints for us whatever is not working or does not add value, so that we can revamp or eliminate it. This Core Type's teaching ability can help us attain a wider perspective, so that we have an easier time emotionally releasing whatever no longer works well in our lives and work. The Sage's natural detachment makes us less hesitant to let go of whatever is superfluous, whatever hampers efficiency, productivity, and a profitable bottom line. However, this level of detachment however can overdestroy, because what makes sense in theory does not always translate well to real life. If the Sage has not sufficiently factored in human issues, it may let go of the wrong things. This Core Type may not have a sense of the unintended side effects that its seemingly logical destruction could have. The Sage's apparent lack of caring also can have an adverse effect on working relationships, eroding the emotional glue necessary to hold workgroups together during stressful times.

Destruction and the Core Cultures

The *Innocent* Core Culture works with the force of Destruction when it bucks itself up, looks difficulty in the eye, says "We can do that!," then lets go of whatever, or whoever, no longer works well. This kind of workplace fears loss of what currently exists in the organization, for example, a pleasant working environment. It will rarely go willingly into the Destruction phase of change, where it has to surrender what it has worked so hard to attain. This culture has less tolerance for difference than many other kinds of work environments, so it will sometimes eliminate anything that or anyone who is too different from the norm. Such conformity in turn puts the damper on risk taking and innovation.

The *Orphan* organization assumes that the process of Destruction is a way of life, and that its organizational purpose is to defend against this constant force in order to survive. It will go out of its way to smash rose-colored glasses or any other illusions, insisting instead that all staff look squarely at whatever can go wrong. It meets Destruction almost as an ally, an old companion. In high-level Orphan organizations, barriers within the organization are removed in an effort to get everyone to work together against a common enemy or threat. However, destruction can wreak havoc in this culture when all staff members are just looking out for themselves. Barriers are then thrown up and people assume a defensive, first-strike posture towards internal or external threats. In these cases, fear removes the possibility of connectedness and morale seriously erodes.

The *Seeker* Core Culture will not allow dependency in staff members. It encourages truth-telling, and the kind of candor which challenges little lies, convenient untruths, and conformity. Unfortunately, connectedness among staff members is sometimes the casualty of focusing on separate areas of specialty. In many Seeker organizations, the bridges to collaboration collapse from neglect and non-use. Another factor that can adversely affect this kind of workplace is holding stubbornly to a particular cherished truth — usually the one that its top researchers have here-to-fore promoted. Micromanagement or any threats to worker autonomy are also destructive forces in this culture.

The *Jester* organization blasts through difficulties, untruths, and illusion with the humor and sharp wit of its staff. It quickly lets go of what is not working. Sometimes too quickly. The Jester culture delights in destroying old paradigms, cultural beliefs or conventional approaches — anything that no longer works, or that doesn't work fast enough. Sometimes, however, this lightning approach can cause the premature death of worthwhile projects due to neglect, distractedness, lack of focus or confusion. I've seen Jester cultures where the quick intelligence and biting humor it so prizes eroded good communications and connection between workers. Everyone was trying to one-up each other with verbal barbs that cut too close, drew some blood, and set up the need for retaliation.

Caregiver workplaces support the spirit of sacrifice. Putting clients' needs first winds up piercing through a lot of organizational posturing. It also clarifies the real priorities of this organization. Everything else is secondary, and can be let go of. Client service determines what needs to be done, how much needs to be done, and where money and time need to be spent. All other activities are superfluous. The major problem with Caregiver cultures is that they tend to devour the very people upon whom they depend to do the work. In treating staff members so poorly, low self-esteem and low morale become a drain on the organization's success. Caregiver systems can destroy themselves by squandering human resources and also by not wisely stewarding their physical resources.

The *Warrior* organization uses the force of Destruction to wipe out the competition. The characteristic toughness of these kinds of workplace cultures serves to eliminate weakness in individuals and teams. However, its fierce focus can cut two ways: it gives an intense energy to all activity, and it eliminates diversity of opinion. The Warrior system has a tendency to let go of too much, be too Spartan, too tough, too "lean and mean." Particularly under stress, this kind of organization will drive its staff very hard, almost like an enforced march. It also may let go of the wrong things. For example, communication training may be considered a frill, yet be precisely what is needed to break down barriers and build internal bridges. Excessive boundaries and competitiveness within the Warrior cultures tend to destroy cohesion and obstruct the flow of information. Another debilitating tendency in this culture is its tendency to punish mistakes — thereby suppressing the risk taking so necessary to inventiveness.

Magician cultures enjoy challenging the accepted paradigms of their industries and societies. This includes not only products and services, but also ways people are to work together. This culture empowers employees so as to discourage dependence. It expects everyone within it to function fully, and does whatever it can to help workers and leaders alike let go of their own limiting beliefs about their capabilities. This kind of organization can border on the arrogant, by not sufficiently recognizing the contributions of the past to today and tomorrow. This workplace's desire to live in the future — that is its own particular vision of the future — often clouds its clear view of both the past and present day reality. Trying to do too much too fast is also a negatively destructive tendency in Magician cultures, as it can cause the whole system to collapse.

In its best form, the *Ruler* culture eliminates instability and chaos. It cuts through confusion and anarchy, putting order and stability in their place. The Ruler organization eliminates waste and inefficiency by instituting better procedures and policies. It also does not hesitate, when necessary, to release unproductive employees. The very best forms of this kind of workplace institute "sunset" time frames, which serve as self-regulating mechanisms so that all policies must be actively reinstated when their terms run out. The amount of structure in Ruler organizations can be overly burdensome, and not allow for timely course corrections. Although difficult for all cultures, rapid change is experienced as particularly debilitating in this kind of work environment.

The intensity of the *Lover* organization and its fierce commitment to its mission can destroy both internal and external barriers that impede this system's work. The internal intimacy common to these organizations often serves to remove personal and professional barriers among its staff. (This can be good or bad.) The zeal in this culture can be excessive, devouring those who work within it. The Lover organization needs to have structured, regularly scheduled staff meetings and evaluations so that it is forced to notice, confront, and "weed out" what is not working well. Probationary periods and firings are a must in order to counter-balance a tendency for people to cloy to each other and their cause. If these precautionary measures are not institutionalized, conflict will erupt when it is well past healing. These work environments are too easily ripped apart by divisions among the staff where hatred becomes as strong as the love that first held them together. Although less visible, another potentially destructive force in Lover systems is the exhausting intensity of day-to-day work.

In the *Sage* culture, pettiness and conflict are not tolerated. A strength of this kind of workplace is its detachment from specific outcomes and its ability to let go of specific results. Its scientific, research approach to problems serves to remove attachment to particular paradigms and ideas. The Sage organization's cool-headed evaluation and analysis gives it an edge in sorting out truth from fiction. Moreover, the detachment that is characteristic of such cultures allows them to easily let go of anything that is not working well. This reflective workplace enjoys studying itself so that it can determine what needs improvement. Unfortunately, this system's lack of emotion can work against it, destroying the interpersonal connections that are necessary for any organization's long-term success. Another potentially destructive aspect in the Sage culture is its tendency to be hypercritical, thereby eroding trust and cohesion among staff members.

CREATION

Creation is the bursting forth of new life, seemingly out of nowhere. Creation chooses from thousands of latent possibilities and says "Yes!" to one. It births something, which then forces change throughout the whole system to make room for this additional form of life. In sharp contrast to the force of Destruction, most of us tend to be quite enthusiastic about this aspect of change. Creation is the embracing life force: it ranges from birthing a child to having a great idea. Creation takes the form of a flash of insight, inventing a new product, revitalizing an old one, designing new systems, and the architecting of buildings or organizational structures. Creation also happens when we add new staff, thereby forming a whole new field of interactions and personal chemistry.

A lack of the creative force translates to barrenness: no innovation, no spark, no vitality, boredom. However, overcreation can quickly bypass Sustenance and turn into Destruction. For example, we can overcreate something that is harmful to us, ranging from cancer cells to the excessive production or marketing of a too-costly product. Overcreation also happens whenever we have insufficient commitment or ability to support what is being created. A common example in organizations is the frustration people feel when they have one brainstorming session after another, yet no ideas ever come to fruition. It doesn't take long for participants to become cynical and stop creating altogether. "What's the point?" they rightfully ask.

Creation and the Core Types

The *Innocent* inside us acts as a creative force by offering a fresh perspective by having us see things as if for the first time. Seeing things in new ways, with new eyes, allows inventiveness, a "rebirthing" of what has gotten old and stale. By and large, people love the Innocent's optimism and hope. This trait can open doors for us, for example by drawing investors during the formative stages of a new venture. The Innocent can also bring into being nonrealistic, impractical things, which we then naively expect to do well in the marketplace. The world may not be ready for the utopian vision, or such idealism. The Innocent can also get us into trouble when it overcreates, becomes overwhelmed, yet cheerfully denies that we are in over our heads.

The *Orphan* creates new life whenever it encourages us to share our full selves, both our strengths and weaknesses. By having us be vulnerable in this way, the Orphan makes possible a whole new way of interacting, for in an environment of trust and compassion, the force of creativity can flourish. The Orphan also generates strong new life by making certain that whatever is newly created will survive the birthing process. It helps us face unpleasant problems — the equivalent of watching to make certain the baby is in the right position so that it can survive its delivery into the world. The Orphan names all the things that can go wrong and makes certain we have backup plans. By naming constraints and limits, it helps us determine which, of all the many possibilities available to us is the one most likely to make it from conception to delivery. The Orphan can also create negatively by imagining more obstacles than are real, augmenting fears, or increasing blame and alienation in a work-place.

The *Seeker* contributes to Creation when it has us speak the truth as we see it. This part of us is willing to examine new para-digms that shake up our worldviews and open us to new possibili-ties. Seekers also create whenever we contribute our own unique gifts, skills, and perspectives. By not holding back, by participating fully, the Seeker helps expand our world so we can bring into reality the ideals we are seeking, even within the context of the current community, workplace, or project team. Also, the Seeker creates something new whenever it has us follow our instincts to a new world, which exists at first only in our mind as an ideal. This is true up to a point, after which the Seeker overcreates by continually chas-ing rainbows, the perfect mate or job, and illusive ideals. This Core Type can produce negative situations by saying more than others can understand, want to hear, or are capable of handling.

The *Jester* loves creating new ideas, and playing at innovation and brainstorming. It enjoys looking at things from a totally new, different, even "upside-down" perspective. The Jester believes that if the first thing doesn't work, the next one or the next one is likely to. The Jester in us is capable of rapid-fire idea generation, a constant stream of free association. It also uses its irreverence to help us find fertile soil for conception that others overlook as taboo or untried areas. A negative aspect of Jester's free-form creative style is its ten-dency to believe that more is better. Therefore, the Jester often has us moving on to the next idea before the first has been tested, thereby overcreating as we leap from one idea to the next.

The *Caregiver's* creative strength can be seen easily in its physi-cal manifestations. This Core Type asks us to give birth, literally, from our own bodies. The Caregiver uses the sweat of our brow, the strength of our muscle, the depth of our hands-on experience to craft, construct, produce our work. The Caregiver's creativity is practical, useful, ready-to-wear. This part of us puts aside our own needs until the new life, project, or idea sees the light of day. The Caregiver can overproduce by bringing in too many children, pro-jects or ideas, when it cannot possibly provide sufficient care for all of them. This part of us can easily become overextended so that we cannot pay adequate attention to what we have brought into the world.

The *Warrior* contributes intense focus, discipline, and a roll-up-your-sleeves attitude to the creative process. It was probably the Warrior who said that creativity is 1 percent inspiration and 99 percent perspiration. The Warrior is the part of us that is willing to do all the nonglamorous detail tasks and follow through — without which creation would never become reality. The Warrior also helps us break through barriers to creation, such as writer's block, by making us keep at it until the words start to flow again. It gives us the discipline we need to follow through on any act of creation, for example fleshing out a report from an outline. The Warrior can create negatively by having us build bigger, better weapons than our opponents, thereby creating an escalation of conflict, for example, a counter-marketing campaign that drains a disproportionate amount of the organization's resources for a dubious return.

The *Magician* creates by connecting inspiration and practicality, the poles of "heaven and earth." It tries to have us build the best of all possible worlds by bridging the past and the present to a compelling vision of the future. Magicians try to transform ourselves and our workplaces from the inside out. This Core Type contributes synergy to the creative power of change. Creative magic may look easy, but it is very hard work, requiring the full cooperation of body, mind, and soul. The Magician is the part of us that believes we are inherently co-creators, that we really are just "naming" and helping to make visible (unfold) that which already exists. The Magician can create negatively by using our powers selfishly, by forcing our will on others, by charismatically promoting our ideas over others, or by creating situations that inadvertently cause harm.

The *Ruler* establishes the stable, peaceful environment that permits the flowering of thought, artistic, and entrepreneurial endeavors, and that funds creative efforts, such as scholarships, exploration and research. The same is true of us internally: we can only create successfully when we have a baseline of order in our lives. We can only make headway creatively if, for example, we have a place to work where we can find our files from one day to the next. The internal Ruler also acts as our benefactor, providing us with sufficient resources. The Ruler can also overproduce structure, layers of bureaucracy that are excessive "fat," or a workday schedule that is too full, rigid, or compulsive.

The *Lover* in us is highly attuned to the creative, regenerative power of Nature. It makes us fall in love, for example, with an idea that puts our mind so on fire we can barely sleep. It draws us to embark on new creative endeavors, no matter how difficult. The Lover's generative force pulls us magnetically, making us dive headlong into our work, to commit to it with all our heart. It makes us love the act of creation as dearly as the results. The Lover also shows us the beauty of all creation surrounding us. It urges us not only to smell the roses, but to indulge all our senses, in this way providing the emotional fuel necessary for our journey through the often difficult process of creativity. The Lover can create negatively by blurring the line between us and what we produce in our own image. It can also overcreate, losing itself in its own perpetual creative process, and in this way withdraw from the real world.

The *Sage* creates by sitting quietly in the center of activity, observing all that is going on, determining the point of leverage, and then moving to open a small but optimum window for change. In this way, the Sage allows us to produce great results with little effort expended outward. Actually, it takes a great deal of effort to remain quiet long enough to create in this powerful way. The Sage helps us stay still so that we can hear what we are really thinking, remember things that are germane to this issue, and get flashes of insight. The Sage's gifts of meditation, contemplation, dispassionate observation, and discernment all strengthen our generative efforts. The Sage undercreates when we do not intervene to stop our workplace from creating something that is not in its best interests. The Sage's calm also may mean that we tolerate, and thereby contribute to the continuation of, a level of chaos that exhausts and frightens coworkers who are not so detached.

Creation and the Core Cultures

The *Innocent* Core Culture tends to favor creating more of what has worked before, or products that are similar or compatible, or that support already existing lines. This kind of workplace goes to great lengths to establish stability, security, a family feeling, trust, and a strong foundation upon which the work itself can then rest. The best forms of the Innocent organization use their fresh perspectives, hope and enthusiasm as creative forces, to bring themselves into a new, revitalized life.

In the *Orphan* organization, its realistic perspective and its ability to make money are creative forces. This culture fosters resilience and toughness in workers. It makes certain that all its efforts are properly funded. This kind of workplace establishes its own security, as it does not believe in luck or good fortune. Unfortunately, the Orphan work environment can also produce paranoia, that is, it sometimes sees problems where none exist. Its "us versus them" perspective sometimes creates unnecessary distance between individuals and groups that should be cooperating.

The *Seeker* organization focuses on creating identity and meaning. Diversity of opinion is a highly generative force in Seeker workplaces. They can become more innovative when they make links between highly competent people who otherwise would just go their own ways. Seeker systems do well when they deliberately establish conditions for synergy and promote cross fertilization of ideas from different disciplines. These organizations get into trouble when they create classism or friction among their members, based on their differing expertise. Such divisiveness throws up barriers to the creative force.

Jester workplaces tend to be highly inventive, "idea-a-minute" cultures. Laughter is a creative force here, puncturing seriousness and shaking things loose. Jester organizations support mistakes and "fast failures" as an integral part of the birthing process. Moreover, this culture rewards people according to their quick intelligence and inventive powers. At times, however, this kind of workplace has a tendency towards overcreativity. Little gets implemented when Jester systems become overwhelmed with their many wonderful ideas. Their overly fast pace of creativity often means that they are too front loaded with possibilities and have too little focus on actual productivity or achieving results.

In the *Caregiver* organization, harmonious working conditions are created by like-minded souls who gather for the same mission. The genuine care they bring is itself, a creative force. For example, Caregiver systems manage to create health, community, hope, or skills where there were none or little before. This kind of workplace rewards good ideas for improving services and work processes. Often, it is as if the Caregiver organization just keeps adding and altering work "ingredients" until the recipe is just right. Unfortunately, these good-hearted cultures can sometimes give away everything they have. I frequently see Caregiver organizations produce excessive demand on their system, for example by making certain that all potential clients who are entitled to a free service know about it.

Warrior organizations create a winning spirit and a drive to excel. They establish standards that employees must meet to prove and define their competencies. These workplaces create clear lines of authority so people know who is in charge of what, and who to listen to under which circumstances. Warrior systems do whatever they can to establish efficient work processes and on-time delivery. They engender pride in their staff. Moreover, they keep raising standards in order to create higher levels of excellence. Warrior cultures try to take themselves and everyone within them to a higher playing field. (The word *compete* means "to fly with.") Unfortunately, this tendency can have negative effects. It sometimes creates internal divisiveness as people try to outproduce each other. In the worst cases, this competitiveness can create antagonism and barriers where none existed before. This, then, obstructs the creativity and life flow of the organization.

Magician workplaces tend to be highly creative cultures where innovation is wedded to outcomes. They often are on the cutting edge, conceiving entirely new products, markets, or services. Moreover, by expecting people to work together differently, these work environments provide the conditions for dialogue — the passing through of spirit. When this culture is obstructed from reaching its goals, it is flexible in generating new strategies. In the best Magician organizations, a real balance is achieved so that employees can bring their full selves to work and also "have a life" outside it. However, the time is often not yet right for the Magician culture's new creations, and they are stillborn, or can't manage to survive in the present larger environment. Therefore, Magician workplaces need to be certain that they are not creating for the sake of creativity. This kind of organization is most successful when its inventive activity is constantly reassessed for the value it can offer customers.

Ruler systems focus on creating order. Historically, these cultures create the stable conditions necessary for creativity to enter "golden" eras. Just as wealthy kings and queens have traditionally commissioned works of art and science, wealthy Ruler organizations sometimes fund creative research and activities. Ruler workplaces tend to be organized so well that people can find their tools when and where they need them. Fortunately, this system has a tendency to establish more policies and procedures than are necessary. In such cases, the "rule book" just keeps getting bigger, and the people trying to enforce the policies and those regulated by them become increasingly restricted, thereby dampening the creative force.

Lover cultures focus on creating consensus. This produces a unified system where synergy can result, and the mission can more easily be achieved. The strong degree of trust among staff members is also a creative force. Artistic flamboyance and colorful diversity are tolerated, even encouraged, here. Moreover, its flat, democratic structure allows people in Lover organizations to give all they can. Countervailing forces in this kind of workplace include its intensity, which can easily cause exhaustion, and with it a sharp drop in creativity. It is then very hard for people to pick themselves up and regain momentum after the wind has been knocked out of their collective sails.

Sage organizations foster creativity with their calm environments and laboratory work conditions. Here, ideas can bubble up to the surface, as if on a smooth pool, where they can be examined at length. Fact-finding and candid evaluation make certain that creativity is going in the right direction, and that innovative projects will be worthwhile. However, the Sage culture can be overly critical. This tendency often prevents good ideas from getting out of the birth canal. This kind of work environment can also allow too much time for thinking while simultaneously underestimating the time necessary for follow-through on creative ideas.

The final chapter of *Working from Your Core* will discuss how all the material described to this point — the Core Types, Core Cultures, and the dynamic processes of change — comprise a path that can lead you from workplace challenges through learning to Wisdom.

NOTES

1. Carol Pearson and Sharon Seivert, *Magic at Work: Camelot, Creative Leadership, and Everyday Miracles*, Doubleday/Currency, New York, 1995, p. 5.
2. Charles Handy, *The Age of Unreason*, Harvard Business School Press, Boston, MA, 1989, p. 4.

7

Personal and Corporate Wisdom in a World of Change

> So what we have to do with regard to the great wisdom
> from the whole of the past . . . is to assimilate it and go
> onto new and original perception relevant to our present
> condition of life.[1]
>
> — DAVID BOHM

Working from Your Core describes "great wisdom from the whole of the past," as it is encoded in the Core models of human behavior, human systems, and change. Wisdom is practical; it helps us make sound decisions; it gives us depth of insight; it draws upon and helps us interpret our experiences so we can adapt more appropriately in a world of change. The archetypal templates presented in *Working from Your Core* are a bit like a starter kit, a map, a blueprint, or a stepping stone that helps us ease into complex territory. Each Core Type, Core Culture, and process of change makes its own special contribution to the understanding we need to meet our daily work challenges.

INNOCENT
Hope, trust, seeing what is good, enthusiasm

ORPHAN
Compassion, seeing what is wrong, sensitivity to real difficulties

SEEKER
Self-definition, independence, search for meaning

JESTER
Lightness, humor, freedom, inventiveness

CAREGIVER
Kindness, recognizing and sacrificing for what is important

WARRIOR
Discipline, focus, action-orientation, assertion, protection of boundaries

MAGICIAN
Balance, wholeness, healing, synergy, paradigm vigilance

RULER
Stewardship, taking responsibility, maintaining stability and order

LOVER
Capacity to love and commit, to appreciate beauty, intense energy

SAGE
Detached, scientific approach, calm objectivity, keeps overview in mind

---

SUSTENANCE
Knowing what or whom to support, how to support them, and for how long

DESTRUCTION
Knowing when it is time and how to let go of something, recognizing what no longer exists

CREATION
Knowing when it is time for the formation, production of something new, and how to bring it into the world

As you experience the various lessons of each Core Type and Core Culture, you can recognize these distinct aspects of yourself. This last chapter describes the process by which we accumulate such profound knowledge. Specifically, it details a heroic, highly adaptive process of *learning from your Core*; over time this path can lead to personal and corporate wisdom.

The good news and the bad news are the same: on both the individual and organizational level, as far as real learning goes, you are on your own. This is a hard truth for most of us to swallow. By and large, we have become accustomed to quick fixes for our personal or workplace pains. I remember one group of managers, who although enthusiastic about systems thinking, reacted quite angrily when my colleagues and I took them into the less defined territory of "learning organizations." Here they had to design their own projects, had no formulas to fall back upon and no ready answers. We were not prepared for their reaction to (what they perceived as) having the rug pulled out from underneath them. They did not appreciate such a free-fall state of learning, and told us so. As a result, we gained a valuable lesson about how to more gently, more compassionately, bring our clients into such unchartered territory.

STEP BY STEP (AND MIS-STEP): WHAT THE PROCESS OF LEARNING LOOKS LIKE AT WORK

You can use every event at work, every new challenge, every stressful situation to take another step towards personal understanding and adaptation. And, if your organization allows, you can contribute your insights to its success. Figure 7–1 shows how this path to learning plays out, step by step.

As an example of how this process works, let's say I have an employee who has been sullen for the last several weeks. He has become unpleasant in his interactions with his colleagues. People are starting to complain to me. I am annoyed by this distraction, and a bit puzzled about how best to proceed.

Figure 7–1 **Learning from Your Core Flowchart**

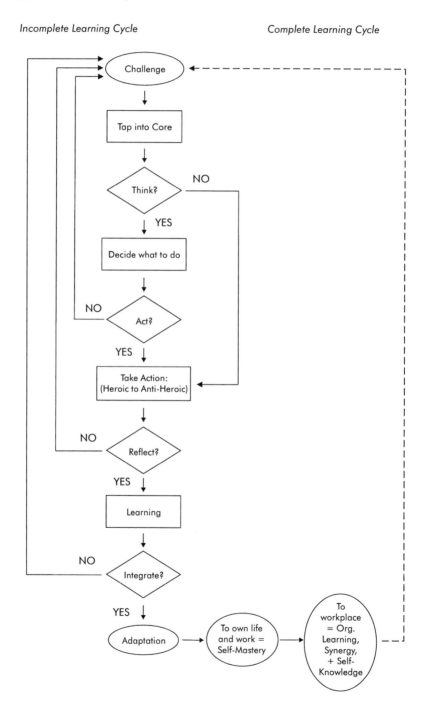

Incomplete Learning Cycle   Complete Learning Cycle

Puzzlement is the beginning of wisdom.

— ERICH FROMM

When met by this or any other *challenge,* I always begin by *tapping into my Core.* I do this whether or not I am conscious of doing so. In my Core the internal advisors present me with a great many possible ways to behave. If I *think* before I act, I will be able to consciously decide what to do. If, however, I act without thinking, if I do an end-run to action, my behavior will be an unconscious reflex, similar to an involuntary body response, neither well considered nor under my control.

For example, my first impulse may be to tell the employee in no uncertain terms to "shape up or ship out." After all, I am the boss. Thankfully, in this case, I take a moment to *decide what to do.* After only a few minutes of cooling down, I decide to bite my tongue and ask a few questions first. In this way, I figure, I may be able to find the underlying reasons for his altered behavior.

I then *take action.* (I could also decide to put off action until a more appropriate time; for example, I might decide to avoid a confrontation because tempers are ready to flare.) My action in this case is to set a time when we can meet to talk about the problem. During our appointment, the employee confesses that he feels overwhelmed because he was not adequately trained for a task I recently assigned him. The employee did not want to appear incompetent and now was in over his head. He is surprised that his difficulties were so evident to the rest of the staff. Now that all the cards are on the table, we can more easily address the situation.

The profoundly happy truth is that we will always have another chance to learn. Always. My actions in this particular case could have been heroic or antiheroic. I could have yelled at the employee or not bothered to speak to him at all. I could have been a model of executive behavior or a real jerk. Fortunately, no matter what I've done, I always have a chance later to step back and *reflect* on what happened, to ask myself some questions. Did I handle the situation as well as I could have? Did the employee respond or not? What did I learn about him? What did I learn about myself — as a manager and as a person?

If I do not reflect for even a moment, I lose this opportunity and am doomed to enter the next work challenge no more skilled than I was the last time. This results in a vicious cycle, a nonlearning loop. However, if I take some time to reflect, I then have the chance to *learn* a lesson about myself in the world, what I might do similarly or differently next time. This increases the self-knowledge and skill with which I meet the next challenge.

There is another step necessary to complete this cycle. I now have the opportunity to *integrate* what I've experienced. To embody it, to make it mine. If I take this extra step, I will be able to make an adaptation in *my own life and work*. Over time, as I continue to integrate what I've learned into my life, I attain *Self-mastery*, the goal of all my journeying.

Moreover, I may have the opportunity to apply my new knowledge to *my workplace*. Whether or not this application takes place is partially up to me and partially up to the organization. For example, if the culture discourages managers from "coddling" workers, I will probably decide not to share my recent experience with other executives. This translates to an increase in my self-knowledge, but not the organization's. If, however, managers discuss such things at our management meetings, several things will happen:

1. I will *increase my own insights* by seeing the experience through my colleagues' eyes.
2. *Synergy* will result as my colleagues and I share this and other experiences.
3. *Organizational learning* will occur as we put our personal knowledge to work for the whole company. In this way, we become more capable — individually and collectively — of meeting the next challenge.

And of course, the next challenge will inevitably come our way, as surely as night follows day, whether or not we have learned from the last one.

LEARNING FROM YOUR CORE

> The manager of the future will merely be a learning guide.
> — PETER DRUCKER

Learning from your Core is an ongoing process of discovery about yourself and your world. It is how you bring the unknown and the unconscious into your awareness, then put what you've learned to some good use. It is also the way we and our organizations adapt to changing environments and evolve over time.

Working from your Core is the best way to respond when you are confronted by a challenge or when you want to move proactively in a new direction. The Core Learning Model builds on the research and discoveries of many other learning theorists, primarily Deming's teacher, Walter Shewhart (designer of the Plan-Do-Check-Act cycle) and David Kolb (whose learning cycle is: doing; reflecting; thinking; deciding). It differs from these and other classic learning models primarily in that it

- is a five-step model that begins the learning cycle in your Core, where your individual identity resides and where your Unconscious and Consciousness meet
- shows how your Core serves as a self-referencing center of gravity for learning
- underscores that learning requires integration and adaptation to be complete
- is structured as a spiral (to represent how learning expands in an ever widening pattern as you integrate more and more of your core wisdom into your life and work), and
- is congruent with an archetypal template that symbolizes a whole, well-balanced, comprehensive, and therefore, transformative learning process.*

---

* The *Working from Your Core* learning spiral also forms a *magic circle*: an archetypal template that represents self-healing, integrity, completeness, and personal power. It symbolizes the way the whole individual can connect to the sacred whole. This design makes certain you gain knowledge by starting in the center of who you are and then moving outward to touch each aspect of you, as symbolized by the four directions. For more information on how to use this model, turn to Appendix C.

The Core Learning model reflects an important truth: how we are changed by what we learn, how it makes us *larger*. This five-step process allows you to access knowledge and talents you may not even know you have. The good news is that, although this path is not easy, over time it becomes increasingly more efficient. What was seemingly insurmountable before becomes doable. Moreover, you will no longer be stuck in a rut; you will never have to enter another experience at the same level again.

These five steps represent a complete and *virtuous* cycle. Every time you are faced with a new problem, there will quite literally be more of you to meet it. Learning from your Core charts a map to survival and sanity. (Insanity has been defined as doing the same thing over and over, while expecting different results.) The Core model, then, is a sane, practical, highly adaptive way to respond to changing circumstances and stressful situations (Figure 7–2).

Here's how it works. Our automatic, first response to any challenge is to *Tap into our Core (Step One)*. This is a given. It is an involuntary, instinctive response to anything out of the ordinary, including any stress, threat, desire, attraction, stimuli, or "irritation of doubt"** that takes us out of our comfort zone. Like all other living organisms, we move into the world around us from our identity, from who we are. Biologists call this principle self-referencing, a learning trait that is "fundamental to all self-organizing systems."[2] Self-referencing is a survival mechanism that organizes our lives, that literally keeps us from falling apart. It allows us to maintain our integrity, to stay who we are by responding to changes only in ways that are congruent with our core identity. It prevents us from changing randomly. Thanks to self-referencing, princes become frogs (and vice versa) only in fairy tales.

Our next step, if we have sufficient presence of mind, is to *Think (Step Two)*. Unfortunately, under the kind of stress many of us

** Charles Sanders Pierce, the founder of pragmatic philosophy, coined the phrase: "The irritation of doubt causes a struggle to attain the state of belief. . . . Doubt is an uneasy and dissatisfied state from which we struggle to free ourselves and pass on to the state of belief. . . [which is] a calm and satisfactory state. . . . We cling tenaciously, not merely to believing, but to believing just what we do believe." ("The Fixation of Belief," *Popular Science Monthly* 12, November 1878.)

Figure 7–2 The Core Learning Model

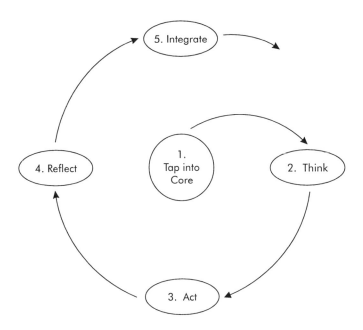

endure as we career through our daily work load, we sometimes bypass thinking entirely, moving quite unconsciously directly into action. This nonadaptive behavior is even subliminally encouraged in many workplaces. "Just do it!" we're told by advertising, and often by our bosses. "Nothing to it, but to do it," say the motivational speakers. But if we pause and think, even for a moment, we more fully engage our cognitive control powers. Then we are able to make better decisions and move more decisively into the world to implement those decisions.

We must *Act (Step Three)*, both because that's what we get paid for and because experience is how we *test* ourselves and the world. Personal experience is the only way we can test truth, the only way we can discover reality for ourselves. As Moshe Feldenkrais, founder of the ground-breaking body therapy, said: "Learning is a crystallization of experience."

After we act, we need to *Reflect (Step Four)* so that we understand what happened this time, how we can improve what we do next time, and the implications and possible applications of what occurred. And lastly, it is only if we *Integrate (Step Five)* these valuable lessons into our lives and work, only if we make adaptations, that we can complete the cycle and enrich ourselves or our work systems. If we forego this final step, it is as if we had purchased the mega-bucks million dollar winning lottery ticket, then accidentally threw it out in the trash.

The five-part Learning from Your Core model describes a transformative path by which we can progressively alter our lives and work. All five steps are indispensable to our success. The Unconscious alone is dreamy, ineffective, not entirely of this world. Our conscious minds by themselves spin frantically in perpetual loops of their own making. Our thinking becomes effortful, dry, and also ineffective. Action alone is mindless and soul-less; to quote Shakespeare's ill-fated Macbeth, "full of sound and fury, signifying nothing." This is why so much effort in the workplace — busy work, or work done under high stress — has to be redone. Reflection alone translates to paralysis. And, of course, without the other steps, there is nothing at all for us to integrate. Any of these steps alone is less than ordinary; a few of them together, quite ordinary. However, when all of them are put together, they can produce extraordinary results.

Sometimes even miracles.

There is a way to further optimize this process, bringing us even closer to Self-mastery and Wisdom. And it takes so little time. We can consciously deepen this Core learning process if we deliberately continue to "connect the dots" between each step and the Core (Figure 7–3). Behaviorally, this is done quite simply: by breathing slowly and deeply, and by staying inwardly quiet as you proceed through each step. (See Appendix C for a more detailed, step-by-step description of this learning process.)

Conscious breathing has an immediate positive effect on our bodies, minds, and souls. It serves as a healing balm, an antidote for our workplaces' continual fight or flight stressors. Our bodies and minds tend to overrespond to threats in ways that are quite dysfunctional for modern living. In truth, our nervous and hormonal systems have not evolved much beyond that of our cave dwelling

Figure 7–3 Continually Connecting with the Core

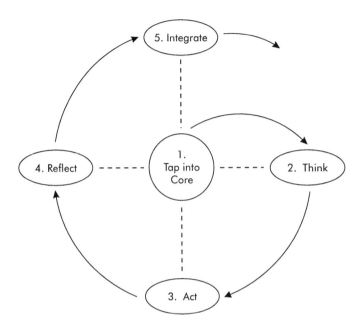

ancestors. This means that they automatically kick into full gear under any stress, treating your five o'clock deadline as if you were being chased by a saber-toothed tiger. By breathing your way through this Core learning process, you can reverse this dysfunctional stress reaction.[†] After a bit of practice, you will soon find that you stay stronger and more alert at work, and that act more calmly and intelligently in a crises. (It is amazing how much better the brain works with a sufficient supply of oxygen.) Using these techniques while working is a bit like putting yourself in training to become a

† There are a great many relaxation/breathing techniques you can use as well as numerous books written on the subject. You will probably find it an excellent long-term investment to take a class and master a technique that suits your life/work-style. An easy technique for destressing, moving out of the panic zone, and getting your mind refocused is to slowly breathe in to a count of four and then breathe out to a count of four. Try it. An example of an energizing breath that counteracts fatigue is to breath in to a count of four, hold (without tensing your body) for a count of five, and then release slowly to a count of seven.

long-distance runner rather than a sprinter. This deliberate process of continually connecting with the Core will provide you with more options for survival at work. And, an added benefit: you will have some energy left at the end of the day.

When you reconnect the dots between steps one and two, pausing for a moment to become still, rather than agitated while you're thinking, the Core will respond by giving you even more ideas about how to handle things. Your inspiration will be drawing from a larger pool of possibilities. For example, you can deliberately consider, then choose, which of the Core Types might be most helpful in a given situation. If you reconnect with the Core when you move into action, whatever you do will have more resonance, like rich overtones from a well-tuned musical instrument. Your actions will be more decisive, coordinated, and meaningful, more certain to be congruent with your values and identity. This not only will make your work more satisfying; it also will increase its efficiency, because less of it will have to be redone.

When you consciously connect the dots between step four and the Core, your understandings about this particular challenge will be enriched as you reflect upon this particular incident. Moreover, you will find yourself remembering similar prior experiences, relevant readings from management literature or today's international news, or ways other of the Core Types might have handled this situation differently.

Finally, when you reconnect the last step with the Core, you will become more aware of the full range of possible ways to integrate this life lesson. You will be more likely to see a practical application that might not have occurred to you otherwise. With this step, you can weave this last experience into the whole fabric of your knowledge. You will become more wise.

It is important at this point to acknowledge that what is drawn here is a flat model, and real life is neither flat nor linear nor smooth. You probably will find that when you experiment with the Core Learning Model, oftentimes these steps occur almost concurrently. On really fast-moving days, you may need to think and reflect, for example, while you're continuing to act. At those wilder than normal times, this model can still help by serving as a checklist that

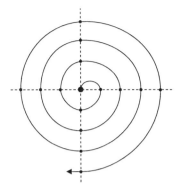

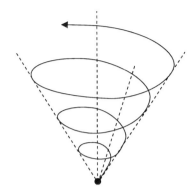

Figure 7–4   The Spiral of Learning

Figure 7–5   Your Core serves as a self-referencing center of gravity

reminds you to touch all the bases as you run around them towards home plate.

The Core Learning model describes a virtuous, upward spiral of learning (Figures 7–4 and 7–5). Your Core serves as your own self-referencing center of gravity. The more conscious you make this usually unconscious process, the more satisfying (comprehensive, resonant, in-depth) your work will become. At first it is extremely difficult to alter doing business as usual. To stay fully with your Self requires effort, vigilance, and definitely courage, as you set your own pace despite the craziness around you. However, you will quickly find that the payoff is well worth that effort.

FROM LEARNING TO WISDOM

When does learning become Wisdom? When you act from the quiet Core, that still place inside you, your own inner center of gravity, you are well on the road to becoming more wise. This is because the Core connects you to a great source of profound knowledge. The Core is where the mind and will of God whisper to you, giving you insights, knowledge, and guidance that you could not attain any other way. In your Core lives that wisest part of yourself that watches what you are doing, processes what happens to you, notices what you think and how you feel, and remembers what you dreamed about when you were sound asleep last night. This Witness part of you functions much like a driver behind the steering wheel of your actions and thoughts.

When learning becomes a way of being, a way of moving through life, it becomes Wisdom. In *Learning as a Way of Being*, Peter Vaill describes this state as "an authentic way of living and working, thinking and feeling, in the world of permanent white water." Vaill says we experience this permanent white water "as confusion and loss of direction and control, as a gnawing sense of meaninglessness." He argues that learning is a natural state, that it is critical to our successfully navigating our current "complex and unstable environment," and that our natural learning abilities have been "profoundly suppressed and distorted by the highly structured learning practices of institutional learning."[3]

As a natural state, learning is available to us all the time. I like to think of life itself as a full-time school, with a constantly evolving curriculum of courses. The transition to Wisdom happens when we spend less of our time in what I call the "2 × 4 school of learning." When we first begin our heroic journeys, it seems as if only crises can get our attention. We have to be hit over the head with the emotional equivalent of a 2 × 4 wooden board for us to notice whatever is right in front of us. And, if we are very resistant, armored, deluded, or arrogant, sometimes only tank-equivalents rolling over us can get our attention. I have observed that a person's willingness and ability to learn is something of a paradox: people who are the most open, humble, and understated about their accomplishments seem to be both the most wise and the most likely to continue gaining knowledge and skill in new areas. They have firmly established themselves in an upward spiral of learning.

I will never forget when I first experienced this insight. I was a recent college graduate. My advisor and favorite teacher, Dr. Duncan McNab, asked if he could introduce me to the famous pianist and his friend, Alfred Brendel. McNab said that Brendel was eager to meet me. I was incredulous. Our first conversation consisted of Brendel's grilling me regarding a psychological issue about which he felt I had some expertise. I had just heard Brendel play and could barely contain my admiration for his extraordinary talent. But he was so humble and unaffected — and eager to learn — that he put me completely at ease. Soon we were great friends. That evening I learned a lesson that has stayed with me ever since. As it says so succinctly in the Sri Guru Gita: "One who thinks he knows not, knows; one who thinks he knows, knows not."[4]

We always have a choice to learn or not learn. As we continue with our life studies however, we move from having to learn primarily through difficulties that confront us, to eventually seeing everything and everyone as our teachers. As we become more wise, a blade of grass pushing through a crack in the sidewalk can have a message for us. Listening carefully to Mozart can teach us about the genius of enthusiasm. Dreams can bring messages from your psyche that powerfully inform your waking day. You may open a book to a phrase that contains the perfect answer to a problem you've been stewing about. In short, when you see learning as a natural state, and life as the schoolroom, when you actively seek to be taught, with humility and gratitude for your many teachers, you are clearly on the path to Self-mastery.

Another important step on this path is to realize that, on some level, you have created everything that's in your life right now in order to learn and evolve. This is a really tough, often unwelcome, lesson. The ancient Alchemists, who attempted to transmute themselves so they would become less like lead and more like gold, said it this way: "It is true without lie, certain and most veritable, that what is below is like what is above and that what is above is like what is below, to perpetrate the miracles of one thing."[5] They believed that whatever was inside us would be reflected in our outside world, and vice versa.

Although this perspective may seem entirely too cosmic at first glance, it is, at a minimum, an excellent idea with which to play. It can help you recognize whatever you've contributed to a given situation. If you are having a fight with someone at work, for example, he or she may indeed be acting like a jerk, *and* you probably have something valuable to learn from this colleague. A perspective that produces profound knowledge is to assume that you have attracted this person to you to reveal and heal this very same part of you that is quite obvious in this other unpleasant person but hidden deep inside you, out of your view. Try it. You'll be amazed at what you discover.

> Through learning, we re-perceive the world and our relationship to it. A learning organization is a place where people are continually discovering how they create their reality and how they can change it.
>
> — PETER SENGE

The fact that we are at least partially responsible for creating our experiences is one of the main reasons work is so central to attaining Self-mastery and Wisdom. Not only is the work changing us. Not only are we changing it. We also are working on and changing each other. A great teacher once described it this way. When asked how he helped his followers along the spiritual path, he replied that he actually did very little. He just put them all together, like rocks in a bag, and let them wear off each others' rough edges. Work is a great place to have our rough edges worn off. Work has the capacity to either humanize us or dehumanize us, to turn us into heroes or antiheroes. When we view work as an arena for learning, we can use it as a path home to our Core.

The Core Types contribute to Wisdom by teaching us that, when pressed, we do have the inner courage we need to meet life's challenges and learn from them. The dragons we meet along the way are then transformed from our enemies into our teachers. This is as true of inside teachers as outside teachers. When inner enemies/teachers, such as our own fear, anger, pride, envy, worry, emerge into our view, we can take a step back, and ask ourselves, "Why am I feeling or thinking this way; what does this negative thought or feeling teach me?" We can ask ourselves, "How does this limit my life; how does it hold me back; how do I hurt myself when I feel and think this way?" Interestingly, good follow-up questions are: "How does this *serve* me; how have I used this anger (fear, envy, etc.) in the past as a survival technique?" (For example, what was an excellent survival strategy as a child may be maladaptive as an adult.) "Do I really still need to act or think in this way? How is this inner state trying to move me on?"

These often-rejected parts of ourselves are our very own children, our mental and emotional creations. We feed them all the time with our actions and thoughts and feelings, then turn around and expend a lot of energy trying to keep them out of sight. It is an exhausting, self-perpetuating, downward spiraling process. Wisdom comes when we attain higher levels of our Self *by first moving into and through the lower aspects of ourselves* so that we can access all that raw, wonderful, repressed energy. Another way to think about this process of Self-mastery is that it is similar to our consciously transforming waste material into fertilizer so the crops can grow abundantly.

> Wisdom is the skill we gain when we penetrate to the very core or essence of matters. It is a highly creative and connective way of processing knowledge that distills out essential principles and truths. Wisdom tells us what to pay attention to. . . . Wisdom is the truth seeker and pattern finder that penetrates to the core of what really matters.[6]
>
> — VERNA ALLEE

WISDOM, WHOLENESS, AND HEALING

Great understanding comes when we see the world and ourselves as we really are — the best and worst parts — whole, connected, integrated, "holy." The Core model helps us in this endeavor by giving us a view of the world and ourselves. Each Core Type and Core Culture has its own theory of the world. Each process of change helps us move through that world we think we live in so that we can better adjust to it. Each of these archetypes has just its own fragment of the total picture. However, when taken together, they give us a more true and comprehensive picture of reality.

David Bohm believed that reality is not fragmented, but rather whole. Indeed, he argued that the fragmentation "of cities, religions, political systems, conflict in the form of wars, general violence . . . is the response of this whole to man's action, guided by illusory perception, which is shaped by fragmentary thought." He asked that we pay attention to our "habit of fragmentary thought" so that we could stop it. Bohm felt that when we approached reality as a whole, its response would be whole.[7] He even considered that the wholeness of reality traversed the illusory veil of time and space, and that shifting our paradigm could help collapse those effects in our work and lives that appear to be separated in time and space. As Barbara Shipka says: "Wisdom considers past, present, and future."[8]

Our habit of fragmentation leads us to compartmentalize everything. We try to separate our lives and work. We tend to think of our organization's departments before we think of the whole organization. Often we act as if our minds and bodies don't know how to speak to each other. We do not really understand how connected we are to our coworkers, or how much these relationships affect everything we do. We have been taught again and again to see only separation; we are rewarded for measuring parts rather than stepping back to view the whole. Learning from the Core, however, takes us in an entirely different direction. It can be defined as the act of moving out of fragmentation into wholeness, out of separation into relationship. Wisdom is one of the fruits we enjoy when we think of reality as a whole.

We can easily see the problem of fragmentation in our daily work. Let's say you are trying to make an important decision. You've been struggling for some time. You just can't figure it out. You will know you've finally made the right choice when your whole self says "Yes!" (or "No!") together. This whole self includes your body, mind, heart, will, and soul: every part of you consulted, in agreement, aligned, ready to launch into action. Each part of you has its own special form of knowledge. When we put them all together, we are much more likely to act wisely.

Of all the forms of knowledge available to us, the one that most of us are cut off from is our body wisdom, which is also the most primal and honest. Our bodies cannot lie. They tell us what we are really feeling, when we are excessively stressed, when we should "go for it," and when we should run for cover instead. Our bodies provide the connection to our deepest intuitive knowing. Yet we often ignore our bodies' messages, pushing ourselves to the point of breakdown.

BODY WISDOM

I have been very fortunate in having teachers who have shown me how to access profound knowledge though the body.‡ In fact, my forays into this arena have been both soul and body nourishing, not to mention, mind-boggling, and have significantly improved my work and life. I think the time is rapidly approaching when more and more people, both inside and outside the workplace, will benefit from such body-based disciplines.

In *An Unused Intelligence: Physical Thinking for 21st Century Leadership*, Andy Bryner and Dawna Markova describe physical thinking, which helps us *incorporate* our learnings, anchor them, and *embody* them. Physical thinking helps us become more flexible while we still stay centered and strong. It moves us to vitality and away from stress-induced rigidity. Bryner and Markova say that physical thinking, or embodied learning, is powerful for two reasons. First, it changes the context of our thinking. A changed context can change our perceptions, then our behavior, then our beliefs. Second, it taps into natural or species wisdom that is encoded in each of our bodies.[9] Bryner and Markova have dedicated themselves to helping others access their own physical intelligence.

Embodied learning helps us make sense of things. The Cartesian mind/body split makes us insane (from Latin, meaning "not healthy"). Due to our body/mind fragmentation, we tend to make the same mistakes over and over. This is true for both individuals and corporate mind/bodies. We think or talk or just work faster when we would benefit much more from listening to the internal voices that are screaming for attention. When we ignore these messages, we pay a great price. The body acts out in stress when we ignore what it has to teach us. The cost of this rejection of body wisdom in the workplace is staggering. Indeed, stress-related illnesses are estimated to cause three-fourths of the sick days in America.

---

‡ I have been privileged to apprentice for many years with traditional Reiki Master Julia Carroll, to work extensively with Andrew Hahn, and also to learn from Judith Swack and Kathy Eckles. These fine people have given generously of their time and talent to teach me their ways to access body intelligence and to guide my own forays into this rich territory.

A TECHNIQUE FOR TAPPING INTO BODY INTELLIGENCE

Find someone who is willing to do this body intelligence experiment with you. Ask your partner to hold his or her arm straight out to the side. Stand directly in front of this person with one hand resting on their relaxed shoulder and your other hand resting just below the elbow on their outstretched arm. Give your partner the following instructions: "To give me a 'yes,' your arm will become like steel. To give me a 'No,' your arm will relax, even if you consciously try to keep it up."

Muscle test your partner by putting a steady pressure on his or her extended forearm. Say, "Give me a yes." Test. The arm should feel strong. Press again and say, "Give me a No." Test. The arm should feel significantly weaker, and you should be able to press it down while applying the same amount of pressure as you did before. Ask some simple questions that can be answered with a yes or no, or test for the veracity of very simple statements (for example, have the person say "My name is _____.") If the forearm tests strong for BOTH the "yes" and "no" responses, have your partner take some relaxing breaths and say, "I choose to unblock." If your partner's responses still seem confused, have him or her drink a bit of water.

The next step is to ask your partner to hold a resistance. Muscle test. Zip Up your partner's energy field by moving your hand 3 inches to 6 inches in front their body — starting from below the crotch and moving to the lower lip. Muscle test. Zip Down by moving your hand from the person's lower lip to below the crotch. Muscle test. Your partner should test strong on the Zip Ups and weak on the Zip Downs. Always finish with another Zip Up, in order to increase your partner's energy. (Note: You can do this Zip Up technique for yourself whenever you need an energy boost.)

Now try the Meridian Flush. Have your partner relax both arms. Stand to his or her side. With your hands 3 inches to 6 inches from the body, simultaneously move your hands from below the crotch to the lower lip (in front) and from below the base of the spine over the top of the head to the upper lip (in back). Always move your hands away from the body as you circle back and down to repeat the Zip Up technique. Do as many repetitions as necessary until your partner feels rejuvenated. Then it is your turn! Enjoy.

Thanks go to Drs. Andrew Hahn and Judith Swack for permission to reprint this material.

THE ALTERNATIVE TO LEARNING

We always have the choice, at any given moment, of learning or not learning. We tend to hold onto our mild-discomfort zones rather than venture too far into unknown territory. This is very understandable. This process of gaining "innerstanding" often demands that we move from our attachments, limitations, and blind spots through some suffering before we arrive at healing or joy. It is painful to have our dearly-held illusions stripped away. It is small wonder then that learning our life lessons is sometimes referred to as the hero's journey. It takes guts. And sometimes, en route, you may feel as if those guts are being ripped out. But the alternative — staying stuck where you are — actually is much worse.

Roberto Assagioli describes how the emotional disorders of the average person are more serious and intense, "more difficult to bear and for doctors to cure" than those temporary reactions, the highs and lows, that are connected with Self-realization. These, he said, are merely "by-products of an organic process of inner growth and regeneration."[10] According to Assagioli, the outcome of this journey to self-realization is an increasingly integrated personality that has access to the wealth of all the inner realms.

Because we often are afraid to move out of our comfort/discomfort zones, the heroic Core Types help us meet our specific fears with specific forms of courage. The alternative to learning is a steady erosion over time of ourselves. The downward spiral of nonlearning results in unhappiness, fragmentation, emptiness, hardness, self-hatred, and an inability to receive or give love and care. Learning humanizes us; it makes us full. The alternative is to retreat from Life, to withdraw and diminish our own life force.

Rudolph Steiner described this antilife process as *calcification*. Indeed, I see much of corporate life as unnecessarily hardening our bodies, minds, and souls, desensitizing us so we can complete our work without fuss. Steiner's view was both colorful and memorable. He felt that humanity was being fought over by the protective Archangel Michael and an unholy alliance of the daemonic Ahriman and Lucifer. He said, "while Lucifer sucks the juice out of the lemon, Ahriman presses it out, thereby hardening what remains." Not a pretty picture. What remains, Steiner warns, is only the "soul-less husk of a human being."[11] Against these two negative forces stands the formidable Michael. I find it no coincidence that Michael is often depicted in mythology as a heroic figure who is battling a dragon.

Our real-life role in this epic mythological battle is *to learn*: to move toward Life rather than away from it. Whenever we choose to become more whole, rather than ignore our feelings or physical knowing, we are actually transforming and making allies of our own inner demons. And better yet, with each individual insight, we can chalk up another victory not only for ourselves, but also for the evolution of humanity.

Another contribution we can make to this epic battle is for us to "de-calcify" our organizations. Many of our workplaces suck the juice, the life, out of their people. Indeed, I believe this situation has reached crisis proportions, that the evolutionary gap between individuals and traditional workplace systems, some of which operate like repressive governments, seems only to have widened in recent decades. Often we feel as if our choices are to revolt, flee, or submit. The question I present is: How can we contribute our own knowledge to our organizations so that they too evolve? The answer is twofold: (1) summon your own courage and do your own learning so that you survive despite your surroundings, and (2) wherever possible, institute systemic learning efforts that tap into and move your organization from its own Core.

Although the task of making our workplaces more wise seems daunting, it is not impossible. Remember, the world is changing, and change is on the side of learning and evolution. Studies by physicists and biologists have described "phase transitions," a phenomenon where an organism moves from a relatively disordered to a much more ordered state. For example, in an embryo, a very small group of "organized" cells determine the development of the many other undifferentiated and unordered cells. The same phenomenon has been documented in human systems, where more harmony and order can be generated by a very small percentage of the group. For example, one study of eleven cities demonstrated significant reductions in the rate of serious crimes when just 1 percent of the population were actively meditating.[12]

We can no longer separate our work from the rest of our lives. We have tried that for a long time. It hasn't worked very well. A few years ago I came across a statistic claiming that the overwhelming majority (90%!) of Americans believe they have a *personal relationship* with God. This data argues for a more commonsense approach to the workplace; one where, instead of desensitizing workers, we support each other in strengthening our connections to our own personally-defined, self-rejuvenating, spiritual base.

This approach would result in a very different way of working. We would increasingly tap into our personal and collective Cores. Our individual and collective efforts would reinforce each other. And the organizations that supported workers in this way would benefit from a reduction in stress and a surge of creativity and productivity. Indeed, such a conscious connection to the whole could result in "a miracle of one thing," and the Wisdom we need to thrive in a world of change.

Wisdom is the unburdening of yourself and your organization from any kind of calcification. It is getting rid of what is not yours: limiting identities, false assumptions, outdated beliefs that are layered over you, covering your true nature. As we and our systems gain insight, we will find ways to break out of our own restrictive shells into the light of day. We will emerge from our cocoons and take flight into our own evolution.

WISDOM IS NOT THE END OF THE JOURNEY

> Call it by any name, God, Self, the Heart,
> or the Seat of Consciousness, it is all the same . . .
> the very core of one's being, the center,
> without which there is nothing whatever.[13]
>
> — RAMANA MAHARSHI

Wisdom, although a great treasure, is not the end point of your learning journey. Wisdom is in service of something greater — the Life Force itself. Wisdom brings us to happiness: Joy, Peace, Contentment, the juice of life. This is why great beings have told us that

"Happiness is the very nature of the Self; happiness and the Self are not different."[14]

The entirety of *Working from Your Core*, and all the archetypes described herein, are in service of the Life Force. These models of human behavior serve us *and* the life force by helping us become more alive. They move us out of our limitations into fullness. Out of separation into connection. Out of fragmentation into integration. Out of isolation into relationship. Out of our warring parts into a more peaceful, harmonious whole. Out of calcification into vitality. Learning is whatever moves us in the direction of saying "Yes" to Life, to Love, to the Self. Wisdom is cooperating fully with that life force, and saying "Yes!" to wherever it takes us.

Wisdom, then, is what the Self comes to understand about itself. As you become increasingly comfortable with the fact that your life is a continuous cycle of learning, you will be able to rest more frequently in that wonderful state that is the end of all your striving.

You will have come home.

NOTES

1. David Bohm, *Wholeness and the Implicate Order*, Routledge, New York, 1980, p. 24.
2. Margaret Wheatley, *Leadership and the New Science: Learning about Organization from an Orderly Universe*, Berrett-Koehler, San Francisco, CA, 1992, p. 94.
3. Peter B. Vaill, *Learning as a Way of Being: Strategies for Survival in a World of Permanent White Water*, Jossey-Bass, San Francisco, 1996, pp. 42–44.
4. Swami Muktananda, "Sri Guru Gita," *The Nectar of Chanting*, SYDA Foundation, South Fallsburg, NY, 1972, verse 40, p. 18.
5. Stanilas Klossowski de Rola, *Alchemy: The Secret Art*, Thames and Hudson, London, 1973, p. 15.
6. Verna Allee, *The Knowledge Evolution: Expanding Organizational Intelligence*, Butterworth-Heinemann, Boston, 1997, p. 44.
7. David Bohm, p. 7.
8. Barbara Shipka, *Leadership in a Challenging World: A Sacred Journey*, Butterworth-Heinemann, Boston, 1997, p. 169.
9. Andy Bryner and Dawna Markova, *An Unused Intelligence: Physical Thinking for 21st Century Leadership*, Conari Press, Berkeley, CA, 1996, pp. 8–9, 26–28.

10. Roberto Assagioli, *Psychosynthesis: A Collection of Basic Writings*, Penguin/Arkana, New York, 1965, pp. 52–53.
11. Richard Leviton, *The Imagination of Pentecoast: Rudolf Steiner and Contemporary Spirituality*, Anthroposophic Press, Hudson, NY, 1994, p. 220.
12. Maharishi Mahesh Yogi, *Creating an Ideal Society: A Global Undertaking*, MERU, Seelisberg, Switzerland, 1977, p. 8–9.
13. Ramana Maharshi, *The Spiritual Teaching of Ramana Maharshi*, Shambhala Dragon Edition, Boston, 1972, p. 91.
14. Ibid., p. 11.

Epilogue

While finishing this book I suffered a life trauma. My beloved relationship of fifteen years, which I treasured beyond words and which I was certain would last until the end of my days, itself ended just as this manuscript was due. The reason I am closing *Working from Your Core* with this extremely personal note is that I gained some insights about the Core, wisdom, identity, and relationship that I felt were important to pass on to you.

For months after the separation, I was alternately in shock and severe emotional pain. Much of the time I could barely function. The blow was staggering to me. It was as if my life was a large crystal bowl that had been dropped onto a tile floor where it shattered into thousands of pieces. I felt paralyzed, stuck in time, watching and rewatching the accident and its aftermath. I knew that I could never put the pieces back together. I was unable to move and had not a clue about what to do next. My life was broken beyond fixing.

After a couple of months, I went to a meditation center where I hoped to restore my body, mind, and spirit. There in the middle of the morning chant, I gradually felt my shocked body melt, relax, ease. It was as if, in one golden moment, all the parts of me that had fragmented came back together to inhabit the same body. My contracted lungs released. I could breathe again. Then a line in the chant caught my attention; it spoke directly to the image of my shattered life, making sense of all I had undergone: "Just as water merges in the ocean, milk in milk, ghee in ghee, the space inside the pot in the space outside when a pot is broken, so the individual soul merges in the universal soul."

Apparently my life had reached a point where it had to be "broken" if I was ever to move on. But I just couldn't see it. Carl Jung once said that the hardest task we ever have to accomplish is to first recognize, then withdraw, our projections onto others. These projections can be either positive or negative. I had developed a pattern of willingly sacrificing my time, effort, and energy to support people I admired and/or loved. However, when I did not sufficiently value myself, those to whom I was so devoted tended over time to value me less. The truth is they were just reflecting back to me my own lack of self-worth.

We all have to learn our major life lessons in different forms, from different people, in different settings until we really "get it." Everything I had learned about self-worth to this point had only been practice. This was the relationship that mattered most to me. I loved this man with every fiber of my being. Consequently, I was devastated by the separation; it went to my *identity*. Who I was. What I was worth. Even whether my life was worth living.

There are times, in both the lives of individuals and organizations, when we are blasted apart and have to go about the job of redefining ourselves, starting with the core of our being. Scientists have discovered that living systems, when put under such life-threatening stress, have the capacity to *self-organize*, that is, to reorganize themselves to a more adaptive and complex level. We have the ability to literally *reform* and *transform* ourselves into different expressions. Perhaps the old nursery rhyme was wrong. My guess is that Humpty-Dumpty actually put *himself* back together again, not as Humpty Dumpty, most likely, but as something better. Something not so fragile. And he stopped hanging out on ledges.

I too am in the process of reorganizing. At such critical junctures we can make a *quantum leap* in learning because a window opens to expose self-knowledge that can be life-altering. We gain "in-sight." A veil lifts; we can see ourselves, and therefore others, more clearly. However, we can only lay claim to this wisdom by paying an extremely high price: by being willing to surrender our familiar, comfortable lives for new, as yet completely undefined, ones.

Now, it is probably true that if I had been less resistant, less willful, I would not have had to suffer so much. I had avoided this particular lesson until it reached crisis proportions. Such times are, of course, quite dangerous. Like Samson, we wake up to find that we are shackled in chains and then choose, at some level of our being, to bring the roof down upon ourselves.

We can just as easily fall to the depths as rise to new heights at these difficult times. We can hold on to hope and love, or we can lose our courage, collapse, give in. I must confess that, despite all the support I have from family, friends, and a wonderful spiritual community, despite all the gifts Life had showered upon me, there was a pivotal moment when I seriously contemplated ending my own life.

It is very hard for me to write these words. It is painful for me to admit that I fell into such despair. But at the time I truly felt that I had already lost my life. I was in the throes of a profound existential crisis. For a critical moment I completely lost faith in myself, love, life, and God.

Upon reflection, I understand that thoughts of ending one's life are *symbolic* and therefore best viewed archetypally. (To act on them is a tragic misunderstanding.) Our life force is calling us, from the depths of our being, to end some aspect of our lives. Something central to our existence is no longer working. Some debilitating belief, relationship, or habit must be destroyed. The "dark night of the soul" I experienced served as a turning point for me. It was truly the end of my old life and the initiation into my new one.

Now that I have begun the process of rebuilding, I realize that, in some profound way, *my identity has shifted*. It is as if the center of my being has moved slightly to the side (or slightly down or up), and I am now revolving from an entirely different gravitational center. An earthquake has changed my inner landscape beyond recognition. I am no longer the same.

One thing I have learned in this process is that it is *extremely* difficult to self-reference at times of existential or spiritual crisis. My experience is that I have been "emptied" of what previously defined me. Now everything — every belief, idea, personal value, relationship — is up for grabs and must be reexamined. As I move slowly back into the world, I feel as yet quite loosely formed, vulnerable and exposed to the elements, deliberately staying open to life's messages for me. As my Core reforms, I will eventually be able to redefine the rest of my life and work in ways that are integrated with this new identity.

As I emerge from this personal crisis, I find myself reflecting more upon the parallel life-altering, spiritual crises that I have seen organizations undergo. They too have times when their inner and outer landscapes change suddenly, when the organizational center of gravity fundamentally shifts. Often these crises are responded to with self-destructive, semisuicidal moves: haphazard reorganization, sudden layoffs, deep budget cuts, desperate mergers, dramatic shifts in the workplace culture. Usually these reactions occur without revisiting, rethinking, or redefining the organizational Core. It is no surprise then that such times of spiritual crisis can easily trigger a downward, life-negating spiral for the whole system. However, when we understand that what is really happening is an archetypal call to end the system's old life and create a new one, we can use these crises to propel us instead through the dark passageway into a revitalized organizational Core.

I certainly don't know what or whom my new life will contain. I don't know its likely shape or size. What I do now finally recognize, is how, on an unconscious level, I had actually *asked for* this shift.

It happened this way.

At the beginning of this year, I came across a quote that I loved. I typed it in large letters and placed it on my desk so I could look at it many times a day. It read:

> O Self of all,
> I take refuge in You.
> I ask nothing of You.
> Grant me whatever boon you choose.
> I will be totally content
> with whatever you give me,
> whether it be pain or pleasure.
> Do whatever You will,
> but keep me in Your presence.

I now understand that I was experiencing a "soul call." I was shouting "Yes!" to the life force. During such times, we give life a

green light to employ every tool at its disposal, including every archetypal process of change — be it destruction of what we hold dear,
the sudden creation of enticing new opportunities, or some sustenance we have always craved — to move us towards life and away
from calcification.

In my case, I think it was a matter of misalignment. My soul
wanted something different out of life than my heart, body, will,
emotions, and conscious mind. It led me down a path that I never,
in a thousand years, would have chosen. It had more courage,
strength, wisdom, and foresight than all the rest of me. (See the song
I wrote a full month before the crisis began.[3]) I have learned, without a doubt, that the soul is quite willing to sacrifice anyone and
anything that stands between it and its home, the greater life force.

Another significant insight I gained from this difficult time has
to do with *relationship.* Our connections with others are greater than,
and form the context for, our own individual heroic journeys. It is
true that we self-reference and move into life from our own Cores,
but we always do so in relationship to other people and our environment. Life is a complex dance with others. We fill a variety of
archetypal roles for each other, each playing a part that needs playing. In this way, we help each other learn and evolve.

We are all separate, unique individuals *and* an integral part of
an interwoven fabric. Bohm was right: we are not fragmented. In
reality we are joined, whole. Relationship is what saves us, all the
time, but most obviously during times of crises. It provides the stage
upon which, and the actors with whom, we daily perform the scenes
from our personal stories. The invisible netting of relationship also
keeps us from falling through the holes of illusion and loss of faith
into despair and oblivion. This primacy of relationship was an ab-
stract concept for me until I experienced how people gathered and
wove themselves so beautifully around me when I temporarily lost
myself. I know now, with utmost certainty, that we never journey
alone.

The people listed on the next page came to my aid when I fell
apart. They demonstrated to me that relationship not only provides
a strong external infrastructure that sustains us, but that it also
forms an "inner-net" in which we live, breathe, move, dream, and

hear each other's calls for help. These profound, invisible threads of connection are the key to our survival as individuals and as a species. Each person contributed a vital gift to me: ranging from regularly checking in on me to giving timely advice and good counsel, taking me out for lunch or a night on the town, holding me while I wept, treating me to a Reiki healing session, helping me financially, providing work leads, and much more. Each name on this list contains a story of compassion, concern, and care. (My apologies go to other friends, relatives, and members of my community who would have helped me in a heartbeat had they known my circumstances.)

Very special thanks go to . . .

My ever-supportive family: Mom and Dad, Dorothy, Irene, Tom and Mary Lou, and cousins Nancy, Myra, and Al. My great friends, colleagues, and neighbors: Julia Carroll, Kathy Eckles, Andrew Hahn, Prema Popat, Kevin Bourne, Kathleen and Daniel Bowman, Anne Bardake, Ann Rahimi-Assa, Linda and Joe Miller, Sukanya Ray, Charles Dietrick, Judith Lieberman, Bill Tasso, Lynn Collins, Margaret Peloquin, Padma Morel, Marlene Palmer, David Boor, Karen Speerstra (and all the Sophias), Laurie Lippin, Josephine Withers, Steve Cavaleri, Cathy Bourne, Barbara Curcio, Connie Barber, Dorrett Hope, James Galvin, David Wolfe, Laurie Burgess, Michael Bailet, Glen Koocher, Brian Finne, Peter Selby, Ben Orofano, Nick Monsarrat, Deborah Barlow, Mark Allin, Fred Reed, David Fearon, Stanley Bartlett, and the many caring members of my meditation community, Reiki community, and the "unlimited connection" therapy study group.

These, then, are the insights I recently bought at what seemed to be an excessively high price — my old life. Yet even now I suspect that some day I may be able to look back at this crossroad with clearer eyes, a lighter heart, and the understanding that my soul actually made a good bargain, after all.

Consequently, despite the recent difficulties I have encountered on my own personal journey, I do not hesitate to urge you forward on yours. You will carve your own unique path as you make your way "home." You can be wiser and braver than I was. You can meet change with courage, simply by accepting it as a gift from life.

I now know that when you claim your internal heroism, when you allow yourself to love and be loved, when you approach learning with joy and change with acceptance, you will be rewarded with the multifaceted treasure of wisdom. For I have learned that when you embrace life, it enthusiastically embraces you back, filling every corner of your being and spilling over with its richness.

So, don't hold back. The journey is well worth it. Godspeed.

NOTES

1. Swami Muktananda, "Sri Guru Gita," *The Nectar of Chanting*, SYDA Foundation, South Fallsburg, NY, 1972, verse 162, p. 51.

2. Swami Muktananda and Swami Chivilasananda, *Resonate with Stillness: Daily Contemplations*, SYDA Foundation, South Fallsburg, NY, May 21, 1995.

3. To illustrate how powerful and irreversible this "soul call" was, I want to share a song that I wrote a full month *before* my life fell apart. One morning I awoke with the music and words to the line: "You are a long way from home." I was surprised at the message. My life was just fine, I thought. As if to contradict myself, the rest of the song formed immediately. I wrote down the words. The song is as beautiful as it is disturbing.

What is this voice inside my heart that calls me to the morn'
That wings me to and from the land where shim'ring dreams are born?
What is this voice that whispers soft, that sings so sweet, so low:
"You are a long way from home."

What is this voice inside my mind that trembles so with fear
Whenever darkness covers me and shadows hover near?
What is this voice that torments me, that takes from me all hope?
That says: "You'll never find your way home."

What is this voice that tells my eyes to stare into the cave?
That urges me inside, saying: "Take heart now, be brave.
Behind this great deep darkness a greater light dies glow,
This is your way home."

What is this voice inside my heart that says: "I've never left your side.
My life pulses through your veins, your life echoes mine.
How could I ever forget you when you are to me my own?
YOU ARE HOME.

— SHARON SEIVERT, "What Is This Voice?" © 1997

Appendix A
The Elements of Success

The Elements of Success is a systemic approach to organizations that is easy to understand and apply. It describes the underlying fields that unify and "organize" all organisms, including our workplaces and ourselves. Any system that ignores (or overemphasizes) any of these essential aspects of itself will become out of balance. This can result in serious malfunction under stress. This model is particularly useful during times of significant change and high stress, when we seek to regain, and then keep, our balance.

This model is based upon the cross-cultural metaphor of the five elements, long used to describe the building blocks that make up all living systems. It can be visualized as a compass that helps us stay on course, or as a Medicine Wheel for our self-healing, or as an alchemist's Magic Circle, where we change lead to gold.

Both individuals and organizations are more than the sum of their parts. When a system maintains a dynamic balance among the five elements, it functions as a well-coordinated whole and grows in a more healthy, resilient, and integrated way.

The Core Types and Core Cultures that have been the topic of *Working from Your Core* originate at our Core (the first element) and are reflected in each of the other elements, as described in the following chart. You will quickly note the relevance of these elements to the Core Learning model, which helps learning become more comprehensive by making certain that all of the Elements of Success have been included in the learning process.

***Table A–1 The Five Parts of Complex Systems
(from most obvious to most subtle)***

	Organization	Individual	Core Types and Culture Can Be Seen in	Classical Direction/ Element
5	Structure	Body	Work processes, work space, policies; clothing, walk, facial expressions, etc.	Earth/North
4	Interactions	Emotions	Way workers interact with each other; what emotions and interactions are permitted; external relationships and internal emotions	Water/West
3	Motivation	Will	Clarity of mission, priorities, behavior, level and kinds of activity, focus, power and empowerment	Fire/South
2	Vision	Mind	Beliefs about the world, others, meaning of work, self, etc.; inspiration	Air/East
1	Core	Soul	Ethics; integrity and integration; values; what is considered "right"and most important; the self-referencing center that holds us together, from which we learn and grow	Ether/Center

The Five Components of an Organization

5. *Structure.* Work processes, organizational structure (formal and informal), policies, procedures, physical resources (including finances), physical environment.

4. *Interactions.* Relationships with internal and external customers, teamwork, communications between individuals and departments, respect, trust, information flow.

3. *Motivation.* Mission, energy, power issues, conflict, competition, recognition and rewards, how individual work has meaning in context of whole system.

2. *Vision.* Shared beliefs, inspiration, hope, optimism regarding future, innovation, ability to learn and adapt, scanning the environment for change, clear-sightedness.

1. *Core.* Cultural identity, "gravitational center" of organization, ethics, the "why" of organization's existence, who we are together, what we have in common. The self-referencing center of the organization.

The Five Aspects of a Whole Person

5. *Body.* Physical form, personal health, personal resources (including finances), the externally visible aspects of a person, individual structure, order, and habits.
4. *Emotions.* Ability to work with others, maturity of relationships, emotional depth, range, appropriateness, and self-control ("emotional intelligence").
3. *Will.* Self-discipline, focus, desires, personal mission, "fire in the belly," energy, how conflict handled, how get what one wants, a can-do attitude, personal power.
2. *Mind.* Personal beliefs and worldview, optimism, creativity, willingness and ability to learn, ability to direct mind, individual knowledge, and capabilities.
1. *Soul.* The individual spirit; the most constant, genuine aspect of a person; feeling "at home" in oneself; being "centered," unflappable, content, calm, grateful, and happy.

Looking at Core Types through the lens of the five elements of success can help us understand why they are so pervasive throughout a living system. These are not just a role or robe you can put on. However, by experimenting with them, by paying attention to them, you can initiate a spiral of learning where you can become what, at first, you only pretend to be.

For example, let's say your internal Warrior is somewhat weak and reactive. By paying attention to other good Warriors around you, you can call up that understanding within yourself. You can try on that role, much as a child pretends when playing grown-up. And by so doing, you can awaken that higher form of the archetype inside you so that it can begin its teachings.

In this case, you can start by imitating the Warrior walk (5). Through your body awareness, you will quickly start to "feel" what it is like to be strong, focused, assertive (4). The next time you are confronted by a bully, you are more likely not to shrink away or lash out. That is, you will behave like a more mature Warrior (3). This successful action is likely to cause you to think more like a Warrior, to mull over the Warrior beliefs and worldview (2). Then you will realize that this is indeed an integral part of you, and you can "own" this part of yourself at an identity level (1).

The above-mentioned material has been excerpted from the upcoming *The Elements of Success*. Please do not reproduce or copy it without permission. If you would like more information on this model or the instruments used to assess the Elements of Success in individuals, leaders, or organizations, please contact the author.

Appendix B
How We and Our
Organizations Really Learn

> Only by emphasizing autonomy, including intrinsic identity, the primacy of action, and the critical role of values, can we regain the full capacity for learning and development. And, as part of the bargain, we may also regain the humanity that we are in danger of losing if we do not say good-bye to the era of the machine.*
>
> — FRED REED AND SHARON SEIVERT

Autognomics, the study of how autonomous, intelligent systems learn, defines learning as the ability of an intelligent system to adapt to a changing environment while self-referencing, that is, maintaining its core identity. (The word *autognomic* means "self-knowing.") As a science of learning, autognomics dances happily with the mythology of the hero's journey because both assert that to find your best self, you must choose your own path of learning.

This fledgling science of learning comes to the rescue of anyone who was ever been chastised — in school or life — for coloring outside the lines. Autognomics combines the biological concept of autopoiesis, the pragmatic philosophy and semiotics of Charles

* For more information on autognomics refer to Chapters 12 and 13 in *Managing in Organizations That Learn*, Steven Cavaleri and David Fearon, Eds., Blackwell Business Books, Cambridge, MA, 1996, or directly contact The Autognomics Institute, 32 Williams Avenue, Mystic, CT 06355.

Sanders Pierce, with the mathematics of axiology (a scientific theory of value designed by Robert S. Hartman).[1] Learning, according to autognomics, is knowledge the intelligent system gains about itself by interacting with its environment, *not* what it is spoon-fed by teachers or experts. Autognomics reframes learning as an inward view of one's self rather than an outward-directed view of the world. It states, quite heretically, that intelligent systems do *not* perceive what is out there. Rather, we meet what is outside us with who we are (what we already think and value), thereby actively filtering — actually choosing — our perceptions. This is true of frogs, princes, and organizations alike. Autognomics supports the many sages who have contended throughout the millennia that we simply can't see what we don't believe. As Eugene Pendergraft, a founder of the Autognomics Institute, stated so succinctly: "Men labor under a mistake, under the inherited idea that they receive rather than create information."[2]

Autognomics contends that perception is not a "rational" process in which we take in what is objectively out there, but rather that perception is how we interact with and make judgments about our environment. We interact with our world, that is, learn, by either intrinsically, extrinsically, or systemically "valuing" whatever we meet in it. *Intrinsic* valuing is the direct experience of the intelligent system. *Extrinsic* valuing happens when we value something or someone for its qualities, for example, as being either good or bad. Finally, we can evaluate something via a system of thought, or laws, or policies; this is systemic valuing. A mix of all three provides the best learning. Unfortunately, as a society we have overrewarded systemic valuing (probably because we fervently hope theories will help us predict what's going to happen next). Unfortunately, this reliance has removed us from the primary form of learning that is associated with our direct, personal experience.

Autognomic theorists state that, in general, we should begin our learning with intrinsic valuing and move from there. This is true for both individuals and organizations. This is a particularly good policy as the world changes more quickly, because concepts (extrinsic) and laws (systemic) are becoming obsolete more quickly. Intrinsic valuing needs to be re-emphasized because it is the form of learning that can help us adapt the most quickly.

Autognomics has many implications for organizational learning, because it challenges us to first discover our organization's identity and intrinsic values before we muck about, applying some expert's theory about how the organization should be changed. We discover our workplace's identity by becoming aware of aspects of the organization (such as organizational culture and beliefs) that are typically hidden from our view and that serve — whether or not we are conscious of them — as the foundation for the organization's self-referenced learning process. Any attempts to change an organization without first understanding its identity, without allowing it to self-reference, will result in a lot of effort, little learning, and no successful adaptation.

Autognomics consultant Fred Reed argues that our shared misconception about how we and our organizations learn has profoundly deleterious repercussions.

"The fallout from this mistake is staggering: individuals, organizations, and societies are led to oppressive and sterile notions of learning, development and action. At stake is not simply a matter of reducing education and training costs or raising corporate profitability. Effective learning is not just desirable, it is the key to our survival."[3]

In biological terms, learning requires experience and internalization. It also requires that the organism retain its identity, that is, not come apart at the seams. According to autognomics, such learning begins in *personal experience* (First: "The fire burned my hand"), then moves to an *extrapolation from that experience* (Second: "If I put my hand in the fire, I will be burned), to a *system of thought* (Third: "Anyone who puts his hand into fire will get burned.") All three levels of learning are important.

However, as a species we have tended to overemphasize systemic learning and forget to tap the rich vein of our own personal experience. We go to libraries to research the excellent ideas of others, rather than sitting quietly to discover what WE really think about that topic. We hire outside experts to enter our workplace cultures and "fix" them according to some model they have just written about.

Instead, the theory of autognomics urges us to learn from our Core.

NOTES

1. Fred Reed and Sharon Seivert, *Managing in Organizations That Learn*, Steven Cavaleri and David Fearon, Eds., Blackwell Business Books, Cambridge, MA, 1996, chapter 13.
2. Eugene Pendergraft, "The Future's Voice: Organizing Principles for the Information Age," Unpublished manuscript, 1993.
3. Fred Reed and Sharon Seivert, "The Implications of Autonomy for Learning in Organizations." In *Managing in Organizations That Learn*, Steven Cavaleri and David Fearon, Eds., Blackwell Business Books, Cambridge, MA, 1996, p. 402.

Appendix C
The Five-Part Learning Model

Table C–1 The Five-Step Model of Learning and Working from Your Core

Steps	When you find yourself faced with a challenge:
1. Tap into Core	Breathe. If possible, become silent inside and out. Become aware of the options that your unconscious is presenting to you. Notice images that pop into mind, memories that surface ("This reminds me of that person. . . ." or "I remember the time when . . ."), a relevant quote from a great book, a song with pertinent lyrics, etc. Become aware of what you're feeling. Even if it's unpleasant (anger or fear), or fuzzy and undefined — just take note. This will give you data about the real size, shape, and nature of this particular challenge.
2. Think	It's always best to think before acting, even if for just a moment. In order to slow yourself down to do this, steady your breathing. This reverses any panic impulses by signaling your body that this challenge is not an emergency (even if it is). Moreover, in this way your brain will get the oxygen it needs to work clearly, and the bridge to your Core remains intact. With the benefit of both your conscious and unconscious minds, you will have more options to choose from, and can better decide: (a) what you're really up against, and (b) what to do about it. If possible, determine which of the Core Types and processes of change might be most helpful in this situation.
3. Act	Take action. While acting, gather immediate feedback as you go along, i.e., observe yourself (what you're thinking and feeling) and also others' reactions to your actions. Course correct, as necessary. If possible, breathe steadily while acting. This will keep your mind and emotions more clear, and the link between them intact. It also will allow for more maneuverability in the situation and better recall afterwards, when it's time to reflect.

continued

Table C–1 (continued)

Steps	When you find yourself faced with a challenge:

4. Reflect	When the challenge is over, take a moment to reflect:
	  Contemplate: What did you learn? (If possible, make notes.)
	  This is the time to give yourself feedback and to solicit feedback from involved parties.
	  Answer questions such as:
	    What do you think went well and what did not?
	    How did you feel before, during, and after you acted?
	    What conclusions can you take from this situation?
	    What might you do differently the next time a similar situation occurs?
	  Also decide if there is any follow-up you need to do.
	
	Note: Reflection can also be done in the middle of action, allowing insightful course correction to occur.

5. Integrate	Integrate what you've learned, where applicable, into your life and work.
	  If possible, see where you can use your learning to help your workplace.
	  In order to determine where this learning might be useful, think of similar situations.
	  If possible, talk with others about your learning; this increases your insights and produces synergy.
	  Stay alert for opportunities to put this new learning to good use — for yourself, others, and your workplace.

Here's an example of how this optimal learning process works.

Suzanne is an advertising executive in a midsize firm. At the beginning of this learning cycle we find her sitting at her desk, staring out the window. She's faced with a challenge that has her temporarily stymied. She is in charge of designing an ad campaign for a local restaurant, but she's been uninspired for days. However, fifteen minutes into watching the world go by, a terrific idea suddenly pops into her head (Step One).

She thinks about this idea for a few more moments, looking at it from all angles. She writes the key idea down, drawing a mind map. It actually becomes better with examination. "Yes, this could work!," she hears herself saying (Step Two).

Suzanne turns to her computer and spends the next several hours outlining the campaign. The next day, she talks to her colleagues. They think the idea has great possibilities. A small team with the necessary skills is put together, and the group begins to run with the project. A mockup of the components of the campaign is produced, and a meeting is scheduled with the client (Step Three).

Suzanne presents the proposed campaign to the owners of the restaurant for their feedback. By and large, they like it a lot, although they suggest a few minor changes. After these are made, the agency runs a focus group. Only a few people show up, so another focus group has to be scheduled. The next group responds well to the suggested ad campaign. And, they too have some feedback for improving it. Again, the project team makes the suggested improvements. With these alterations complete, all signals are go, and the ad campaign begins. The day after the campaign is officially launched, Suzanne sets an hour aside to make notes on what went well, what held the project up, and where the obstacles and breakthroughs occurred (Step Four).

With the above notes as reminders, Suzanne is able to apply what she learned to the next ad campaign. In addition, she and her colleagues review the whole experience at their weekly meeting. The fact that the first focus group was a flop is discussed, ideas for improving the feedback process are tossed around, and some changes are made in how the agency schedules its focus groups (Step Five).

Index

Page numbers in *italics* denote figures; those followed by "t" denote tables

325

Butterworth–Heinemann Business Books . . .
for Transforming Business

5th Generation Management: Co-creating Through Virtual Enterprising, Dynamic Teaming, and Knowledge Networking, Revised Edition,
  Charles M. Savage, 0-7506-9701-6

After Atlantis: Working, Managing, and Leading in Turbulent Times,
  Ned Hamson, 0-7506-9884-5

The Alchemy of Fear: How to Break the Corporate Trance and Create Your Company's Successful Future
  Kay Gilley, 0-7506-9909-4

Beyond Strategic Vision: Effective Corporate Action with Hoshin Planning,
  Michael Cowley and Ellen Domb, 0-7506-9843-8

Beyond Time Management: Business with Purpose,
  Robert A. Wright, 0-7506-9799-7

The Breakdown of Hierarchy: Communicating in the Evolving Workplace,
  Eugene Marlow and Patricia O'Connor Wilson, 0-7056-9746-6

Business and the Feminine Principle: The Untapped Resource,
  Carol R. Frenier, 0-7506-9829-2

Choosing the Future: The Power of Strategic Thinking,
  Stuart Wells, 0-7506-9876-4

Cultivating Common Ground: Releasing the Power of Relationships at Work,
  Daniel S. Hanson, 0-7506-9832-2

Flight of the Phoenix: Soaring to Success in the 21st Century,
  John Whiteside and Sandra Egli, 0-7506-9798-9

Getting a Grip on Tomorrow: Your Guide to Survival and Success in the Changed World of Work,
  Mike Johnson, 0-7506-9758-X

Innovation Strategy for the Knowledge Economy: The Ken Awakening,
  Debra M. Amidon, 0-7506-9841-1

The Intelligence Advantage: Organizing for Complexity,
  Michael D. McMaster, 0-7506-9792-X

Intuitive Imagery: A Resource at Work,
  John B. Pehrson and Susan E. Mehrtens, 0-7506-9805-5

The Knowledge Evolution: Expanding Organizational Intelligence,
  Verna Allee, 0-7506-9842-X

Leadership in a Challenging World: A Sacred Journey,
  Barbara Shipka, 0-7506-9750-4

About the Author

Sharon Seivert is the President of The Great Work! Consulting Group, a consortium of freelance business consultants assisting leaders and work-groups in building healthier and more effective workplaces. She advises cultural shift initiatives, including workplace assessment and implementation plans. Seivert also facilitates nondirective executive coaching, leadership development, and team building, and trains other professionals in the uses of the material she has developed.

Seivert has extensive leadership and consulting experience in a wide variety of industries, with a primary focus on health care. She served as CEO of Central Minnesota Group Health Plan, a staff-model, consumer-owned HMO. Seivert secured the capital, facilities, staff, and contracts necessary to launch this HMO start-up which achieved fiscal break-even at 3000 members (an industry record that still stands today). During her time at CMGHP, she was elected to the Board of Directors of the Group Health Association of America.

Sharon began her work in the health care field as Director of a three-county family planning center, where she established an on-site clinic and reduced per-patient cost by two-thirds. For her community contributions and work accomplishments, she was named Minnesota's Outstanding Young Career Woman

Seivert also worked for many years as a senior management consultant with a total quality management firm (the Lynnette Yount Associates) and served as vice president of Meristem, a nonprofit think tank. It was here that she and President Carol S. Pearson began their work together.

Seivert's writings include chapters in *Managing in Organizations that Learn* (Blackwell Business Books, 1996.) She is also co-author, with Carol Pearson, of *Magic at Work: Camelot, Creative Leadership, and Everyday Miracles* (Doubleday/Currency, 1995) and *Heroes at Work: A Workbook* (1988/1989).

Sharon was trained as a musician and continues song-writing to this day. She claims that music and Reiki — a gentle healing technique in which she is a traditional Master — help keep her a bit more sane and a lot more in touch with her own Core.

To receive more information on consultations, seminars, executive coaching, organizational assessment, speaking engagements, or training and certifications in the use of this material, please write:

Sharon Seivert, President
The Great Work! Consulting Group
Ten Magazine Street, #1004
Cambridge, MA 02139